International trade and global development

Jagdish Bhagwati with J.J. Palak and Jan Tinbergen at the symposium

International trade and global development

Essays in honour of Jagdish Bhagwati

Edited by

Ad Koekkoek
and
L.B.M. Mennes

London and New York

382
I 617

First published 1991
by Routledge
11 New Fetter Lane, London EC4P 4EE

Simultaneously published in the USA and Canada
by Routledge
a division of Routledge, Chapman and Hall, Inc.
29 West 35th Street, New York, NY 10001

Phototypeset in 10pt Times by
Mews Photosetting, Beckenham, Kent
Printed and bound in Great Britain by
Biddles Ltd, Guildford and King's Lynn

British Library Cataloguing in Publication Data

International trade and global development : essays in
    honour of Jagdish Bhagwati.
    1. Economic conditions. Related to foreign trade
    I. Bhagwati, Jagdish II. Koekkoek, Ad. *1949–* III. Mennes,
    L.B.M. (Loet B.M.)
    382
    ISBN 0–415–05535–0

Library of Congress Cataloging in Publication Data
has been applied for

Contents

Contents

Part III Foreign investment

Part IV International economic co-ordination

Tables

About the contributors

V.N. BALASUBRAMANYAM did his postgraduate work at the University of Chicago and the University of Illinois. He holds a BA (Hons) and an MA degree from the University of Mysore, India, and AM and PhD degrees from the University of Illinois. Prior to going to the USA he was a Junior Economist with the Committee on Indo-Japanese collaboration attached to the Indian Planning Commission, with Professor Jagdish Bhagwati as his Research Director. Currently he is Professor of Development Economics in the Department of Economics, Management School, Lancaster University. His publications include *International Transfer of Technology to India*, *The Economy of India*, *Meeting the Third World Challenge* (with A.I. MacBean) and *Multinational Enterprises in the Third World*.

ELIAS DINOPOULOS is an Associate Professor of Economics at the University of Florida. He earned his BA degree from Harvard College in 1979 and his PhD degree in economics from Columbia University in 1985. He taught at Brown University and Michigan State University, and he visited the University of California at Davis. His research interests include the area of political economy of trade restrictions, of commercial-policy theory and of high-technology trade and investment. He has published in several journals including the *American Economic Review*, *Review of Economics and Statistics*, the *Journal of International Economics*, and *Economics and Politics*.

ROBERT C. FEENSTRA is an Associate Professor of Economics at the University of California, Davis, and a Research Associate of the National Bureau of Economic Research. He is editor of *Essays in International Economic Theory*, by Jagdish N. Bhagwati, and co-editor of the *Journal of International Economics*. He has published about twenty journal articles on international trade theory and policy, and has edited two conference volumes dealing with empirical studies of trade policy.

JEFFREY FRANKEL is Professor of Economics at the University of California, Berkeley, and Research Associate of the National Bureau of Economic Research in Cambridge, Massachusetts. From July 1988 to January 1990 he was Visiting Professor of Public Policy at the Kennedy School of Government, Harvard University. From August 1983 to August 1984 he served at the President's Council of Economic Advisors in Washington, with responsibility for international economic policy. He has also had visiting appointments at the International Monetary Fund, the Institute for International Economics, the Federal Reserve Board, the World Bank and Yale University. Professor Frankel's research interests include international macro-economic policy co-ordination, the workings of the foreign exchange market, Japanese financial liberalization, and worldwide financial integration. Recent papers include 'International macroeconomic policy coordination when policy-makers do not agree on the model' in the *American Economic Review* (June 1988). Monographs include *The Yen/Dollar Agreement: Liberalizing Japanese Capital Markets*. Frankel is also co-author (with R. Caves and R. Jones) of *World Trade and Payments* (5th edn, January 1990). He was born in San Francisco in 1952, graduated from Swarthmore College in 1974, and received his PhD from Massachusetts Institute of Technology in 1978.

BRIAN HINDLEY is Senior Lecturer in Economics at the London School of Economics. He was born in England and received his secondary education there, but then attended the Universtiy of Chicago (AB 1961; PhD 1967). Among his recent publications are 'European Community imports of VCRs from Japan' in the *Journal of World Trade Law* (March–April 1986); 'Trade in services within the European Community' in Herbert Giersch (ed.) *Free Trade in the World Economy* (1987); 'GATT safeguards and voluntary export restraints: what are the interests of developing countries?' in the *World Bank Economic Review* (September 1987); 'Service sector protection: considerations for developing countries' in the *World Bank Economic Review* (May 1988); and 'Dumping and the Far East Trade of the European Community' in *World Economy*, (December 1988).

AD KOEKKOEK, born in 1949, is Senior Lecturer in International Economics at Erasmus University Rotterdam and Senior Policy Adviser at the Ministry of Foreign Affairs of the Netherlands. He received his MA degree in economics, *cum laude*, in 1971, from Erasmus University. He spent two years as a visiting lecturer at the University of Lagos, Nigeria. He obtained his PhD in 1989 on the subject of developing countries and the Uruguay Round. He has published on matters of trade structure and trade policy in various journals, such as *Weltwirtschaftliches Archiv*, *World Development*, *World Economy* and *Journal of World Trade (Law)*. He is co-editor of a special issue of *Journal of Common Market Studies* on the effects of '1992' on developing countries (forthcoming, December 1990).

LOET MENNES is managing director of the Netherlands Development Finance Company (FMO) and Professor of International Economics at Erasmus University Rotterdam. For many years he was a director of the Netherlands Economic Institute which he left in 1988. He has (co-)authored and (co-)edited books on economic integration, spatial planning, investment planning, European trade policies and project appraisal. He has published articles in journals such as *Econometrica*, *Weltwirtschaftliches Archiv*, *Journal of International Economics* and *Journal of World Trade Law*.

JAMES RIEDEL is Professor of International Economics at the Johns Hopkins University School of Advanced International Studies in Washington, DC and consultant to the World Bank. He has been visiting scholar at Nuffield College, Oxford, and visiting fellow at the National Centre for Development Studies, Australian National University. He has written numerous articles on international trade, international finance and economic development. He is contributor to *The Protectionist Wave* (forthcoming), a co-editor of *The Direction of Trade Policy* (forthcoming) and co-author of *Macroeconomic Crises and Long-term Growth in Turkey* (forthcoming).

H. ONNO RUDING was born in the Netherlands on 15 August 1939. He got his MA in Economics at the Netherlands School of Economics (now Erasmus University) in Rotterdam in 1964 and his PhD *cum laude* in 1969 on a thesis entitled: 'Towards an integrated European capital market?' From 1965 to 1970 he worked at the Ministry of Finance in the Hague as head of the division of international monetary affairs. Thereafter (1971–6) he joined the Amsterdam–Rotterdam Bank in Amsterdam as a joint general manager. From 1977 to 1980 he served as an Executive Director of the International Monetary Fund (IMF) in Washington, DC. From 1981 he was a member of the Board of managing directors of the Amsterdam-Rotterdam Bank until he was appointed Minister of Finance of the Netherlands in November 1982. In this capacity he served until November 1989. From 1985 to 1989 he also acted as Chairman of the Interim Committee of the IMF. Dr Ruding has written extensively on international and national monetary subjects and on European integration. In 1981–2 he was a member of the Board of Foster Parents Plan International.

MOHAMMED ADAYA SALISU holds a BSc (Hons) and MSc degree from the University of Maiduguri, Nigeria. He wrote his MSc dissertation on 'A short term planning model for Nigeria'. He is Lecturer in Econometrics and Mathematical Economics at the University of Maiduguri in Nigeria. Currently he is a Teaching Associate in the Department of Economics, Management School, University of Lancaster, and is completing his doctoral dissertation on 'Oil and the Nigerian economy'.

LEO SLEUWAEGEN is Associate Professor at the University of Leuven in Belgium and holds the chair of European Integration and Corporate Strategy at Erasmus University in the Netherlands. His research and publications are in the fields of industrial organization and international business. His current research focuses on the implications of the European 1992 programme for European industrial organization.

L. ALAN WINTERS studied at the University of Bristol, from which he joined the Department of Applied Economics, Cambridge, to work on the Cambridge Growth Project. While in Cambridge he obtained his doctorate, became a fellow of Fitzwilliam College and was a founding director of Cambridge Econometrics Ltd. In 1980 he returned to the University of Bristol as a university lecturer in economics. Between August 1983 and December 1985 he worked as an economist in the World Bank and in 1986 he joined the University College of North Wales where he is now Professor of Economics and Chairman of the School of Accounting, Banking and Economics. He is Co-Director of the International Trade Programme at the London-based Centre for Economic Policy Research. From August 1990 he will be Professor and Head of the Department of Economics at the University of Birmingham. Alan Winters' writings have mostly been in international economics. They include the following books: *An Econometric Model of the Export Sector*, *International Economics*, *Europe's Domestic Market*, *Primary Commodity Prices: Economic Models and Policy*, and many journal articles and chapters. His current research covers international trade policy, agricultural policy and European integration.

MARTIN WOLF is Chief Economics Leader Writer of the *Financial Times*, London. Born in 1946, he was educated at Oxford University, where he obtained an MPhil in economics at Nuffield College, Oxford. In 1971 Mr Wolf joined the World Bank. In 1981 he joined the Trade Policy Research Centre as Director of Studies. In 1987 he joined the *Financial Times*. Apart from numerous articles, mainly on trade matters, his publications include *Textile Quotas against Developing Countries* (co-author Donald B. Keesing), *Costs of Protecting Jobs in Textiles and Clothing*, *India's Exports* and *Global Implications of the European Community's Programme for Completing the Internal Market*.

KAR-YIU WONG is Associate Professor of Economics at the University of Washington, USA. His dissertation, written under the supervision of Jagdish Bhagwati at Columbia University, analysed the interrelationship between international trade and factor mobility. Since then he has become a specialist in this field. His research interests extend to other areas such as USA–Japan trade and military relations, strategic government policies towards international factor movement, commercial policy under incomplete markets, political economy of trade policies, and the economic reforms in China.

HIDEKI YAMAWAKI is a research fellow at the Wissenschaftszentrum Berlin, where he is currently engaged in corporative research on European, American and Japanese market dynamics and corporate policy.

Acknowledgements

We want to express our gratitude to the editor of *Weltwirtschaftliches Archiv* for allowing us to reproduce Jagdish Bhagwati's article 'Is free trade passé?, to Basil Blackwell Inc. for allowing us to reproduce Jim Riedel's article 'Strategy wars: the state of debate about trade and industrialization in developing countries' from James Riedel and Charles Pearson (eds) *The Direction of Trade Policy*, and to the editor of *World Economy* for allowing us to reproduce Martin Wolf's article 'Why voluntary export restraints? An historical analysis'.

Preface

On 8 November 1988 a solemn ceremony took place in the great hall of the Erasmus University Rotterdam where the University's seventy-fifth *dies natalis* was celebrated. The second co-editor of the present volume had the great honour to address Professor Jagdish Bhagwati of Columbia University with the following words:

> By virtue of the powers invested in us by statute and in accordance with the decision of the College of Deans, I hereby confer upon you, Jagdish Bhagwati, the title of *Doctor honoris causa*, together with all the rights which statute and custom attach to this degree.
>
> As token and proof thereof, I present you with the corresponding charter, duly signed and sealed, and clothe you with the cappa.

The many reasons why it was thought very appropriate to confer an honorary degree upon Jagdish Bhagwati were summarized in the usual 'laudatio':

> For more than twenty-five years Professor Jagdish Bhagwati has made major contributions in international economic theory and in development economics. This has resulted in more than twenty-five books, authored or edited by him, and in more than 200 papers published in all major economic journals. Professor Bhagwati's contributions are masterly combinations of economic theory, empirical validation and policy debate. They relate to four major areas: commercial policy, international factor mobility, domestic development problems and international problems.
>
> In the theory of commercial policy Jagdish Bhagwati has formulated the generalized theory of distortions and welfare, where a considerable body of literature on the welfare economics of trade was unified in seven major propositions. Other major contributions in this area relate to the theory of immiserizing growth and its application; the

equivalence of tariffs and quotas; the theory of the optimum subsidy; project evaluation, effective protection and domestic resource costs; and directly unproductive profit-seeking activities.

The second area is that of international factor mobility with important and innovative contributions to subjects such as international migration, the welfare-theoretical aspects of the brain drain, trade and welfare in the presence of foreign factors of production, foreign investment, and international trade and comparative advantage.

The third area is that of national development problems. In this respect it must be emphasized that for Jagdish Bhagwati the objective of development always was the elimination of poverty. Growth was seen by him as an instrumental variable. Also in this area Professor Bhagwati has made valuable studies on topics such as regularities and explanations of a country's economic structure, technological development and employment, and in particular the theory of transfers and welfare, where the well-known 1929 debate between Keynes and Ohlin on reparation payments by Germany was taken as a point of departure, leading to a brilliant analysis of the so-called transfer problem.

The fourth and last area is that of international problems. Here Professor Bhagwati's contributions relate to, among others, the tying of aid, the substitution between foreign capital and domestic savings, and the relation between food aid, agricultural production and welfare.

One of Professor Bhagwati's major achievements is precisely in this field of international economic problems. Professor Bhagwati is the principal intellectual advocate of liberalization in the modern industrial and trade sectors of an economy. His highly scholarly and influential contributions in this respect are on the relative merits of import-substituting and export-promoting development strategies, demonstrating the great net benefits of non-distorting neutral export-promoting policies.

In his research activities Professor Bhagwati has co-operated with a number of other economists. In honouring Professor Bhagwati, we also honour his colleagues. I would like to mention three of them: T.N. Srinivasan, the late Harry Johnson and Professor Mrs Padma Desai, his wife, who is with us today.

Ladies and gentlemen, I will try to summarize the relevance of Jagdish Bhagwati's numerous contributions to economic science by referring to his last book. It is a small book, called *Protectionism*.

We are now in the middle of the Uruguay Round of the Multilateral Trade Negotiations. These negotiations concern the developing countries deeply. The threat of protectionism has resurfaced; it will continue to do so, also or precisely, when the European Common Market will be completed in 1992. This tide of protectionist sentiments and legislation has to be stemmed, in order to give hundreds of millions of poor people a small opportunity for a somewhat better life.

Fortunately, there are major new interests and forces, but in particular new ideas in the theory of commercial policy that strengthen the ideological power of anti-protectionism. For this purpose we have to reform and strengthen the institutional framework, national and international, to harness these pro-trade interests and contain the forces of protectionism more effectively. This calls for continuous information by economic science.

Already for many years Professor Jagdish Bhagwati has provided such information, characterized by theoretical brilliance and thorough empirical analysis. In this way he has served economic science and, by fighting protectionism, mankind. For these reasons, the Erasmus University Rotterdam honours him today.

On the occasion of the awarding of the honorary doctorate to Jagdish Bhagwati the Department of International Economics of the Erasmus University organized a symposium with the title International Trade and Global Development, where some of the papers in this volume were first presented. To do full justice to the breadth of Professor Bhagwati's interests we tried to cover a wide spectrum of topics in international economics, namely trade policy in general, trade policy and development strategies, trade policy and direct foreign investment and international economic co-operation. We were very happy with the instant willingness to contribute of Giorgio Basevi, Jim Riedel, Onno Ruding, Leo Sleuwaegen together with Hideki Yamawaki, and Alan Winters. Their papers are included in this volume, except for Giorgio Basevi's, whose paper on international monetary co-operation, unfortunately, was already committed for publication elsewhere.

Of course, four papers do not make a book. So we tried to increase the number of papers in line with our aim of covering a wide area of international economics. We are very grateful therefore that so many distinguished authors were willing to join our enterprise. It is a reflection, we think, of the high esteem in which Jagdish Bhagwati is held by the community of international economists. Altogether the authors represent a group of admirers of Jagdish, who were, or would like to have been, also his students.

We have subdivided the volume into four parts of rather different size. The introduction comprises two papers; the main part on trade, protection and political economy consists of no less than five papers;

the third part on foreign direct investment has three papers and the fourth part on international economic co-ordination contains just one paper. This somewhat uneven distribution is mostly because of the differences in attention given to the various subjects during the symposium. Trade policy was indeed the main subject, followed by foreign investment and international co-ordination. For the last subject two contributions were planned; unfortunately, one did not materialize.

We shall now briefly present the various contributions: Onno Ruding, who was at the time Minister of Finance of the Netherlands and Chairman of the International Monetary Fund (IMF) Interim Committee, deals with the international economic environment from a practical policy point of view. In his contribution, the Minister supports further attempts to achieve substantial trade liberalization during the present Uruguay Round of the General Agreement on tariffs and Trade (GATT). Dr Ruding also discusses the present way of co-ordinating macro-economic policies. In fact he criticizes the decision-making in the G5/G7 framework, which he characterizes as 'too much politics and too little economics'. Instead he proposes to strengthen the position of the IMF.

We are glad we were allowed to reprint Professor Bhagwati's article, in which he extensively reviews the case for free trade in the light of the many recent developments in the theory of commercial policy, especially in view of the so-called strategic trade policy considerations which have been advanced over the last couple of years. He argues that, whereas the incorporation of imperfect competition into the theory of international trade augments the case for departures from free trade, the incorporation of political processes weakens the case. He thinks the latter are more interesting and compelling, whereas the former are subject to many difficulties on their way from theory to real-world application.

Alan Winters considers the question whether current protectionism, given its specific nature, is amenable to GATT-based processes. In his analysis he distinguishes high-track and low-track protectionism. The former is the visible one, often leading to bilateral solutions. The latter refers to the biased use of formally impartial procedures. Professor Winters is more optimistic about the chances of reducing high-track protectionism than low-track protectionism, because of the risk of 'rationalizing' existing codes, i.e. in his words: 'to fit GATT around the facts'.

Jim Riedel discusses the 'victory' of outward-oriented over inward-oriented development strategies. In particular, he pays attention to two aspects of the debate about these strategies: the infant-industry argument, for which he finds little support, and export pessimism, with regard to which he stresses that, traditionally, import demand elasticities are underestimated, because in the estimation process export supply from developing countries is assumed to be infinitely elastic. Any doubts Jim Ridel may have about the relevance of outward orientation are reserved for the case of Africa.

Martin Wolf describes, in his inimitable way, the history of voluntary export restraints (VERs), starting in the 1930s. Points of departure for his discourse are on the one hand Jan Tumlirs' rather negative assessment of VERs and on the other hand Jagdish Bhagwati's more optimistic interpretation of VERs in terms of the porousness of protection. His own position can best be summed up by quoting two of the propositions he makes: 'A VER here and a VER there and pretty soon you will have real protection' and 'The road to hell is paved with good intentions'.

Robert Feenstra compares tariff-rate quotas and quota auctions in relation to adjustment assistance. Quota auctions imply the reversal of the transfer of rents from the importer to the exporter, in which case trade partners cannot be expected to remain passive. The advantage of tariff-rate quotas would then be to preserve part of the original rent transfer and to use the revenue collected for adjustment assistance.

Brian Hindley discusses whether national policy regarding international trade in services should be subject to the discipline of the GATT, in particular from the point of view of developing countries. He argues that services trade liberalization, even unilateral, would be to the developing countries' advantage. Of course, he adds, it would be in their interest if they could exact a price from the developed countries in the Uruguay Round negotiations for opening up their markets in services.

Leo Sleuwaegen and Hideki Yamawaki discuss intra-firm trade decisions of Japanese multinationals. In their theoretical framework they explicitly look at the role market imperfections, such as protectionism, play here. They find, *inter alia*, that Japanese parent-firms, compared with US firms, import relatively less from their foreign affiliates and strongly direct their intra-firm exports to their foreign distribution subsidiaries. There is evidence, though, that this kind of intra-firm trade will reduce in magnitude and be substituted by local manufacturing.

Elias Dinopoulos and Kar-yiu Wong deal with direct foreign investment, not as a means of circumventing protection, but rather as a way of defusing the threat of protectionist action. Professor Bhagwati called this sort of investment *quid pro quo* direct foreign investment. They carefully analyse various policies, for both the importing country and the exporting countries, in the context of protectionist threats and *quid pro quo* direct foreign investment, which can improve the national welfare of both the importing and the exporting country.

V.N. Balasubramanyam and M.A. Salisu focus on Bhagwati's thesis that countries pursuing an export promotion strategy are, *ceteris paribus*, likely to attract more foreign investment than countries following an import substitution strategy. They do indeed find substantial empirical support for this proposition on the basis of a cross-section regression over thirty-eight developing countries for the period 1970–80.

Jeffrey Frankel takes up the second point made by Minister Ruding: the G7 co-ordination mechanism. He explains that the present mechanism is vulnerable to serious obstacles of three sorts: compliance, inflation-fighting credibility and uncertainty. Professor Frankel argues that co-ordination should involve an explicitly agreed and publicly announced intermediate target and that this should be a nominal variable. He concludes that the nominal intermediate target to which countries should best commit is one that does not even appear on the current G7 list at all: nominal gross national product.

To round off this volume, Professor Bhagwati, at our request, has agreed to present some comments on the various papers.

Ad Koekkoek
L.B.M. Mennes

Part I
Introduction

1 Improvement of the international trade environment in order to stimulate economic growth in developing countries

H. Onno Ruding

INTRODUCTION

I am pleased to have this opportunity to address this symposium, organized in honour of Professor Bhagwati, who is no doubt one of the most distinguished international economists alive and who is one of the few people who continuously publish theories about trade policy with a clear message for politicians. That is why I gladly accepted the invitation to open the symposium. I should like to focus on the positive effects of an improvement in the international trade environment on economic growth in developing countries.

A recent study by the staffs of the International Monetary Fund and the World Bank concludes that protection in industrial countries reduces national income in developing countries by almost twice the amount of the official development assistance that is currently provided. Liberalization of trade is therefore of the utmost importance for the growth prospects of developing countries. Although aid remains important, especially for the low-income countries, it is obvious that it cannot substitute for the beneficial effects of trade liberalization. At this point I should also point out that trade liberalization is no zero-sum game. Industrial countries have gains to expect from liberalization too, although this is not necessarily the case for specific non-competitive sectors.

In general, the effective rate of assistance in industrial countries is high for temperate zone agricultural products and for manufactures, including the most unsophisticated forms of processing such as crating and packaging. This affects production decisions in developing countries, constituting a brake on investments in the field I mentioned and stimulating developing countries to invest in those products that are the least affected by protectionism. This leads to a production bias in developing countries in favour of those products that are neither substitutes for temperate climate agricultural products nor manufactures that are subject to tariff escalation and other forms of protectionism. Protectionism in industrial countries thus reduces developing country investments in areas of true comparative advantage and potential growth sectors. Of course, developing country policies must also be taken into account. Protectionism in developing countries themselves, directed both against other less developed countries and against industrial countries, is often very high. In addition, bureaucracy in developing countries often acts as an impediment to trade.

It is encouraging to note that awareness in developing countries of the beneficial effects of trade liberalization has increased. Many developing countries are executing adjustment programmes with the support of the IMF and the World Bank. These programmes often incorporate changes in trade policy in addition to measures which increase the efficiency and responsiveness of the economy as a whole. Because it is important that these positive developments are accompanied by policy changes in developed countries, I should now like to go into somewhat more detail with respect to two sectors where industrial country protectionism is particularly damaging to growth in developing countries: agriculture and manufactures.

AGRICULTURE

Agricultural policy in the main Western trading blocs provides most of their farmers with high and stable 'guaranteed' prices for their products based on import barriers and subsidies. It also leads to excess supply and, as a consequence, for Third World farmers, most prices are lower and less stable than the prices Western farmers get for their products. This bias creates an incentive for farmers in industrial countries and a disincentive for Third World producers. Certainly, industrial country agricultural policies provide a source of cheap food for food-importing developing countries. The growth of agricultural production in developing countries, however, is much lower than it could have been. Third World dependence on Western food sources is unnecessarily large.

In this connection, it should also be pointed out that developing countries have often pursued the wrong policies by favouring industrial sectors above agriculture and by keeping domestic agricultural prices low. Artificially low prices have a destructive effect on the development of agriculture in developing countries. In some of these countries such a policy is based on domestic political rather than economic grounds, i.e. to subsidize the urban population at the expense of the rural population.

MANUFACTURES

In my intervention in the Development Committee of the World Bank at the IMF in Berlin this year I said that industrial country protectionism constitutes a major disincentive for developing countries to opt for a more outward-looking strategy. Industrial country trade barriers are, on average, higher on imports of manufactures from developing countries than on those from industrial countries, even when one takes the various Generalized Systems of Preference into consideration. Most-favoured-nation tariff rates tend to be higher on products exported mostly by developing countries.

Furthermore, there are relatively more non-tariff barriers on exports of developing country manufactures than on those of developed countries. Finally, industrial countries often do not charge each other the most-favoured-national tariff rate. This is because of bilateral and plurilateral agreements among industrial countries. Such agreements based on reciprocal concessions are now in force between the European Community and the European Free Trade Association and between Australia and New Zealand, and there soon will be one between the USA and Canada. The absolute level of protection is not increased by these arguments, but the relative access of third countries is smaller, leading to a diversion of trade. According to a recent World Bank study, most EFTA countries have applied rates three to four times higher for developing countries, reflecting the duty-free treatment of most manufactured goods traded between the EC and the EFTA.

An important impediment to growth in developing countries is industrial country tariff escalation. Restrictions in imports increase with the degrees of processing. The effective rate of assistance for processing is therefore higher than the tariffs indicate because it measures the influence of protection not on the whole product, but on value added in a production process. The result is that processing takes place in industrial countries, while without escalation of protection it might in many cases have taken place in developing countries.

LIBERALIZATION

The negative effects of protection in industrial countries on growth in developing countries lead to the following recommendations for liberalization.

First, the escalation of protectionism must be tackled; any negotiating process that leads to an abolishment of tariffs on raw materials while leaving the protection on manufactures based on these raw materials intact, must be avoided.

Second, we should limit the possibilities for an industrial country to protect its market solely against one or more developing countries; I think we should progressively eliminate the use of individual quotas, selective safeguards, voluntary export restraints and orderly market arrangements. Neither should we use anti-dumping rules and counter-vailing measures for protectionist purposes; only in clear cases of dumping should anti-dumping measures be used.

Third, all countries must have the opportunity to call upon effective dispute settlement procedures. It should be possible to adopt the results of dispute settlement independently of the goodwill of the country accused, thus resulting in rapid implementation, following the old Roman law principle *nemo iudex in sua causa*; this should also hold good in international trade. In order to increase the attractiveness of the General Agreement of Tariffs and Trade for developing countries, developed countries should abide by panel conclusions against them. To this end, some form of pressure from the GATT, authorized by consensus among all GATT contracting parties that are not directly involved, could be helpful. Even better would be binding rules, and a strong organization that is capable of making individual countries stick to these rules. This would take us further away from the consensus formula which has retarded liberalization processes for so long. We must not forget that the idea of the International Trade Organization (ITO) which would provide the appropriate institutional machinery for fast liberalization, was blocked by the USA; this should not prevent us from trying to build the GATT into the strong organization that the ITO never had a chance to be.

Fourth, protection on products exported in significant part by developing countries must be lowered. I mentioned the textiles and clothing sector. There should be no misunderstanding about the eventual abolition of the Multi-Fibre Arrangement. An agreement could involve a transitional period; it should also specify the conditions under which all protection in textiles and clothing could be abolished, one of which is intellectual property protection for designs.

Fifth, liberalization in the agricultural sector is necessary, and the Common Agricultural Policy will have to be adapted further for this purpose. The size of agricultural production should be strongly determined by market factors; production must be more clearly based on comparative costs. This means that further reductions of support are called for. Support for incomes of farmers in unfavourable conditions during a transitional period should be much more in the form of decoupled income support, with as little connection as possible with production levels. Direct income support would not stimulate production and could reduce budgetary expenditures compared with the present system; the way that the EC system of variable levies is applied insulates Community market prices from the outside world and therefore is neither an optimal way of adapting to world market developments nor a good way to accomplish market access.

Sixth, the liberalization of services, in particular of financial services, is important; foreign financial institutions can be a major force for modernization of financial services, a field in which developing countries all too often suffer from inefficiency. Of course, we should have an open eye for the concerns that these countries may have about the effectiveness of prudential supervision and of monetary policy, and the vulnerability of their own banking industries. In this area technology transfer and management techniques have a major role to play. Developing countries deprive themselves of major benefits if they do not participate in the overall liberalization of services in the GATT.

Seventh, we should move away from bilateral trade deals and concentrate on strengthening the multilateral trade system.

Eighth, we should be watchful for a new phenomenon identified by Professor Bhagwati as voluntary import expansion, which in my view is only useful in trade deals with State Trading Countries.

Finally, we should strive for a better balance of obligations in the GATT and towards a more selective application of discriminatory treatment in favour of developing countries. The developing countries that profit substantially from international trade should integrate to a greater extent into the GATT than is the case at present. A policy for graduating out of the Generalized Systems of Preference should be based on objective criteria such as per capita income; Western trade policy concerns should, not, of course, be among the criteria for graduation.

It goes without saying that the GATT Uruguay Round provides an excellent opportunity to accomplish substantial liberalization in the areas I have just mentioned.

CO-ORDINATION OF MACRO-ECONOMIC POLICIES

Whilst we know that in principle it may be asserted that protection leads to welfare losses for all concerned and liberalization, even when unilateral, increases welfare, we also know how impervious politics are to economic reason, being governed by a different kind of rationality. The very process of negotiation creates vested interests. Those who negotiate may listen more to their self-interest, which is very narrowly defined, than to economic reason. Economic theory and practice, however, have a major contribution to make towards creating an environment in which political perversity does not find nourishment. I speak of the maintenance of a healthy macro-economic setting and, in particular today, of the contribution that can be made to this by the international co-ordination of national macro-economic policies.

The fact that the risks of resort to protectionist measures have not yet declined can be seen as a reaction against the appreciable increase of interdependence of national economies in recent years. In this respect, close co-operation between the IMF, the World Bank, the GATT and the Organization for Economic Co-Operation and Development (OECD) is necessary. Systematic informal consultations and exchange of information between these organizations can be useful.

Interdependence not only creates opportunities but also increases vulnerability. We must do all we can to resist the defensive reaction of diminishing vulnerability by protection. On the contrary, we must cultivate the opportunity to gain from interdependence by enhancing international co-operation. Effective co-ordination of macro-economic policies, means not only bringing existing imbalances into a more sustainable pattern but also conducting policies that foster more long-lasting stability. Since trade is so closely related to stability, international policy co-ordination could help to revitalize the international economy and create a surge of activity in the developing world. But the co-ordination should be focused on long-term developments, on the fundamentals of the economies and on structural policies.

Today too much emphasis is given to the short-term, to cyclical developments, to exchange rates and to performance indicators. This holds in particular for the recent co-ordination policies within the compass of the G7. These policies, though at certain moments very useful, contain too much politics and too little economics. At present the G5/G7 tend to preempt and politically bias the decision making process in multilateral institutions, like the GATT, the IMF, the World Bank and the OECD, which lost some of their direct influence in recent years, especially because of the rise of the G5/G7.

For the moment, focusing on the IMF, I see clear advantages for a stronger position of this Bretton Woods institution in the process of international economic policy co-ordination and of efforts to improve the international monetary system as well. Multilateral organizations such as the IMF have very capable experienced staff and these form important engines for co-operation. But most of all, by means of a multilateral institution like the IMF, co-ordination can be based on clear-cut rules which apply to everyone on the same footing, in contrast with the small group talks and informal transactions that are usage in the

G5/G7. Codified rules are particularly important for small and less powerful countries. The inclusion of these countries in international economic policy co-ordination is important for a broad support of common policies, and in this sense is also vital for the long-term success of international co-ordination.

In this way policy co-ordination can contribute to a healthy world economic environment, in which trade can play its role without being undermined by protection measures. It is partly due to Professor Bhagwati that today there is consensus of opinion about this aim among most economists.

2 Is free trade passé after all?

Jagdish Bhagwati

INTRODUCTION

Let me first express my great pleasure in being awarded the Bernhard Harms Prize. In the field of international economics, it is now recognised as the profession's most notable award.[1] I feel honoured to join today the distinguished economists who have preceded me as recipients of this prestigious prize.

It would be logical for me to celebrate this occasion by addressing the great issue that led Adam Smith to give simultaneous birth to both economics and international economics. This is the issue of free trade or what we now call the theory of commercial policy. This is undoubtedly the area to which I have given my reflection and research in the last three decades: here lie certainly my own comparative advantage and indeed the reason for today's ceremonial occasion.

But the subject deserves scrutiny also because the question of free trade has now returned to centre stage. This is not simply because, since the 1970s, protectionist *demands* have increased, as certainly the beleaguered executives and administrations of the European Community and the United States know. It is also because the resistance to the *supply* of protection by these executives may have been imperilled by careless and incomplete assessments of recent developments in the theory of commercial policy itself.

These developments, as I shall argue presently, are by no means one-sided in strengthening the analytical case for departures from free trade. One set of developments, addressed to the incorporation of imperfect competition systematically into the theory of international trade, does indeed augment the conventional case for such departures by focusing on market imperfections and failure. However, another set of developments, addressed to the more fundamental task of incorporating into the theory 'political' processes such as rent-seeking and other unproductive (what I call directly unproductive profit-seeking, i.e. DUP) activities, generally weakens the case for such departures.

But the former set of developments has achieved greater currency recently. This is only partly because they are more conventional in scope and hence more appealing to the economist's taste. In replacing the perfectly competitive by the imperfectly competitive assumption in formal modelling, utilizing the new theoretical tools from the theory of industrial organization, they amount to fitting an old bicycle with new wheels, whereas the other pro-free-trade set of developments, belonging to the new and unconventional field of political economy, constitutes a greater intellectual challenge: it amounts to taking the old bicycle down a different road.

But a key explanation also must be found in the fact that interests require the legitimacy that ideology provides. Protectionist forces, as they gathered strength in the 1970s, were looking precisely for the *coup de grâce* to free trade that a 'new' and 'more appropriate' theory of trade would provide. The trade-theoretic analysis incorporating imperfect competition in product markets seemed to provide exactly that since, as should be immediately obvious, such models of imperfect competition in repeated applications demonstrated the possibility of improving welfare by departing from free trade. And, if this fact itself could somehow be construed as a departure from what the theory of commercial policy taught, and hence as a 'new' and radical development that made the 'old' theory obsolete, the result could be electrifying. As it happens, reality has turned out to be not too far from this outlandish scenario.

It should suffice, for my purposes, to quote the latest and apparently the most meticulous and carefully crafted statement on this subject by Paul Krugman, my distinguished student at Massachusetts Institute of Technology who succeeded me in my chair there, and a leading proponent of these important developments. Writing in the new *Journal of Economic Perspectives* of the American Economic Association, where research findings are disseminated to the wider community of economists and policymakers, Krugman has this to say:

> the case for free trade is currently more in doubt than at any time since the 1817 publication of Ricardo's *Principles of Political Economy*. . . . In the last ten years the traditional constant returns, perfect competition models of international trade have been supplemented and to some extent supplanted by a new breed of models that emphasizes increasing returns and imperfect competition. These

new models . . . open the possibility that government intervention in trade via import restrictions, export subsidies, and so on may under some circumstances be in the national interest after all . . . free trade is not passé, but it is an idea that has irretrievably lost its innocence. Its status has shifted from optimum to reasonable rule of thumb. There is still a case for free trade as a good policy, and as a useful target in the world of politics, but it can never again be asserted as the policy that economic theory tells us is always right.

(Krugman 1987: 131–2)

This is surely puzzling. Not merely does the post-war theory of commercial policy, which I and others helped to shape during the 1960s and 1970s, show plainly that 'import restrictions, export subsidies, and so on, may under certain circumstances be in the national interest'. It shows also, at great length, that one cannot assert that free trade is 'the policy that economic theory tells us is always right': this is surely the core contribution of the post-war theory of distortions and welfare.[2] Moreover, the post-war theory of commercial policy goes beyond both these propositions to alert the analyst and the policymaker that, even when departures from free trade are justifiable, it is necessary to distinguish between policy interventions that are merely beneficial and those that are maximally useful – a prescription more often ignored than respected by some of the recent proponents of the theory of imperfect competition in international trade. For the sophisticated economist, who seeks to influence his nation's trade policy, some of the key questions to answer after these theoretical developments have been (i) what, in *theory*, is the nature of the appropriate intervention when departures from free trade (and domestic non-intervention) are justifiable and (ii) whether, as a matter of *empirical judgement*, your country's reality fits any of the numerous theoretically possible cases where such appropriate intervention is desirable.

Let me simply stress therefore that those who see the developments based on imperfect competition as 'radical' and 'new' in their implications for the scientific corpus of the theory of commercial policy are either unfamiliar with that theory or forgetful of its central tenets. Indeed, the recent models of imperfect competition are analytically seen best as augmenting the number of cases where the invisible hand falters and where therefore a benign government (in our conventional theory of economic policy where the government is simply and totally the puppet of the economist, speaking with his voice and acting to his command) can act to national advantage, through appropriate (domestic or trade) policy interventions. These added cases are perfectly compatible with, and indeed fit neatly and without surprise or paradox into, the impressive corpus of theoretical principles and framework that emerged as the theory of commercial policy during the post-war period.

Given then the misassessments and misconceptions that facilitate the protectionist capture of the theoretical developments based on imperfect competition,[3] and the comparative neglect of the important countervailing contributions made by the theoretical developments based on political economy, there is no task more compelling than to take a careful, scholarly look at where we should now properly stand on the issue of free trade. This, I propose to do now.

I shall consider the classical theory, the post-war contributions and the recent developments, in turn. At the outset, however, permit me to make an important, indeed a critical distinction between free trade for one and free trade for all, i.e. between *unilateral* and *universal* free trade, drawing essentially on the theory prior to the post-war period.

FREE TRADE FOR ONE

The distinction between unilateral and universal free trade is critical whether one is thinking of trade policy simply from the viewpoint of a single country's national advantage or whether one is considering the rather different question as to the nature of a trade regime for nations in the world economy. Thus, in the former case, one can ask: should a country embrace free trade even if others do not? In the latter case, however, one may consider whether a regime, such as that provided by the General Agreement on Tariffs and Trade, should involve free trade by all.

The question of regimes is a recent one. The question of a suitable trade policy for national advantage, by contrast, is a time-honoured one since the days of Adam Smith. And the answer to the latter has, for nearly two centuries, been in favour of unilateral free trade. It is important to understand exactly why.

The precept of unilateral free trade should be seen as a blend of theory and empirical judgement about the relevance of that theory and the irrelevance of the exceptions to the theory's conclusions.

The theory

Central to the theory is the notion that, given external trading opportunities, specialization and ensuing exchange would ensure gains from trade among nations engaged in voluntary transactions. It is easy to see this today. But when the early economist propagated this notion, it was in contradiction to the dominant doctrine of mercantilism.

The new science of economics focused on trade as an opportunity to specialize in production, undertake exchange of what one produced efficiently for what others produced efficiently and wind up in consequence with more rather than less. A policy of free trade would guide the nation to an efficient utilization of this trade opportunity. In essence, as post-war theorists of international trade would clarify, free trade would maximize returns by efficiently utilizing two alternative ways of securing any good: (i) through specialized production of other goods then exchanged in trade for the goods desired, and (ii) through domestic production of the desired goods oneself. Free trade would ensure that these two alternative techniques, trade and domestic production, were used efficiently, i.e. in such a mix as to produce equal returns at the margin.[4] Two critical assumptions underlie this neat conclusion – and the classical economists were cognizant of them in their own way.

First, free trade guided one to the efficient outcome only if the price mechanism worked well. Prices had to reflect true social costs. Thus it was understood, particularly after the writings of List, that infant-industry protection could be justified. In modern language, if there were future returns that could not be captured by the infant industry but would dissipate to others in the country, this market failure justified protection.

Equally, if the country's trade in a sector was large enough to confer on it the ability to affect its prices, then John Stuart Mill warned that a tariff could enable the country to restrict its trade and gain more, exactly as a monopolist can increase profits by restricting his sales. Hence this came to be known as the 'monopoly power in trade' argument for protection.

Second, the external trade opportunity had to be assumed to be independent of one's own trade policy. Suppose that, by imposing tariffs, you could pry open the protected markets of your trading partners. That could conceivably justify the use of tariffs. Unilateral free trade in that event would not be desirable. Even Adam Smith was aware of this possible qualification. Indeed, he considered [5] the question at some length:

> The case in which it may sometimes be a matter of deliberation how far it is proper to continue the free importation of certain foreign goods is, when some foreign nation restrains by high duties or prohibitions the importation of some of our manufactures into their country. Revenge in this case naturally dictates retaliation, and that we should impose the like duties and prohibitions upon the importation of some or all of their manufactures into ours. Nations accordingly seldom fail to retaliate in the manner.
>
> There may be good policy in retaliations of this kind, when there is a probability that they will procure the repeal of the high duties of

prohibitions complained of. The recovery of a great foreign market will generally more than compensate the transitory inconvenience of paying dearer during a short time for some sort of goods. To judge whether such retaliations are likely to produce such an effect, does not, perhaps belong so much to the science of the legislator, whose deliberations ought to be governed by general principles which are always the same, as to the skill of that insidious and crafty animal, vulgarly called a statesman or politician, whose councils are directed by the momentary fluctuations of affairs, When there is no probability that any such repeal can be procured, it seems a bad method of compensating the injury done to certain classes of our people to do another injury to ourselves, not only to those classes, but to almost all the other classes of them.

His scepticism on this case for retaliatory protection would be shared later by Alfred Marshall and indeed many others at the end of the nineteenth century. They recognized the theoretical possibility but none the less propagated the wisdom of unilateral free trade in practice.

Empirical judgement and the nineteenth century British debate

In the end, the intellectual case for free trade, and that too as a unilateral policy, had to rest on the empirical judgement that these exceptions were unimportant, if not theoretical *curiosa*, and further that, even if this were not so, protectionist policies based on them were likely to cause more harm than good.

This resort to empirical judgement is evident in the remarkable debate that ensued at the end of the nineteenth century when Britain, in relative decline as Germany and the USA rose in economic stature, found its longstanding unilateral free trade policy in serious jeopardy from 'reciprocitarians' who sought to match foreign tariffs with their own as a way of prying open foreign markets. The arguments marshalled at the time against the reciprocitarians, by statesmen and economists wedded to unilateralism, consisted of the following.[6]

1 The belief in the folly of protection was so complete that it was felt by many that the grievous losses on its practitioners would in themselves suffice to chastise and then induce them to embrace free trade in the end.
2 Others believed that the success of free trading Britain would set an example for other nations, ensuring diffusion of free trade policies.
3 Richard Cobden, the great crusader for repeal of the Corn Laws and adoption of free trade, went so far as to argue that insisting on reciprocal tariff reductions would only serve to make the task of free

traders abroad more difficult by implying that free trade was really in the British interest rather than their own.

4 Equally, many felt that reciprocity was not an effective instrument for securing tariff reductions abroad simply because Britain did not have the necessary economic power.

5 In addition, some feared that Britain itself was more vulnerable to retaliation than other countries.

6 Marshall even suggested that infant-industry protection justified some of the foreign tariffs of Britain's new rivals, so that reciprocity aimed at opening foreign markets was inappropriate.

7 Finally, several economists at the time were convinced that, however sound the rationale underlying the use of tariffs for reciprocity aimed at opening foreign markets, the policy would wind up being captured by protectionists and political interests.

Thus Marshall, after observing the American experience with protection which reinforced his scepticism of rational tariff intervention, felt that 'in becoming intricate it (i.e. protection) became corrupt, and tended to corrupt general politics'.[7] This was undoubtedly an early manifestation of the recent developments in the theory of political economy and international trade which replace the orthodox view that governments are benign and omnipotent with the view that their policies may reflect lobbying by pressure groups. This may lead to defects in the visible hand that outweigh ones in the invisible hand for which remedy is sought, an issue I shall consider below.

FREE TRADE FOR ALL

But this prescription of free trade as a unilateral option, popular among economists, has had little appeal outside the nineteenth century British experience. In fact, mutual and symmetric access to each other's markets, i.e. universal rather than unilateral free trade, is the guiding principle in practice. It is also embodied, in essence, in GATT's functioning, for GATT is a contractarian institution, with symmetric rights and obligations for members.

Trade regimes and free trade everywhere

As it happens, the question of which rules a trade regime should have for member states has a distinct answer in the theory of trade in favour of universal free trade. It is to be found in the cosmopolitan (as distinct from the nationalist) theory of free trade. If we apply the logic of efficiency to the allocation of activity among all trading nations, and not merely within our own nation state, it is easy enough to see that it yields the prescription of free trade everywhere. For that alone would ensure that goods and services were produced where it was cheapest to do so. The key to this conclusion then must be the notion that prices do reflect true social costs, just as it is the key to the case for free trade for one nation alone. If then any nation uses tariffs or subsidies, protection or promotion, to drive a wedge between market prices and social costs rather than to close one arising from market failure, then surely that is not consonant with an efficient world allocation of activity. The rule then emerges that free trade must apply to all.

Where therefore the nationalist theory of free trade glosses over the use of tariffs, quotas and subsidies by others, urging free trade for a nation regardless of what others do, the cosmopolitan theory requires adherence to free trade everywhere. The trade regime that we construct must then rule out artificial comparative advantage arising from interventions such as subsidies and protection. It must equally frown upon dumping in so far (and only in so far) as it is a technique used successfully for securing an otherwise untenable foothold in world markets.

National advantage and free trade everywhere: Darwinism and 'fairness'

But, even within the perspective of national advantage, it is possible to contend that unilateral free trade is politically imprudent, likely to imperil the free trade policy itself, and hence must yield to symmetry of surrender by protectionists everywhere.

This is because the unilateralist prescription is at variance with the intuitive Darwinian rationale for free trade. Think of the issue in the context of others using export subsidies while we keep our markets open and you can see immediately what I mean to convey. It is hard enough to cope with the demise of an industry in pursuit of the gains from trade if the foreigner has a market-determined advantage. But if he is backed by artificial support from his government, that is likely to raise angry questions of 'fairness'. And it surely does.

While, therefore, an economist is right to claim that, if foreign governments subsidize their exports, this is simply marvellous as we get cheaper goods and we should unilaterally continue our free trade policy, he must equally recognize that the acceptance of this position will fuel demands for protection and imperil the possibility of maintaining the legitimacy, and hence the continuation, of free trade. A free trade regime that does not reign in, or seek to regulate, artificial subventions will probably help to trigger its own demise. An analogy that I used to illustrate this unhappy 'systemic' implication of the unilateralist position in conversing with Milton Friedman on his celebrated *Free to Choose* television series is imperfect but still apt.[8] Would one be wise to receive stolen property simply because it is cheaper; or would one rather vote to prohibit such transactions because of their systemic consequences?

We have here therefore a prudential argument for universal free trade even from the vantage point of *national* advantage. It buttresses the *cosmopolitan* argument for devising a world trading order that defines and seeks the principle of free trade for all with provisions such as those permitting the appropriate use of countervailing duty and anti-dumping actions to maintain fair competitive trade.

In fact, it is notable that, as nations have turned to freer trade, they have simultaneously tended to adopt and strengthen the provisions and processes for maintaining fair trade. Historically this happened in the 1930s in the USA as, in the aftermath of the disastrous Smoot–Hawley tariff, the country moved to what would turn out to be a half-century of trade liberalization. It is also true today in the developing countries such as Mexico which are shifting under IMF and World Bank prodding to a slow renunciation of their autarkic attitudes and policies. The important question, which I cannot consider adequately today, is how we can prevent these 'fair trade' processes from turning, via capture by protectionist forces, into *de facto* instruments of protection as they have in recent times.[9]

THE POST-WAR THEORY OF COMMERCIAL POLICY

The major post-war developments in this theory of commercial policy were to appear principally from analysis addressed to the two exceptions to the case for free trade for national advantage that I explained above: (i) market failure represented by the infant-industry argument; and (ii) the presence of monopoly power in trade. The former would lead to the influential theory of policy intervention for an open economy in the presence of distortions; the latter would pave the way for a systematic analysis of strategic trade-policy initiatives. In both cases, however, the developments can be argued as having strengthened the case for free trade, but in a subtle and sophisticated sense. Let me explain.

(i) The new theoretical developments showed that the traditional case for protection when markets failed, as was the case for infant-industry protection, was weaker than had been thought. An appropriate tariff could improve welfare over free trade; but the more appropriate optimal policy intervention was a domestic one, targeted directly at the source of the market failure. The first best policy intervention in the case of domestic distortions (i.e. domestic market failure) was domestic; the tariff would only be a second-best policy. Tariffs were appropriate only when there was a foreign distortion: they were the first-best policy only when there was a monopoly power in external markets. Tariffs were thus demoted to a more limited role than in earlier theorizing.[10]

(ii) But even this 'monopoly power in trade' argument was called into question. It required the presence of non-negligible market power in international markets. The scope for its application was therefore limited to cases where significant market shares obtained and entry was difficult.[11] But, more seriously, the use of tariffs to exploit monopoly power opened up the distinct possibility of retaliation, a possibility that had only been underscored by the inter-war experience and the apparent reaction to the Smoot–Hawley tariff. Early theorists conjectured that, even though a country may reap a short-term advantage by exploiting with a tariff its market power, retaliation would leave all worse off. Later analysis, however, showed that an ultimate net gain, despite retaliation, could indeed be demonstrated as a possibility.[12] Therefore while retaliation could not be demonstrated as definitely ruling out final gain to a country adopting a tariff to exploit its monopoly in trade, that it could immiserize it and indeed others as well was also analytically established, calling into doubt the wisdom of even this time-honoured exception to the argument that a free trade policy would maximize a nation's welfare.

I have interpreted both these developments, the former already remarkable in its impact and the latter prescient in its introduction of later strategic analysis, as strengthening the pro-trade ideology. It is fair to say, however, that they, and especially the former, could well have been regarded in a different (but unsophisticated and wrong-headed) light as strengthening the protectionist hand instead. For, if you were to read the massive literature that grew up on the theory of distortions and welfare during the 1960s and 1970s, you would have found repeated analysis of market failures of one kind or another. Since some of the recent proponents of imperfect competition seem to suffer from amnesia even about matters only a decade old, it is necessary to recall the many contributions to the analysis of market failures arising from monopoly, factor market imperfections (such as monopsony, exogenous and endogenous wage differentials, and sticky wages), increasing returns etc. that dominated the post-war analysis of commercial policy. If you then came away with the impression that market failure was all-pervasive, and that free trade made little sense, you could be excused. But you would also be betraying yourself as a careless economist who missed the central overriding pro-free-trade message: that domestic market failures were best dealt with, not by trade-policy interventions, but by choosing domestic policies tailor-made to assist and countervail the market failure as its source.[13]

RECENT DEVELOPMENTS: POLITICAL ECONOMY AND DIRECTLY UNPRODUCTIVE PROFIT-SEEKING ACTIVITIES

But if the case for free trade was strengthened in this subtle fashion, it was to be assisted yet further by important developments in the theory of commercial policy that came from the direction of political economy in the late 1970s.

You will recall that the post-war theory of commercial policy had shifted the focus away from protection for all market failures to domestic intervention (and hence continued free trade) for all failures of domestic origin (i.e. for domestic distortions). But this left intact the case for *appropriate* intervention in all cases of market failure. And underlying this case was the view of the conventional theory of economic policy that the state was merely and exclusively an instrument for executing the policy recommendations of the economist, with no will or character of its own: what I have recently called (Bhagwati 1989) the puppet government assumption where the economist pulls all the strings according to instructions yielded by his policy analysis. Therefore, the case for free trade could be strengthened yet further if we could argue as follows.

1 Market failures were unimportant and/or self-correcting, hence needing no intervention at all.
2 The puppet government view was an irrelevance and, when it was replaced by a more realistic view of the government as affected by pressure groups, the intervention was likely to be, not appropriate in keeping with the economist's recommendations, but perverse instead.
3 The cost of such perverse interventions was greater than conventional analysis suggested, once the costs of intervention-induced unproductive DUP activities were taken into consideration.

Let me address each of these arguments in turn.

The theorists of commercial policy have not generally been associated with the first line of defence of free trade above. Admittedly, some subscribe to the witticism that externalities, and hence promotion rather than *laissez faire* as the policy prescription, are the last refuge of the scoundrels, and others to its sequel that they are the *first* refuge instead.

But many would be prepared to concede that externalities may well be important. Nor is it possible to find many adherents of the view that the Coase theorem's scope is sufficiently great to internalize all important externalities.

By contrast, the theorists of commercial policy have explored systematically the latter two lines of inquiry distinguished above, each relating to different aspects of political economy, and both leading to a possible new defence of the merits of free trade.

Many recent theoretical writings on trade policy have replaced the puppet government assumption of endogenizing policy. Thus, governments have been modelled as autonomous agents with objectives of their own: what I call the self-willed government assumption. Alternatively, at another extreme, they have been modelled as simply an arena where lobbies clash over policy: this is the clearinghouse government assumption. In either case, or combination thereof, the government is rescued from its fictitious and emasculated role as the economist's echo or sounding board.

When policy is so endogenized, the possibility arises that intervention, instead of being consonant with the economist's benign recommendations, is perverse. It obviously cannot be argued that this is necessarily, or overwhelmingly, so. But, in the case of tariff policy, a case may be made along the following lines (though I advance no formal proof here).

Recall that, in the absence of retaliation and the presence of 'monopoly power in trade', there is a case for an optimal tariff for national advantage. Heuristically speaking, therefore, we would expect a benign, puppet government to levy higher tariffs on goods in inelastic world markets than on goods in elastic markets. But if pressure group lobbying leads to tariff formation, and if the demand for tariff protection is greater in goods which are in highly elastic foreign supply (e.g. textiles) and hence highly competitive but less in goods with rising foreign supply price where there is therefore 'natural' protection against substantial entry by foreign rivals, the endogenous tariff structure with a clearinghouse government may well be exactly the opposite of that which the conventional economist would like from a benign puppet government.

But the endogenization of trade policy in recent theoretical work has played a substantially more dramatic role in the case for free trade than the foregoing possibility of perverse intervention would indicate.

This it has done by demonstrating that the cost of (erroneous, welfare-worsening) protection is greater, possibly significantly greater, than the conventional theory suggested. This demonstration is a direct consequence of what we now call the theory of DUP activities (Bhagwati

1982a). These are activities which constitute 'unproductive' ways of making an income so that they use resources to produce income (or profit) but no socially valued output. Such DUP activities in trade policy, pertinent to my theme, can be distinguished into two major analytical groups, defining them relative to any given policy of import protection, for example:

1 downstream activities, e.g. lobbying for the premium or windfall rents carried by import quotas (what Krueger (1974) has graphically called rent-seeking) or its counterpart for tariff revenues (what I and Srinivasan (1980) have called revenue-seeking) (these downstream activities can arise whether the protection is exogenous or endogenous, of course); and

2 upstream activities, e.g. lobbying aimed at making (or opposing) protection, since its presence (or absence) will affect the income earned in productive activity (these are of course the activities that result in endogenizing trade policy).

It has thus become customary now to add to the conventional Harberger–Johnson–Meade 'triangle' estimates of the deadweight cost of protection (which have been dismally low and singularly unfit as a weapon to fight protectionism on the ground that it is expensive) two further costs: from the upstream DUP-theoretic estimate of protection-seeking that precedes the protection and from the downstream DUP-theoretic estimate of rent-seeking or revenue-seeking that follows the protection.

Of these two new arguments for augmenting the case against protection by adding to its cost, however, I should now stress that the downstream variety is the more robust whereas the upstream variety raises serious conceptual difficulties which must make us pause. I will explain.

The *downstream* DUP-theoretic costs are certainly an important matter, as is evident even to the naked eye. In fact, they were suggested to Tullock (1967), Krueger (1974) and me (Bhagwati 1973), all of whom have theorized about them, during exposure to rent-seeking and revenue-seeking activities in developing countries. But I must also confess that the body of scientific literature that has now grown up on this theme suggests that the early presumptions in DUP theory that these added costs would be extremely large have given way to more modest expectations for at least two reasons.

First, the earliest estimates, particularly by Krueger (1974) in her seminal work, assumed that rent-seeking would lead to (market value) losses as large as the rent being sought: an eye for an eye, a dollar lost for a dollar chased. This presupposes open competition among risk-neutral lobbyists. But, in reality, the brother-in-law theorem often applies: the brother-in-law usually has a better chance of getting the licence and the rent it fetches, and so it deters others from expending as many resources on rent-seeking as perfect competition would imply.[14]

Second, market losses are not necessarily social losses to society. If the import quotas have strongly distorted domestic allocation to begin with, the market price of a dollar's worth of resources diverted to rent-seeking aimed at the import quotas is not its true social cost at all. In fact, in 'highly distorted' economies, such resource diversion while directly unproductive, may paradoxically improve welfare indirectly.[15] In jargon, the shadow use into unproductive DUP activity could be negative.[16] While there are countless such observations of 'value sub-traction' in productive activities, when social costs and values rather than market prices are used to make estimates, this is undoubtedly an extreme phenomenon. Suffice it to say that the social cost of rent-seeking is likely, in distorted economies, to be below its nominal market cost.

But let me stress that, with both these *caveats* duly noted, this literature does strengthen the anti-protectionist hand.

The *upstream* DUP-theoretic costs would equally suggest an augmentation of the cost of protection. After all, if resources have been used in lobbying for protection, should we not add that cost also to the deadweight cost of protection?

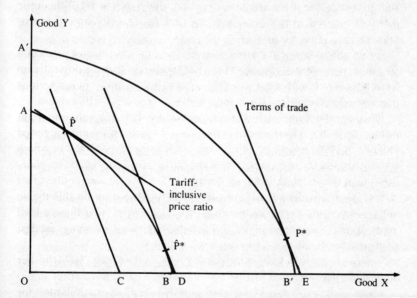

Figure 2.1

This seems logical, at first sight. Thus, in Figure 2.1, once resources have been used up in creating an endogenous tariff, the resources available for productive activity (producing goods X and Y) shrink, and so does the production possibility curve from A′B′ to AB. The given terms of trade, for this small country, define the free trade optimal production at P*. The endogenous-tariff production is at P̂. Now, the deadweight (production) cost of protection is measured in Hicksian equivalent-variational terms as CD, since the production at undistorted terms of trade (*and* with resources lost to lobbying for and against the tariff) would be at P̂*. But if these resources were also restored to productive use, the economy would operate at P*. Therefore the lobbying cost is DE. The total cost of production is therefore

CD	+	DE	=	CE
(deadweight loss)		(DUP-theoretic lobbying cost)		(total cost of protection)

The only question would then seem to be whether empirically DE is a substantial figure. But there is a problem. For, as soon as you endogenize policy upstream, you can lose the degree of freedom to vary policy as in conventional puppet government theory. The optimal free trade policy at P* cannot meaningfully be compared with the tariff at P̂ as in conventional analysis of rank-ordering of policies, for the augmented political-economic system yields the tariff at P̂ as the policy that will emerge in this economy. To take free trade policy at P* as the reference point for measuring the cost of protection is then to impose back on the system a DUP-activity-free economy, wiping out the 'political' part of the economy. This would make as much sense as saying: let us compare P̂ with what would emerge as the equilibrium production if economic constraints were relaxed!

Upstream DUP-theoretic endogenization of policy then raises a fundamental difficulty. The theory of economic policy runs forthwith into what I have called the determinacy paradox: endogenizing (upstream) policy generally removes the degree of freedom to vary policy interventions (Bhagwati *et al.* 1984; Bhagwati 1987).

It is clear to me then that the impulse to add the *upstream-lobbying* costs to the conventional deadweight losses is conceptually treacherous. The implications of endogenous policy modelling of the upstream variety can be fruitfully found instead in other ways which can turn the theory of commercial policy in novel directions. Let me differentiate between two different such ways.

First, while one cannot now meaningfully vary economic policy and rank alternative policies, one can ask other *variational* questions – for example, how will welfare change (from $\hat{P}$ in Figure 2.1) if a parametric change such as improved terms of trade occurs? Thus, whereas conventional puppet government analysis would have rank-ordered different policies as efficient responses to the changed terms of trade, the new endogenous-policy approach would solve for the new policy that would emerge in response to the changed terms of trade and then would be able to evaluate whether welfare had improved or worsened (using the preferred welfare criterion). Prediction rather than prescription would then be the essence of this approach to economic policy.

Second, however, there still remains one key way in which prescription can be rescued from total elimination by the determinacy paradox. Think of variational questions, not from the economic side of the economic model augmented by equations for the political process that endognize (upstream) policy, but rather from the political side. Suppose, for instance, that the spread of ideas and ideology makes the cost of lobbying for a tariff greater: the government, converted to a free trade bias, resists protectionist lobbying more strenuously. We could then analyse the welfare impact in this 'regress' in the production function' for a tariff. Alternatively, imagine that the institutional structure changes, in consequence of a cataclysm such as economic disaster or war, so that the cost of tariff-making changes. Once again, the consequence of this change on welfare could be analysed within the specified model of the economic-cum-political process.

But as soon as you do this, the way opens to ask: if alternative institutional structures which bear on the final (endogenous) policy change could be specified, could we then not rank-order these institutional structures themselves?

There is, of course, the important question of how these institutional arrangements will be chosen in pluralistic societies. If we were to judge one such set to be more conducive to social welfare and hence preferable to another, the question still arises: how will we transit to the preferred set from the one we have as the initial condition? From this perspective, the notion that 'constitutional amendments' should be undertaken to choose and freeze the optimal institutional choice for policy-making may often be only begging the question.[17]

But it remains useful none the less to ask: how would one institutional set-up rank-order *vis-à-vis* another, if we had either in place and no lobbying resources were devoted to changing it (e.g. because the constitution is framed in a way which makes such lobbying too expensive). This may then be regarded as an exercise in the comparative dynamics of alternative institutions, with the question of the transition path from one steady state to another left out of the analysis.

Four examples of such comparative institutional analysis by policy analysts in international trade should illustrate well this new set of developments. Each relates to the effect of alternative institutional arrangements on the degree of protection that will emerge in the economy.

(i) The first example relates to the shift in tariff-making authority from the US Congress to the Executive following the cataclysm precipitated by the Smoot–Hawley tariff in 1930. Nearly half a century of trade liberalization followed. Among the causes cited is the fact that the Congress is necessarily more responsive to constituency pressure for tariffs whereas the executive does not have to be. The institutional change to tariff-making by the Executive therefore shifts the 'supply' of protection by the government to the left and, given any demand for protection by protectionist lobbies, reduces (increases) the protection (liberalization) that will emerge.

(ii) The USA also shifted in 1934 from tariff-making in Congress to 'administered protection' under which protection had to be sought by an industry or firm by going through 'rule-oriented' administrative bodies such as the International Trade Commission which would determine whether, according to the rules defined, the party seeking protection should be granted protection. This meant that the net demand for protection again diminished for subtle reasons. Earlier, congressmen had yielded to constituency pressure to enact, as in Smoot-Hawley, made-to-order tariffs for constituents in a process of log-rolling where each congressman was permitted self-indulgence by the other in an atmosphere of what Schattschneider, the great historian of the Smoot–Hawley tariff, has called 'reciprocal noninterference'. Once the protectionist lobby had to go by the rules, however, the lobbying had to seek changes in the rules themselves. But this then precipitated anti-tariff lobbying, since rule change inevitably attracted such debate and competitive lobbying from mutually opposed pro-trade and anti-trade lobbies. Therefore, with the net demand for protection thus falling under the shift to a rule-oriented institutional structure for tariff-making, the amount of protection actually materializing could be expected to fall, *ceteris paribus.*[18]

(iii) Yet another example is provided by the comparison that Rodrik (1986) has undertaken of tariffs and subsidies as policy instruments for protecting an industry. Now, tariffs are generally considered to be less desirable for this purpose in the conventional theory of commercial policy because they protect an industry by adding a gratuitous consumption cost in the process (Bhagwati and Ramaswami 1963; Johnson 1965). Suppose, however, that we were to allow the protection to be determined endogenously. Suppose next that subsidies are tailor-made for each firm whereas tariffs cannot differentiate between firms and must be given to an industry generally. In that case, the free-rider problem will afflict the demand for tariff protection but not the demand for subsidy protection. The demand for protection therefore will be less in a regime where subsidies are granted than in a regime where tariffs are granted. Therefore, given the same resistance to protection by the government, the protection emerging will be less under a tariff regime than under a subsidies regime. Of course, before anyone rushes in to act on this insight, it should be remembered that (i) even if the protection with tariffs is less, its total cost may be greater because tariffs carry the consumption cost that subsidies do not; (ii) the tariffs may be *supplied* more readily by governments (who see their effects on revenues as beneficial and the loss of revenue from subsidies as a problem instead), and (iii) in reality, tariffs in many countries are adjusted to sufficient detail to be firm specific as required whereas subsidies entirely specific to a firm (as in the case of 'bailouts') are not very common. None the less, the argument illustrates well the kind of question that theorists of commercial policy, as they grapple with the invigorating influx of political-economy-theoretic considerations, are now addressing.

(iv) Finally, it has now become manifest that the institutional structure of 'administered protection' is designed in a fashion that does not balance the protectionist and anti-protectionist forces evenly but is in fact biased in favour of protection. Thus, for instance, the anti-dumping and counter-vailing subsidy mechanisms do not permit the weighing of consumer interests: those are typically left to the end of the process (in the USA, by the President) while the opening salvos in the game are left to be fired only by the industry or firm seeking protection. The failure to have impartial multilateral panels to determine the outcomes of complaints of unfair trading practices such as dumping and foreign subsidies that often lead to protection also facilitates protectionist capture of these 'fair trade' processes.

All of this translates into a greater effective demand for protection, and into more protection *ceteris paribus*. Many international economists (Finger 1982; Willet 1984; Baldwin 1985; Bhagwati 1988) have therefore called for a variety of institutional reforms so as to give pro-trade forces a fairer chance of success than they have had to date.

I have concentrated here on the 'theory of commercial policy' implications of the new developments in the political-economy analysis of international trade. But the prognosis, explanation and prediction components of these developments are equally exciting and can bring altogether new perspectives on old problems.[19]

This can be illustrated well by the recent theory of *quid pro quo* direct foreign investment (DFI) (Bhagwati 1985, 1986). In this theory, DFI is undertaken in response to the threat of protection, not with a view to 'jumping' the anticipated protection but with a view to *defusing* that threat. This reduction of the protectionist threat can follow because either the supply of protection by the host government is reduced due to the 'good-will effect' of the DFI or the demand for it is reduced because host-country firms and/or unions, the agents seeking protection, are co-opted by the DFI into not pushing for protection against foreign competition. For instance, consider the case where Toyota and General Motors have a joint venture in the USA. Toyota makes an otherwise unremunerative DFI which helps GM while the *quid pro quo* for Toyota is that GM breaks ranks with other US car makers later by opposing the renewal of voluntary export restraints (VERs). First-period losses on DFI in the USA (compared with exporting more Toyotas to the USA) are then balanced against second-period gains that follow from the resulting reduction in the probability of renewal of US VERs on Japanese cars.

This type of *quid pro quo* DFI has certainly been manifest in the USA–Japan context recently and has been modelled in the competitive context by Bhagwati *et al.* (1987) and in the oligopolistic context by Dinopoulos (1989) and Wong (1989). It represents an altogether novel way in which political processes play an essential role in inducing profit-seeking DFI. It is an example of the power and originality that the new political-economy-theoretic approach has to offer us.

RECENT DEVELOPMENTS: INCREASING RETURNS, MARKET STRUCTURE AND STRATEGIC TRADE POLICY

To return to the theory of commercial policy, however, the recent developments also include progress from an altogether different direction. Inspired by the theory of industrial organization and new solution concepts in game-theoretic formulation, several trade theorists also turned their attention during the 1980s to models of imperfect competition in product markets, whose rationale lay in the phenomenon of economies of scale (internal to the firm).

Economies of scale, external to the firm but internal to the industry, are compatible with perfect competition. But they can result in loss of convexity with well-known consequences (e.g. Kemp 1964; Panagariya 1980) such as wrong specialization, suboptimality of free trade etc. depending on how precisely increasing returns operate. Such economies of scale can therefore justify an appropriate intervention to assist the invisible hand. Again, careful scholars have known that, when multiple equilibria arise under increasing returns, identical economies can have trade, and indeed beneficial trade; and reversed trade patterns are also demonstrable as possible multiple equilibria (e.g. Kemp 1964).

The recent developments, with similar results, assume on the other hand that increasing returns are internal to the firm. If such returns are large relative to the size of the market, evidently perfect competition will break down (as noted by Sraffa and Kaldor over four decades ago). The resulting imperfect competition can take the form of the large-group or the oligopolistic small-group case distinguished by Edward Chamberlain and Joan Robinson.

The *large group* case is less interesting in terms of its implications for commercial policy. Since Chamberlain's analysis, we have known that the implication of monopolistic competition is that market failure characterizes *laissez faire*. Recent analytical developments, to be attributed most to Helpman and Krugman, drawing in turn on the pioneering work of Lancaster (1966, 1980) on the one hand and Dixit and Stiglitz (1977) on the other, have enabled us to examine the issue more fully. In particular, as Lancaster's neo-Hotelling modelling of taste diversity underlines forcefully, the combination of increasing returns and taste diversity can lead to outcomes where the market leads to a suboptimal result: one where the exploitation of economies of scale in a limited range of products must be set against loss of product diversity, and the market outcome may therefore be improved upon.

But once again, the theory of commercial policy, as it evolved during the 1960s and 1970s, requires us to distinguish between different questions: is free trade better than autarky; is trade policy intervention welfare-improving; and is trade policy intervention the ideal (first-best) intervention or is domestic policy intervention (or a mix of the two) yet better and more appropriate? The general answers here must be that, first, free trade is not necessarily better than autarky (this is simply a further instance of the proposition that free trade and autarky cannot be rank-ordered in the presence of distortions (Haberler 1950), which is in turn explained also as an instance of the theory of immiserizing growth (Bhagwati 1971)) and that, second, trade policy intervention could improve welfare.[20]

But the question of *optimal* policy intervention remains more complex. Since, in an open economy, the variety-cum-increasing returns model of imperfect competition should generally imply both a domestic and a foreign distortion (Bhagwati 1971) it would follow that the optimal intervention would be a mix of trade and domestic policy interventions.[21]

But for all the questions discussed above, it is important to remember that free trade may well have eliminated the problem of monopolistic competition by addding sufficiently to the size of the market in all sectors relative to increasing returns, and that trade restrictions may themselves be a source of the particular market failure for a country. My guess is therefore that few economists are likely to argue for the adoption of policy departures from free trade because of the large-group case.

The matter is somewhat different for the *small-group* case. In oligopolistic markets, where strategic interactions between firms are likely, and firms can earn excess profits, free trade is evidently not optimal. As has been emphasized by Brander and Spencer (1981), in this situation, governmental intervention can shift production and therefore associated excess profits to one's own firms by altering the terms of competition among firms in different countries.

Theoretically, this case is sound. It is not surprising either. With oligopoly, prices do not generally reflect social costs; therefore free trade cannot generally be better than autarky or be optimal.

Strategic interaction amongst firms must also arise; the analysis is more complex than, but none the less, in the spirit of, the pioneering Johnson analysis of strategic interaction of governments. For, in the Johnson analysis, the firms are competitive but the two governments are in strategic interaction (though Johnson's analysis was entirely in terms of Cournot–Nash strategy), whereas now there are at least four actors who can engage in strategic interaction: the two governments and the two firms (though the current analyses usually confine the strategic interaction only to the firms).

These analyses construct simple examples of strategic interaction between firms, with government policy undertaken often as a once-for-all intervention to influence the terms of inter-firm competition, to show how free trade can be improved upon.[22]

There is no denying that, where perfect competition does not prevail, free trade will not be optimal – there is no new insight here, of course. The interesting policy question is rather whether in this class of cases, where oligopoly is important and excess profits obtain, governments intervene to increase national welfare.

The problem here, recognized by some of the more careful analysts of this class of cases, is that the precise intervention that will improve welfare depends critically on the nature of the strategic interaction between the oligopolistic firms. Thus, consider the highly simplified model[23] where two firms, one domestic and one foreign, produce a homogeneous product only for a third market where they may compete. Here, an export subsidy is socially optimal if the firms follow the (Cournot–Nash) strategy where each firm selects its optimal level of output taking the output of the rival as given. But if, in the very same model, we were to assume that, rather than choosing output levels and letting prices adjust correspondingly, the firms engage instead in the (Bertrand) strategy of setting prices and letting outputs adjust to the demands at those prices, the prescription for an intervention turns from an export subsidy into an export tax.[24]

This sensitivity, or lack of robustness, of the policy interventions to the assumptions on the nature of oligopolistic strategic interaction creates information requirements for policy intervention that appear to many of the architects of this theoretical innovation to be sufficiently intimidating to suggest that policy makers had better leave it alone.[25] This viewpoint is further reinforced for them by doubts whether there are indeed (excess) profits to be shifted through such intervention. As Grossman has put it cogently:

> Often what appears to be an especially high rate of profit is just a return to some earlier, risky investment. Research and development expenses, for example, can be quite large, and many ventures end in failure. Firms will only undertake these large investments if they can reap the benefits in those instances where they succeed. Once the market is in operation, we will of course only observe those companies that have succeeded. We may then be tempted to conclude that profit rates are unusually high. But industry profits should be measured inclusive of the losses of those who never make it to the marketing stage.
>
> (Grossman 1986: 57)

The practical application of the new and theoretically valid increasing-returns-based argument for policy intervention to shift profits towards oneself in oligopolistic industries is therefore beset with difficulties.

These are further compounded, as was the classical theoretical prescription for an optimal tariff, by the fact that the new case for export subsidization or import tariffs[26] is equally based on considerations of national advantage and presupposes that foreign governments do not retaliate.[27] As with the unilateral exercise of an optimal tariff to exploit monopoly power in trade, the asymmetric unilateral use of export subsidies or import tariffs in oligopolistic industries to gain competitive edge and possibly shift profits to advantage by a government is, however, likely to invite retaliation from aggrieved trading partners.

In fact, such retaliation is more likely in precisely the knowledge-intensive high-technology industries where economies of scale relative to world markets are presumed by the proponents of these new theories to be significant, for these industries are widely regarded as important in themselves. Their location behind one's own borders is supposed frequently to be a matter of securing broader political and economic benefits, just as manufacturing generally was regarded by developing countries during the post-war years. Foreign governmental intervention, regardless of whether profit-sharing-related advantages exist or not, is generally seen therefore as an attempt to get a larger share of this important pie than is warranted by legitimate market forces. This is surely a major reason behind the sensitivity of the USA on this question as asymmetrical predatory governmental interventions in such industries are alleged for Japan and retaliatory action is sought concerning them.

If such retaliation occurs, then it is not beyond the ingenuity of economists to construct cases where it would still leave the country which initiated the profit-shifting game better off. But, as with the earlier retaliation analysis of the optimal tariff for exploiting monopoly power, the competitive retaliatory policies provoked by attempts at profit-shifting are likely to leave each country worse off, especially if such actions spill over into other areas of trade policy or drag into the game other players simply because of the multilateral aspects of international trade.

To shift the perspective, however, should such retaliation be encouraged, or even embodied in one's national trade policy?

This has been recommended by some who build on Axelrod's (1981) celebrated advocacy of tit-for-tat strategy to induce non-predatory co-operative behaviour (after repeated games) by recalcitrant game players.[28] Under this strategy, the USA would play fair on the first move and then retaliate if Japan next makes a predatory move, matching whatever move Japan makes. The problems with applying such strategies to trade policy are legion and invalidate in my view the relevance of the Axelrod prescription. In particular, bilateral determination of the other player's fairness may be confidently expected to lean towards being self-serving: what is tit and what is tat becomes problematic and contentious. A tat, unfairly alleged, and retaliated against with a tit, will invite resentment and probably generate trade skirmishes rather than take one down the benign co-operative route that Axelrod conjures up for our acceptance. Indeed, in a protectionist climate such as today's, tats are likely to be found readily and charged against successful rivals and the Axelrod strategy is likely to be captured by those who seek protectionism, as is evident from the efforts by US producers of semiconductor chips to gain guaranteed access to Japan markets and to regulate competition in third markets too.[29]

For such reasons, I am strongly opposed to strategic trade policy-making, whether to shift profits to oneself or to retaliate against rivals allegedly doing this. To recapitulate: (i) the case itself is limited to a few sectors where world markets are significantly small relative to economies of scale; (ii) there are theoretical exceptions to it, as with earlier strategic-trade-policy analysis of governmental interventions, once governments can retaliate, i.e. act strategically among themselves; (iii) the information requirements for suitable interventions, regardless of retaliation, are complex and outcomes are unusually sensitive to governments making the correct guesses and choices; and (iv) the protectionist capture of this market is usually easy in the high-technology R&D-intensive industries to which it is allegedly applicable precisely because most governments want these industries because of an implicit belief in the economic and political advantages of having them at any cost, making the resistance to protectionist demands therefore less likely.

CONCLUDING OBSERVATIONS

In conclusion, let me reiterate that certain developments make the case for free trade more robust whereas others make it less so. The former are more interesting and compelling, however, and the latter are subject to many difficulties and dangers as one passes from the classroom to the corridors of policy-making and suggest strongly that common sense and wisdom should prevail in favour of free trade.

The case for free trade, as brought up-to-date from 1817 to 1987, is therefore alive and well. This is not to say that we have not learned its strengths and weaknesses, its nuances and subtleties, with greater understanding in light of the new developments. If we remain convinced of the virtues of free trade, it is then not in the spirit of Robert Frost's affirmation of the virtue of belief:

> . . . why abandon a belief
> merely because it ceases to be true.
> Cling to it long enough, and not a doubt
> It will turn true again, for so it goes.

Rather, it is the spirit of T.S. Eliot:

> We shall not cease from exploration
> And the end of all our exploring
> Will be to arrive where we started
> And know the place for the first time.

NOTES

1 This is the text of the acceptance speech on the occasion of the award of the Bernhard Harms Prize at the Kiel Institute, Germany, on 25 June 1988. I should like to thank Martin Wolf for having long encouraged me to

put the theory of commercial policy in perspective and to evaluate recent developments, focusing on all of them rather than only those related to imperfect competition. I have profited (if inadequately) from the comments received from Richard Brecher, Robert Feenstra, Douglas Irwin, Larry Summers, T.N. Srinivasan, Alasdair Smith, Martin Wolf and Aaron Tornell. I have retained, for publication, the informal lecturing style, keeping references to a minimum. I therefore seek indulgence from many whose work I have profited from over the years but have not given explicit credit to here.

2 As I have argued below, a careful grasp of even the classical theory of gains from trade would not lead one to conclude that 'economic theory' makes free trade 'always right'. I might add also that it is historically inaccurate to think that there has been no loss of belief in free trade as a good policy in practice, i.e. that the premises leading to the case for free trade are not empirically valid. The most compelling such loss of belief occurred, as Hicks reminded us in the 1950s, during the years following the Great Depression, with Keynes among the many converts. Evidently, it made no sense to argue the virtues of a free trade policy in conditions of massive unemployment: market prices no longer reflected social costs.

3 The capture follows from the fact that if it is wrongly asserted that the theorists of commercial policy, who in fact wrote many volumes and over a hundred scientific papers during the post-war period on the appropriate nature of policy intervention and departure from free trade, were *doctrinaire* believers in free trade and that it took the 'new' developments in the 1980s to save us from their unfortunate belief in the virtue of free trade derived from *inappropriate* scientific argumentation, then protectionists will happily reject that important body of scientific work and those theorists and proceed to assert that 'new' and 'more appropriate' theories have 'finally' shown that protection can be scientifically sound and therefore should be pursued.

4 For a formal statement of these theoretical principles, most textual expositions should suffice. See, for example, Bhagwati and Srinivasan (1983: Ch. 17).

5 Cf. Smith (1937: 434–5). In principle, retaliation against exercise of one's monopoly power in trade also implies that the external trade opportunity is not dependent of one's policy. But this question was not raised, to my knowledge, in classical writings and I deal with it later in the context of post-war developments in the theory of commercial policy since it was considered then.

6 For more detailed discussion, see my 1987 Ohlin Lectures (Bhagwati 1988).

7 Cited in Bhagwati (1988).

8 The analogy is imperfect because the systemic effects in the two cases arise from phenomena with altogether different ethical implications. It is apt because the parallel lies in the systemic consequences of the pursuit of immediate price advantage.

9 I have addressed this question at some length in the Ohlin Lectures (Bhagwati 1988).

10 The post-war developments in the theory of commercial policy, as stated here, have been the work of many theorists, including Harry Johnson, T.N. Srinivasan and Max Corden. But they originated in two independent contributions: the *Journal of Political Economy* article of Bhagwati and

Ramaswami (1963) and Meade's (1955) volume on *Trade and Welfare*. For an excellent statement of the basic theory, see Johnson (1965); and for a synthesis and generalization, consult Bhagwati (1971).

11 I should emphasize that economists today would see the applicability of this exception as wider in scope than we believed in the 1950s, extending to industrial products and not just primary products such as jute and oil.

12 Scitovsky (1941) had conjectured the immiserization of all. Using a Cournot–Nash tariff-retaliation model, Johnson (1953) demonstrated the possibility of a final net gain none the less. Rodriguez (1974) showed that the Johnson analysis with quotas substituting for tariffs would restore Scitovsky's conjecture. For an excellent review of this literature, see McMillan (1986).

13 Of course, a trade policy can generally be decomposed into a sum of domestic policies. For example, a tariff of final goods is equivalent to a production tax-cum-subsidy plus a consumption tax-cum-subsidy, as noted in Johnson (1965) and elsewhere.

14 In turn, this presumption itself must be somewhat qualified since there could be resources spent on becoming the brother-in-law: an arduous exercise, I am sure. See also the recent analysis of Hillman and Riley (1989) which casts further light on the issue of how significant the rent-seeking losses may be in practice.

15 See Bhagwati and Srinivasan (1980), in particular.

16 Theoretically, this observation is of profound importance, for it means that, contrary to the practice of Buchanan (1980) and many others in the public-choice school, it is not meaningful to *define* unproductive activities as necessarily welfare-worsening. I have therefore used the adjective 'directly' to qualify these unproductive profit-seeking activities: for, indirectly or in ultimate outcome, they may improve welfare. Hence I use the phrase DUP activities to describe the generic set of activities which use resources and produce income but zero output. On these questions which affect critically the untenable equation of direct and ultimate waste in *both* the public-choice school and the long-standing discussions since Adam Smith and Marx of the concept of unproductive labour and activities, see Bhagwati (1980, 1982a, 1983).

17 Assuming that the 'original' constitution is devised according to one rule or the other is tantamount to assuming a puppet government. It makes approximate sense only in cases where, in a newly independent country, a constituent assembly is devising a Constitution with which the country is to be endowed.

18 See Bhagwati (1988: 42). Nelson (1987) has developed these styles of argumentation on administered protection.

19 There is now a growing body of literature, for instance, on models of tariff-making (Brock and Magee 1978; Feenstra and Bhagwati 1982; Findlay and Wellisz 1982; Mayer 1984), on the endogenous choice between alternative policy responses to import competition (Bhagwati 1982b; Dinopoulos 1983; Sapir 1983) and on the endogenous choice between tariffs and subsidies (Mayer and Rietzman 1987, 1989).

20 Since both foreign and domestic interventions are likely to be involved simultaneously in this case, it should not generally be possible to argue that trade policy intervention by itself would *necessarily* improve welfare.

See Bhagwati *et al.* (1969: Proposition 2).
21 A recent analysis of the nature of optimal intervention in imperfect competition is given by Krishna and Thursby (1988).
22 The question of strategic interaction between an oligopolistic firm and its own government in the game of seeking and permitting protection may lead to pro-free-trade outcomes, however (cf. Tornell 1987).
23 This is originally due to Brander and Spencer (1981), pioneers in this area.
24 This is elegantly demonstrated in the context of conjectural-variation models by Eaton and Grossman (1986).
25 There are informational requirements to be sure, when conventional interventions for market failure are recommended. In this instance, however, we need information on behavioural assumptions which seem hard to track down. Attempts by Rodrik (1987) and others recently to provide guidelines or rules of thumb to make meaningful inferences of this kind are extremely interesting but not persuasive to me.
26 Import tariffs can also shift profits, while gaining for the protected industry economies of scale that give it competitive advantage *vis-à-vis* foreign firms that are then denied access to this segment of the world market (cf. Krugman 1984).
27 Strategic interaction is entirely confined to governments in conventional analysis because firms are oligopolistic.
28 See, in particular, Goldstein and Krasner (1984).
29 For a useful analysis of other limitations of the Axelrod strategy in trade policy-making, see Brander (1986). I should emphasize, in particular, that the Axelrod strategy, as originally analysed, works with two players who are as long-lived as the repeated games they play. By contrast, trade involves typically more than two players and, in democracies in particular, the players change with changes in governments and in bureaucracies.

REFERENCES

Axelrod, R. (1981) 'The emergence of cooperation among egoists', *American Political Science Review* 75: 308–18.
Baldwin, R. (1985) *The Political Economy of U.S. Import Policy*, Cambridge, MA. MIT Press.
Bhagwati, J.N. (1971) 'The generalized theory of distortions and welfare', in J.N. Bhagwati, R.W. Jones, R.A. Mundell and J. Vanek (eds) *Trade, Balance of Payments, and Growth*, Amsterdam: North-Holland, pp. 69–90.
—— (1973) *India in the International Economy: A Policy Framework for a Progressive Society*, Lal Bahadur Shastri Memorial Lectures, Hyderabad.
—— (1980) 'Lobbying and welfare', *Journal of Public Economics* 14: 355–63.
—— (1982a) 'Directly-unproductive, profit-seeking (DUP) activities', *Journal of Political Economy* 90: 988–1002.
—— (ed.) (1982b) *Import Competition and Response*, Chicago, IL: National Bureau of Economic Research.
—— (1983) 'DUP activities and rent seeking', *Kyklos* 36: 634–7.
—— (1985) 'Protectionism: old wine in new bottles', *Journal of Policy Modelling* 7: 23–34.
—— (1986) *Investing Abroad*, Esmee Fairbairn Lecture, University of Lancaster.

—— (1987) 'Directly-unproductive profit-seeking activities', in J. Eatwell, M. Milgate and P. Newman (eds) *The New Palgrave Dictionary of Economics*, London: Macmillan, pp. 845–7.

—— (1988) *Protectionism*, Cambridge, MA. MIT Press.

—— (1989) 'The theory of political economy, economic policy and foreign investment', in D. Lal and M.F. Scott (eds) *Essays in Honor of I.M.D. Little*, Oxford, forthcoming.

—— and Ramaswami, V.K. (1963) 'Domestic distortions, tariffs, and the theory of optimum subsidy', *Journal of Political Economy*, 71: 44–50.

—— and Srinivasan, T.N. (1980) 'Revenue seeking: a generalization of the theory of tariffs', *Journal of Political Economy* 88: 1069–87.

—— and —— (1983) *Lectures on International Trade*, Cambridge, MA. MIT Press.

—— Ramaswami, V.K. and Srinivasan, T.N. (1969) 'Domestic distortions, tariffs and the theory of the optimum subsidy: some further results', *Journal of Political Economy* 77: 1005–10.

—— Brecher, R. and Srinivasan, T.N. (1984) 'DUP activities and economic theory', in D. Colander (ed.) *Neoclassical Political Economy: The Analysis of Rent-seeking and DUP Activities*, Cambridge, MA: MIT Press, pp. 17–32.

—— Brecher, R. Dinopoulos, E. and Srinivasan, T.N. (1987) '*Quid pro quo* investment and policy intervention: a political-economy-theoretic analysis', *Journal of Development Economics* 27: 127–38.

Brander, J. (1986) 'Rationales for strategic trade and industrial policy', in P. Krugman (ed.) *Strategic Trade Policy and the New International Economics*, Cambridge, MA: MIT Press, pp. 23–46.

—— and Spencer, B. (1981) 'Tariffs and the extraction of foreign monopoly rents under potential entry', *Canadian Journal of Economics* 14: 371–89.

Brock, W.A. and Magee, S. (1978) 'The economics of special interest politics: the case of the tariff', *American Economic Review, Papers and Proceedings* 68: 246–50.

Buchanan, J. (1980) 'Rent seeking and profit seeking', in J. Buchanan, R.D. Tollison and G. Tullock (eds) *Toward a Theory of the Rent-Seeking Society*, College Station, TX: Texas A&M University Press, pp. 3–15.

Dinopoulos, E. (1983) 'Import competition, international factor mobility and lobbying responses: the Schumpeterian industry case', *Journal of International Economics* 14: 395–410.

—— (1989) '*Quid pro quo* foreign investment and market structure', *Economics and Politics* 1 (Spring).

Dixit, A. and Stiglitz, J. (1977) 'Monopolistic competition and optimum product diversity', *American Economic Review* 67: 297–308.

Eaton, J. and Grossman, G. (1986) 'Optimal trade and industrial policy under oligopoly', *Quarterly Journal of Economics* 2: 383–406.

Feenstra, R. and Bhagwati, J.N. (1982) 'Tariff-seeking and the efficient tariff', in J.N. Bhagwati (ed.) *Import Competition and Response*, Chicago, IL: National Bureau of Economic Research, pp. 245–58.

Findlay, R. and Wellisz, S. (1982) 'Endogenous tariffs, the political economy of trade restrictions and welfare', in J.N. Bhagwati (ed.) *Import Competition and Response*, Chicago, IL: National Bureau of Economic Research, pp. 223–34.

Finger, J.M. (1982) 'Incorporating the gains from trade into policy', *World*

Economy 5: 367–77.

Goldstein, J. and Krasner, S. (1984) 'Unfair trade practices; the case for a differential response', *American Economic Review, Papers and Proceedings* 74: 282–7.

Grossman, G. (1986) 'Strategic export promotion: a critique', in P. Krugman (ed.) *Strategic Trade Policy and the New International Economics*, Cambridge, MA: MIT Press.

Haberler, G. (1950) 'Some problems in the pure theory of international trade', *Economic Journal* 60: 223–40.

Hillman, A.L. and Riley, J.G. (1989) 'Politically contestable rents and transfers', *Economics and Politics* 1 (March).

Johnson, H.G. (1953) 'Optimum tariffs and retaliation', *Review of Economic Studies* 21: 142–53.

—— (1965) 'Optimal trade intervention in the presence of domestic distortions', in R. Caves, H.G. Johnson and P.B. Kenen (eds) *Trade, Growth, and the Balance of Payments*, Chicago, IL: Rand McNally, pp. 3–34.

Kemp, M. (1964) *The Pure Theory of International Trade*, Englewood Cliffs, NJ: Prentice Hall.

Krishna, K. and Thursby, M. (1988) 'Optimal policies with strategic distortions', NBER Working paper 2527, Cambridge, MA.

Krueger, A.O.(1974) 'The political economy of rent-seeking society', *American Economic Review* 64: 291–303.

Krugman, P. (1984) 'Import protection as export promotion', in H. Kierzkowski (ed.) *Monopolistic Competition and International Trade*, Oxford: Clarendon.

—— (ed.) (1986) *Strategic Trade Policy and the New International Economics*, Cambridge, MA: MIT Press.

—— (1987) 'Is free trade passé?' *Journal of Economic Perspectives* 1: 131–44.

Lancaster, K. (1966) 'A new approach to consumer theory', *Journal of Political Economy* 74: 132–57.

—— (1980) 'Intra-industry trade under monopolistic competition', *Journal of International Economics* 10: 151–75.

Mayer, W. (1984) 'Endogenous tariff formation', *American Economic Review* 74: 970–85.

—— and Riezman, R. (1987) 'Endogenous choice of trade policy instruments', *Journal of International Economics* 23: 377–81.

—— and —— (1989) 'Tariff formation in a multidimensional voting model', *Economics and Politics* 1 (March).

McMillan, J. (1986) *Game Theory in International Economics*, New York: Harwood Academic.

Meade, J. (1955) *The Theory of International Economic Policy*, Vol. 2, *Trade and Welfare*, London.

Nelson, D. (1987) 'The domestic political preconditions of U.S. trade policy: liberal structure and protectionist dynamics', paper presented at the Conference on Political Economy of Trade: Theory and Policy, World Bank, Washington, DC.

Panagariya, A. (1980) 'Variable returns to scale in general equilibrium theory once again', *Journal of International Economics* 10: 499–526.

Rodriguez, C. (1974) 'The non-equivalence of tariffs and quotas under retaliation', *Journal of International Economics* 21: 285–99.

Rodrik, D. (1986) 'Tariffs, subsidies and the theory of the optimum subsidy',

Journal of International Economics 21: 285–99.

—— (1987) 'Imperfect competition and trade policy in developing countries', Harvard University, mimeo.

Sapir, A. (1983) 'Foreign competition, immigration, and structure adjustment', *Journal of International Economics* 14: 381–94.

Scitovsky, T. (1941) 'A reconsideration of the theory of tariffs', *Review of Economic Studies* 9: 89–110.

Smith, A. (1937) *The Wealth of Nations*, Cannan edition, New York (original edition 1776).

Tornell, A. (1987) 'Time inconsistency of protectionist programs', Columbia University Department of Economics Discussion Papers 386, New York.

Tullock, G. (1967) 'The welfare costs of tariffs, monopolies and theft', *Western Economic Journal* 5: 224–32.

Willet, T. (1984) 'International trade and protectionism', *Contemporary Policy Issues* 4: 1–15.

Wong, K.-Y. (1989) 'Optimal threat of trade restriction and *quid pro quo* foreign investment', *Economics and Politics* 1 (July).

Part II

Trade, protection and political economy

3 Perspectives on trade and trade policy

L. Alan Winters[1]

INTRODUCTION

When I was asked to give a paper on trade and trade policy at a conference in honour of Jagdish Bhagwati, not only was I flattered, but I also thought it would be easy. After all, Jagdish is the leading exponent of the policy aspects of trade theory and has been responsible for several fundamental advances in the subject; it must be easy, I thought, to use his insights to interpret current events. In fact, it has not been easy, for I have been faced with the dilemma that academics hate most of all: what to leave out. It would be impossible to draw on all Jagdish Bhagwati's contributions in such a short space – indeed, it would probably be impossible just to list them – and so I have restricted myself to just two broad issues: can the General Agreement on Tariffs and Trade (GATT) address current protectionism and does it matter if it cannot? Even here I have been selective, dealing just with the following questions:

1　Is the growth of international trade sufficient for improvements in welfare?
2　Is a partial liberalization of trade, such as that which the GATT Round could produce, desirable?
3　Given the nature of current protectionism, is it amenable to GATT-based processes?

The last is the most important topic of the paper, and it draws not only on economic theory and hypothesis testing, but also on the political economy of trade policy, another area in which we owe much to Jagdish Bhagwati. My focus is primarily on industrial countries' trade and trade policy, not because developing countries are uninteresting or unimportant, but because the organizing committee wisely asked Jim Riedel to address their issues separately.

TRADE AND GROWTH

The period 1945–73 was a golden age for economic growth in the industrial world. Recovering from the ravages of depression and war, both the incomes and the international trade of the industrial world expanded at unprecedented rates. This experience, coupled with its obverse during the 1930s, has confirmed most economists' belief in the practical importance of the theoretical arguments that international trade bears a fundamental and causative relation to economic growth and welfare. Jagdish Bhagwati is one of the leading advocates of such a view, and I count myself within that school. Thus this paper starts from the position that satisfactory trading relations between nations are one of the most important facets of a prosperous world economy.

Table 3.1 Growth of world merchandise trade and production (average annual percentage change in volume)

	1950–63	1963–73	1973–9	1979–82	1982–6
Exports					
All merchandise	8	9	4	−0.6	4.7
Agriculture	4.5	4	3	2.9	1.0
Mining	7	7.5	1	−7.4	1.2
Manufacturing	8.5	11.5	5.5	2.8	6.3
Production					
All merchandise	5	6	3	−0.2	3.6
Agriculture	3	2.5	2.5	2.1	2.0
Mining	5	5	2.5	−3.8	1.4
Manufacturing	6	7.5	3.5	−0.2	4.3

Source: GATT *International Trade*, various issues; manufacturing, SITC(R) 5–8 less 68

In the post-war period aggregate international trade has grown considerably faster than world output, although not uniformly either through time or across branches of economic activity. Table 3.1 shows that, whereas agriculture, minerals and manufacturing all showed increasing trade–output ratios until 1973 (trade growth exceeded output growth), the rate of increase in the first two faltered as we moved into the turbulence of the 1970s. Manufacturing on the other hand continued its march towards greater openness throughout the period, although it is noticeable that the increases in its trade–output ratio were merely making up previous losses until about 1973. Figure 3.1 shows that the trade ratio fell from around 1.1 in the 1900s (1970 = 1.0) to 0.7 in 1935 and 0.6 in 1945 before rising in the post-war period.

While increasing trade and trade–output ratios have come to be viewed as an indicator of economic health, the necessity of such a relationship is rather difficult to establish in theory. At a positive level, simple models of trade and growth suggest that growth can be either pro- or anti-trade biased, while more complex models, such as those due to Barker (1977) and Helpman and Krugman (1985), based on heterogeneous products, have only a limited domain. Normative analysis provides additional reasons for not using increasing trade ratios as a criterion for the success of the international trading system. In 1958 Jagdish Bhagwati introduced us to the notion of immiserizing growth, whereby economic growth in an individual country had such deleterious effects on its terms of trade that it was a net loser from the process. This is not generally a problem for today's industrialized countries, and in addition, under immiserizing growth, one country's loss is another country's gain, so that an undistorted world cannot lose overall from such growth. A decade later, however, Bhagwati (1968) showed that similar problems could beset a small country with fixed terms of trade if its growth occurred in the presence of other economic distortions. Closely related to the general theory of second-best, this argument showed that if growth exacerbates an existing distortion, e.g. by dragging resources into an already over-expanded sector, it could be harmful.

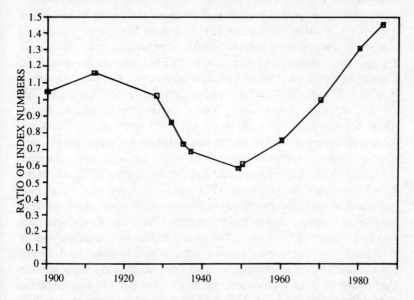

Figure 3.1 Trade/output of manufactures 1900–86, world total (trade/output 1970 = 1)
Source: Maizels (1965) and GATT *International Trade*, various issues

Bhagwati was quick to acknowledge that the 'fault' here lay not with economic growth *per se*, but with the suboptimal economic policies which left the initial distortion untreated. None the less, in a second-best world, the policy implications of such findings could be important. For example, the mere fact that tariff-hopping foreign investment in vehicles and technical progress in agriculture boost European aggregate output is no guarantee that such phenomena are welfare-improving.

Although theoretically less interesting, it is of more practical relevance to extend the notion of immiserization to the growth of exports. Contrary to the apparent beliefs of nearly all governments, not every increase in a country's exports is beneficial. For example, boosting exports by means of export subsidies or of market-sharing arrangements could easily divert a nation's resources from more productive activities. Thus in assessing the attractions of different international trading regimes one should avoid looking at trade growth and should, instead, consider the presence or absence of distortions – especially policy-imposed ones.

These two criteria offer rather different assessments of our current trading conditions. Despite the difficulties of measuring protection, especially that afforded by non-tariff barriers (NTBs), nearly everyone agrees that the last decade has witnessed the widespread application of international market management through NTBs, and the considerable increase in the scope and level of such barriers. For example, early work at the World Bank suggested that in 1983 around 27 per cent of industrial countries' imports were subject to official management of some kind, e.g. quotas, voluntary export restraints (VERs), anti-dumping actions, price agreements etc. (Nogues *et al.* 1986). In the World Development Report 1987 (pp. 142–3) it is suggested on the basis of later data, that 'hard-core' restrictions (quotas, VERs, variable levies and the Multi-Fibre Arrangement) covered 16 per cent of imports in 1986 and that the import coverage of all measures had increased by 16 per cent between 1981 and 1986. Moreover, the rate of increase has certainly not been contained by the standstill and roll-back commitments of the Punta del Este Declaration in November 1986.

Despite such vigorous growth in protection however, the volume of international trade has continued to expand. Particular flows have been severely curtailed by trade restrictions and at considerable loss in economic welfare (see, for example, the World Development Report 1987) but overall international trade has expanded, especially in manufactures. This is particularly true of the exports of Japan and the newly industrializing countries (NICs) which have maintained their phenomenal growth rates whilst bearing the brunt of protectionism.

One interpretation of this growth is that, were it not for the restrictións, trade growth would have been much faster. Another is that much of the growth that has actually occurred is artificial in that it has been induced by the distortionary policies that governments pursue. There is undoubtedly some truth in both these views, but they should be supplemented by a third view that much of the measured protectionism is ineffective in curtailing aggregate imports. This phenomenon was noted by Baldwin (1982), but it was first explained by Jagdish Bhagwati who christened it 'porous protection'. The political pressures for protection are very great and governments are clearly not willing to bear the costs of forever saying 'no'. On the other hand, perhaps the executive branches of government, which have broad responsibilities for foreign affairs and consumers as well as for producers, feel some constraint on the degree of protection they can offer. Bhagwati (1987) argues that one solution to the dilemma is for governments to cheat – to offer protection but not to enforce it effectively. This simultaneously buys off the special interest groups, at least temporarily, while limiting the costs of protection to the economy as a whole. The lack of enforcement can be overt – e.g. the UK quota on footwear imports from China was regularly over-shipped by a factor of 2 – but more commonly it is covert and inherent in the scheme of protection chosen. Most quantitative restrictions are very precise in defining the commodity and countries they cover and thus allow exporters to switch to closed, but unrestricted, substitutes. For example, Yoffie (1983) discusses the attempts to tailor the USA's orderly marketing agreement (OMA) on Korean footwear to the latter's needs. Bhagwati argues that importing country governments may prefer VERs to import quotas precisely because, while both may be porous, the importing government cannot be held responsible for the evasion of a VER. The UK's industry-to-industry VER on footwear with Taiwan suffered growing overshipment in the early 1980s; there were investigations into why, but, unsupported by the government, the UK industry eventually just gave up and abandoned the arrangements in 1985.

One should not conclude, however, that porous protection is harmless – it causes trade diversion and wastes resources in quota evasion (including the relocation of production plants) – but it is perhaps better than 'efficiently enforced protection'. Table 3.2 illustrates two important features of the recent situation. First, manufactured exports from the NICs remained buoyant in the face of protection until 1983, and also subsequently according to the Organization for Economic Co-operation and Development (OECD, 1988). Second, however, the NICs have been overtaken in terms of growth by the newly exporting countries (NECs). Definitions of this last group vary (see Winters 1989) but for our purposes it is sufficient to note that there is another group of

Table 3.2 Manufactured exports of newly exporting countries and newly industrializing countries

	Growth of manufactured exports (per cent per annum)		Percentage share in exports of manufactures of developing countries		
Havrylyshyn and Alikani (1982)					
	1970–9 (value)	1979–82	1970 (all developing countries)	1979	1982
NECs	37.3	16.7	3.2	7.3	8.1
NICs	28.7	10.3	58.0	71.8	67.2
Hughes and Newbery (1986)					
	1965–73 (value)	1973–83	1965 (share in sample of 49 countries)	1973	1983
NECs	16.2	14.3	5.5	5.2	7.9
NICs	19.4	9.9	69.9	82.2	84.8

exporters of manufactures which, *prima facie*, has stepped into the markets forcibly vacated by the NICs. Quite possibly these countries are now industrializing faster because of the trade diverting policies pursued by the OECD.

Although there is circumstantial evidence in favour of the porous protection hypothesis, no final and convincing test is yet available. But even if it explains the experience of the 1970s and 1980s one should not be complacent about the 1990s. Domestic interest groups might come to understand the situation better and demand firmer measures, and we might, anyway, run out of places to divert trade to.[2] A number of governments appear to have begun to reassess the virtues of VERs, and while in some cases the restrictions may just fade away, in others one suspects that they will be replaced by other instruments.

PARTIAL LIBERALIZATION

I have argued that a proper assessment of the trading system should consider the extent and the degree of distortions to international trade. But this is far from straightforward given the present melée of policies and restrictions throughout the world economy. The second-best theory suggests the possibility that the removal or reduction of one economic distortion may be harmful if others remain. Such partial liberalization characterizes all GATT Rounds to date and also in the foreseeable future. Yet in this case I believe that one can be fairly sanguine that second best will not upset the intuitive notion that non-discriminatory partial liberalization is generally beneficial.[3]

First, the liberalization process will eventually lead to a net beneficial position; if progress has to be slow and step by step, better that with the possibility of a few unwittingly harmful steps than never to commence. Second, cross-market spill-overs are not usually very large and so the number of occasions that liberalization in one market is harmful because it affects a second market are few. This leaves, third, those circumstances in which policies and distortions within a single market interact. Here harmful liberalization is conceivable but is also relatively easily identifiable. If trade liberalization is harmful, it is almost inevitably because there exists a distortion which is more efficiently treated by some means other than trade policy. If liberalization points this out to governments and their voters, so much the better, for it makes an approach to the *optimum optimorum* more likely. Bhagwati and Ramaswami (1963) explored these possibilities in a general equilibrium framework twenty-five years ago.

Often the 'other' distortion which renders liberalization harmful is another policy, whose 'treatment' is the perfectly straightforward business of abolition. Otsuka and Hayami (1985), for example, show that the cost of Japan's high rice price policy was around ¥1440 billion (0.7 per cent of gross domestic product (GDP)) in 1980, but that this was cut back to 'only' ¥660 billion (0.3 per cent of GDP) by the imposition of acreage controls to limit the expansion of rice output. Had the acreage controls been abolished by some international agreement, Japan would have been a net loser, but it would be wrong to conclude from this that output controls are rational policies. Similarly, in the trade world, we know that VERs tend to transfer scarcity rents from consumers to exporters. The importing country can reduce these transfers, and hence raise its own welfare, by imposing a tariff. If subsequent liberalization reduces that tariff while leaving the VER intact, the importer loses, but this hardly constitutes a good reason for a general resistance to tariff cuts. In both these cases I would argue that partial liberalization is desirable because it exposes the underlying policy in all its absurdity, and thus encourages genuine reform.

A final argument for partial liberalization (as for free trade itself) is that credible liberalization tends to reduce the scope for direct unproductive profit-seeking (DUP) activity because it restricts the government's discretion over either the height or the nature of its trade restrictions.[4] I can only produce heuristic arguments for this view at present: second best is as relevant with DUPs as without, so that some partial liberalizations could still be harmful. I do believe, however, that

DUPs generally strengthen the presumption in favour of partial liberalization.

Jagdish Bhagwati has been instrumental in the development of the concepts of DUPs and has led us to distinguish between the two important types (see, for example, Bhagwati *et al.* 1984 or this volume, ch. 2). The simpler form is 'downstream' DUPs or 'revenue-seeking', including 'rent-seeking', in which parties compete to capture the rents or revenues generated by an exogenous policy. The most obvious example is Krueger's (1974) discussion of rent-seeking for import quotas. Import quotas create scarcity rents and have to be distributed somehow. If the latter process is not entirely arbitrary but is instead based on some criterion or the other, economic agents have an incentive to arrange their lives to meet that criterion. If this incentive is merely to bribe officials, the economic costs are minor: presumably the most efficient distributors or the agents reaping the greatest benefits from imports will pay the highest bribes and win the importing rights as they should. This is essentially a quota auction but with the revenues accruing privately rather than publicly.[5]

If, on the other hand, the allocation criterion involves, say, expanding capacity, queuing or supplying some other (uneconomic) good, then the economic losses can be heavy, for real resources are absorbed. It is even possible that what Bhagwati calls the 'one-for-one' rule will apply, whereby $1 of rent generates $1 of revenue-seeking expenditure. Although this now seems fairly unlikely (see, for example, Varian 1989 or this volume, ch. 2), any significant degree of rent-seeking can change the ranking of policy options quite dramatically. Return to the example of a VER with a tariff to capture some of the rent for the importing government. If the tariff generates one-for-one revenue-seeking, it adds nothing to national welfare and so its abolition will not be harmful even on immediate criteria. More interesting is Bhagwati and Brecher's (1987) observation that revenue-seeking could explain another of the attractions of VERs to importing governments. If both import quotas and VERs generate revenue-seeking, there is nothing to choose between them in welfare terms: the allocation of the rents between countries does not matter because they are all absorbed by revenue-seeking. Moreover, under certain technological circumstances, or if revenue-seeking exceeds one-for-one, the importing nation may prefer a VER to an import quota because revenue-seeking imposes greater costs on the economy than the rents that it seeks to capture. In this case the right or duty to administer the trade restrictions is a poisoned chalice to be disposed of as quickly as possible![6]

Bhagwati's other type of DUP – upstream DUPs – is more complex

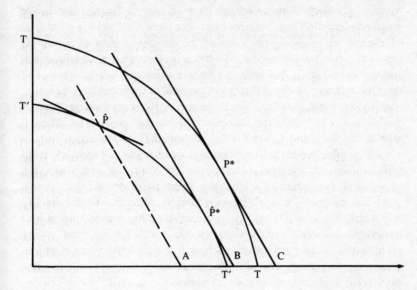

Figure 3.2

and probably more important in industrial countries. It concerns endogenous policy in which the possibility of protection induces political action to create it or influence its level. In this case the policy-making country experiences not only the waste of lobbying but also allocative losses due to the protection that it induces. Figure 3.2, taken from Bhagwati *et al.* (1984), illustrates this. TT represents the production possibility curve without DUP, and T′T′ that allowing for the endogenously determined level of DUP. With free trade, production is at P*, but if the possibility of imposing tariffs is once admitted, lobbying occurs, dragging production onto T′T′ and shifting the domestic price ratio (by an endogenously determined amount) until the final equilibrium is P̂. Bhagwati shows that the losses are decomposable into a part BC due to lobbying (where P̂* is the production point on T′T′ with world prices) and a part AB due to the actual tariff. He also notes the possibility that an endogenous tariff of *t* per cent could be less costly than an exogenous (no-lobbying) tariff of *t* per cent (second best again), but it is clear that the outcome 'no tariff' dominates both.

That lobbying occurs is beyond dispute. For example, Guither (1980) and Body (1984) both draw up long lists of lobbying organizations in the food and agriculture sector with which, as Congressman Finday writes in the Preface to the former book, 'we *must* deal in the legislative game' (emphasis added). Similar groups exist in most industries and in the more concentrated ones we would expect there also to be a good deal of unrecorded lobbying carried out by the managements of individual firms. There is also evidence that lobbying is effective. Casual empiricism and the observation that so many people would be unlikely to spend their time on an activity that was not privately rewarding lead us to that conclusion, but more direct evidence comes from case studies such as that of Petit *et al.* (1987) and statistical analyses such as those by Chappell (1982) and Esty and Caves (1983). Chappell finds some evidence of a relationship between Congressional voting and lobbies' political contributions, while Esty and Caves extend this to relate voting outcomes to resource expenditure on lobbying by pressure groups.

I believe that this analysis has considerable relevance for the GATT. Tariff bindings, while always subject to Bhagwati's second-best reservation, serve to reduce the scope for lobbying, and policy prohibitions, even partial ones such as those on export subsidies and quotas, serve, if they are credible, to reduce it further. On this view the GATT is important because it restricts the menu of policy options open to a government prior to any negotiation it enters into with its domestic pressure groups. That is, like Odysseus, the government may hear the producers sing, but it cannot steer too far towards them.[7]

THE NATURE OF PROTECTIONISM

Viewing GATT as a constraint in domestic policy games helps to explain why protectionism can be so contagious. Bad example and pseudo-legal precedents are important in negotiations, and one act of protectionism can beget many others; governments can no longer argue the force of international constraint if they have conceded protection to other groups or if such constraints are flouted by other countries. Moreover, governments' weakened resistance to protection (an increase in the 'supply of protection' in political market-place terms) can be compounded by increased pressure (demand) for protection if the initial act of protection causes exports to be diverted from restricted to unrestricted markets. De Melo and Winters (1990) analyse such behaviour.

Hamilton (1989) has documented the contagion of protectionism in his so-called 'domino-theory'. During the mid-1970s footwear producers in several industrial countries came under increasing pressure from imports from Korea and Taiwan. Governments resisted most calls for protection until, in 1977, the USA capitulated and imposed an OMA on the two exporters. Within months, Canada, France and the UK had all introduced restrictions of their own. Hamilton also notes a 'reverse domino' during the 1980s as footwear protection was removed. The undoing of trade diversion could explain this, but I do not think that reversing the precedent does: precedent is like innocence – once mislaid, it is lost nearly for ever.

Recent research has drawn a distinction between high-track and low-track protectionism (Finger *et al.*, 1982). The high track is the political one, in which major import-competing interests overtly seek protection from their governments which, in turn, frequently apply considerable political pressure on exporting countries. It is these which lead to acrimonious rows between nations with threats of retaliation and the like. In most cases 'solutions' to these tiffs are found by means of largely bilateral negotiations; imports are curtailed but in a 'politically realistic' way. Sometimes this results just in VERs, e.g. on steel and Japanese vehicles, but in others it also entails an expansion of trade in some other good – a voluntary import expansion (VIE), in Bhagwati's terminology. In either case the 'solution' recognizes the power of certain exporting countries and interests, almost always at the expense of the proponents' consumers and third country exporters. Thus, for example, the argument over US grain exports to Spain and Portugal following their accession to the European Community (EC) was resolved by guaranteeing a certain volume of US sales; the semiconductor case was resolved by Japan agreeing to 'fair and equitable access' for foreign (i.e. USA) semiconductors in Japan and fixing minimum export prices for exports to third markets; and the Korean insurance market was forcibly opened up to US firms without any attempt at a broader liberalization.

Four points are worth noting about these incidents. First, the outcomes are determined almost entirely by political factors and are defined by references to quantities of trade (or companies admitted) rather than to competitive processes. As *The Economist* has observed, the level playing field is no longer sufficient: negotiators now want to ensure that the same number of goals is scored at each end. Second, the incidents reflect an aggressive use of reciprocity: rather than the 'first difference' reciprocity of previous GATT Rounds, whereby countries made balanced reductions in tariffs, we now observe 'levels', or full, reciprocity, where one country threatens to raise its barriers up to or beyond the level that it perceives itself as facing in its negotiating partner. Moreover, such reciprocity consciously spreads the aggravation from one market to another in order to encourage threatened exporters to lobby their government to settle 'reasonably' in the disputed sector.[8]

Third, the reciprocity is used as a lever to open markets up elsewhere, As Bhagwati himself has observed, this is frequently implicitly protectionist and can be quite explicitly so: a US negotiator wrote of one round of bilateral talks, 'On leather, Japan has responded to the GATT panel decision by offering to replace the leather quota with tariffs, but the US has rejected that offer because it would not improve access to the Japanese leather market and in fact could even further reduce our negligible share of the market' (Bhagwati and Irwin 1987). Such market-opening may be preferable to closing markets down, but it is far from economically innocuous: it is potentially trade diverting; it encourages cartels (of a multinational nature); it distorts resource allocation in the exporting country; it offers far more scope for DUP activities as exporters get in on the act; and it subverts export interests from their previously free trade orientation.

Fourth, VIEs have largely been restricted to the USA to date. In part this may reflect economic size – the EC is not often sufficiently unified to act in such a fashion. In the main, however, I suspect that it reflects the USA's more open political system which requires the government to mobilize export interests more explicitly in order to resist protectionist pressures from import-competing interests. VIEs concentrate and identify the export interest concerned and thus make it far more effective politically than that deriving from the general equilibrium export interest that economists see in freer trade. Recently, however, the EC has been pursuing VIE-type agreements with Japan – for example, with respect to whisky and financial services. This suggests an alarming slide towards bilateralism.

What is the prognosis for 'political-track' protection? Its growth suggests frustration with the international trading system on the parts of both domestic interests and governments. Curing the US deficit would clearly release some of the pressure in that country, but the success of the GATT's Uruguay Round also has an important role to play. To the extent that the Round restores governments' faith in the system they will be readier to resist domestic pressure without slipping into bilateralism. But what constitutes a successful Round? Merely enshrining current bilateralism in law through market management agreements clearly would not, but the dismantling of some visible barriers (e.g. in steel and agriculture) plus improved dispute settlement might. All this suggests that the governments should tackle the sensitive topics head-on rather than devote effort to writing ever more complex codes of behaviour, a topic to which I now turn.

Finger *et al.* (1982) describe the second category of trade policy as 'low-track' or administered protection. Following some rather vaguely worded Articles of the GATT, governments use domestic law to define a set of circumstances under which domestic interests will be protected, and a set of procedures for determining whether those circumstances hold. These are the countervailing and anti-dumping duty provisions of the GATT. The legal processes are supposedly fair, but for three reasons the cards are stacked against the consumers and the general interest.

First, there are no penalties for frivolous actions, so that domestic firms may cheaply impose upon their foreign competitors the costs of defending themselves (Bhagwati 1988). Second, the law is defined in terms of injury to producers and trade practices unfair to import-competing firms; nowhere are the benefits of free trade and cheap imports explicitly recognized. Third, a process which involves technical argument in a legal framework favours those groups with the resources to marshall their arguments eloquently and those who are concretely identifiable as having legitimate interests – i.e. producers and factor owners – rather than consumers whose interests are more diffuse and generalized. Only when firms are the principle consumers of a good are anti-protectionist sentiments strongly represented.

These biases are not necessarily accidental. Indeed, Finger *et al.* argue that the *purpose* of the bureaucratic procedures is to obfuscate the granting of protection. The gross transfers involved in protection usually far outweigh the net welfare losses that economists analyse. Thus the various parties to an action have strong and opposing interests. This makes granting protection very risky politically, for it takes on many of the features of a zero-sum game (Thurow 1980). By subjecting it to well-defined legal processes, however, the issue can be both sanitized, i.e. removed from the political arena, and made politically positive-sum. The politicians get the kudos of helping the petitioners but little of the blame for harming the (disenfranchised) consumer: 'after all, the legal process is fair, isn't it?' The net result is creeping trade control, as administered protection – countervailing and anti-dumping actions – becomes more common. The fact that the process is grounded not only in domestic politics but also in domestic law – a sort of capitalized politics – makes it all the harder to tackle.

That recourse has increasingly been made to less than fair value trade laws rather than to political track processes such as Article XIX actions is well known (e.g. Goldstein 1986), and a glance at the press readily shows that the process continues unabated into 1988. What has only recently been documented, however, is that these actions really do have protectionist effects. First, there are a number of biases in the application of EC anti-dumping law which extend the scope of the law well beyond 'honest' dumping (Norall 1986; Hindley 1988). The laws tend, in Finger's (1987) words, to penalize not discriminatory pricing but just low pricing. Second, Messerlin (1989) has shown that the initiation of a dumping action is, on average, associated with a 40 per cent decline in imports within three years. Now this may appear legitimate if dumping has been occurring, but Messerlin also shows that cuts in imports occur where no significant dumping is identified even by the EC's current biased procedures. Many exporters faced with the uncertainty of an anti-dumping action 'settle out of court', by entering price-raising or quantity-fixing agreements. Given the costs and biases involved in fighting a case, this is hardly surprising, and it certainly cannot be interpreted as evidence of guilt.

The 1988 US Omnibus Trade Act illustrates the current vigour of administered protection. GATT legality was apparently not a major issue in the bill's internal discussion, and to the extent that it was raised, it was answered by noting that the bill introduced no *new* violations of the GATT but merely 'tightened up' the administration of existing practice. None the less, the Act gives a significant turn to the protectionist screw as a recent paper by Grinols (1989) shows. Countervailing and anti-dumping procedures have been changed, but the major revisions concern the response to allegedly unfair foreign practices under Section 301 of the Act. For example, actionable unfair trade practices by exporters now include export targeting and failure to provide standards for minimum wages; unfairness determinations are now to be made not by the President but by the US Special Trade Representative, who is much more Congress's creature and who, being actively involved in trade negotiations at all times, will find it most convenient to have his arguments backed by the moral force of 'unfairness'; the US Trade Representative is now formally required to consult Congress and private interests; the executive has much less discretion about whether to act once 'unfairness' has been found; and the Council of Economic Advisors, the Department of Justice and the Budget Office, all of which are, by bureaucratic standards, moderately liberal in outlook, have been excluded from the President's Trade Policy Committee which advises on trade matters.

These changes may increase the pressure for trading partners to eschew unfair practices, but they also increase the pressure and scope to find unfair trade practices with *all* partners and encourage all threatened exporters to agree with some sort of bilateral concession to US interests. This in turn will encourage firms to use the procedures and thus create a new round of protected rents. These rents will become capitalized and spawn interest groups to defend them, and, in particular as they have been achieved by 'legal' means, will become deeply entrenched. Finally, given that high-track protection usually arises from failed low-track actions, one must expect some of the increased activity to spill over into the actively political dimensions of international trade policy.

These low-track procedures have given particular sectors considerable protection and I am afraid that I am not optimistic about them being constructively reviewed in the Uruguay Round. Administered protection uses domestic law to address protectionist pressure from domestic interests, and it is grounded in the mercantilist ethic of domestic output expansion. But this is also the ethic of the GATT. The GATT was not invented as a means to induce trade liberalization, but as a means to codify liberalization that was widely desired and likely to come about anyway. Now that the liberalizing ethic has weakened, the danger of 'rationalizing' the administrative codes in the GATT is that doing so will merely entrench the wrong (mercantilist) model in trade policy determination. The safer approach would be to negotiate the big issues e.g. textiles and agriculture, directly, and leave the administered protection alone. If a few of the big issues are tackled successfully, then executives may be prepared to exercise their vetoes over administrative protection for 'general foreign policy' or 'international trade systemic' reasons. At present, however, any codification of existing practice seems more likely to encourage than to curtail the abuses of the 'fair trade' law.

I have similar feelings about negotiating Article XIX on safeguards in the Uruguay Round. The readiness of importing governments to resort to VERs in response to import surges has led several commentators to argue that Article XIX should be revised to allow countries to achieve their objectives more closely without violating it. In European minds the revision should allow some measure of discrimination and also waive the need for compensation, This, it is said, would bring discipline and legality to what everyone would admit is at present a sub-legal and cut-throat jungle. Hindley (1987), on the other hand, argues that relaxing Article XIX would merely undermine the bargaining power of the exporting countries in circumstances in which protection is inevitable. At present importing governments are uncomfortable with both the non-discriminatory nature of GATT-sanctioned safeguards and the need to make compensatory tariff reductions on other trade. This means that they are prepared to concede quite a lot to developing countries in order to get a VER instead of using Article XIX. To ease the conditions of the latter, therefore, would lower the price in terms of the VER rents that developing countries could extract from the industrial countries when the latter wish to cut imports. Moreover, to the extent that the relaxation of Article XIX reduced the political costs of granting protection it would also weaken the arguments of industrial country governments with their own firms and thus probably encourage more protectionist action. Thus, relaxing the safeguards procedures is a bit like relaxing the interstate speed limit because no one drives at 55 m.p.h. Given that most people are averse to blatant illegality, a limit of 55 m.p.h. perhaps induces an average actual speed of 65 m.p.h. It is not obvious that raising the limit to 65 m.p.h. would leave it there. Rules can affect behaviour even if they are regularly breached, provided that the psychic or political costs of breaching them increase with the degree of violation.

CONCLUSIONS

In this paper a number of current issues in trade and trade policy have been examined. I have suggested that the mere growth of exports is not a sufficient criterion for satisfaction with the world trading system, and have argued that, porous protection notwithstanding, there are strong grounds for concern about recent trends in protectionism. I have also argued that, despite the absence of a theoretically watertight general case, we can be confident that another round of GATT-inspired partial trade liberalization is desirable. Not least of the reasons for this last view is the fact that a GATT Round may curtail some of the DUP activities that currently go on.

The remainder of the paper characterized the protectionist process as a game played principally between domestic interests and their governments. The GATT constrains the latter's feasible set and thus increases its requirements even if these are sometimes violated. While one GATT-inconsistent act begets another, I see no attraction in adapting the GATT in order to validate widespread violations. Even a violated law has some worth, and previous attempts to fit GATT around the facts rather than vice versa have ended up consolidating protectionism rather than controlling it.

Domestic legal procedures have a similar effect. Once a 'right' to protection has been validated by due process, it becomes almost invulnerable to government attempts to abolish it. The abolition of scarcity rents, especially when they have been capitalized into personal wealth, imposes significant losses on someone, and governments hate to appear to be punishing citizens who were doing no more than abiding by the law of the land. For this reason I am profoundly uneasy at the prospect of the Uruguay Round rewriting the provisions on safeguards and less than fair value trade. The most plausible amendments seem likely to make these provisions 'more realistic', which would merely further legitimize protectionism.

I am rather more optimistic about reducing some high-track protectionism through the GATT. Such protectionist arrangements are visible, almost all are GATT inconsistent and subject to increasing concern over their costliness and arbitrary distributive consequences. If governments can only bring themselves to negotiate directly on some of these issues and leave writing new legal codes until later, then we might indeed see some progress in the Uruguay Round. Moreover, once we have a direct success, it is possible that the executive arms of government would be more prepared to halt the insidious creep of administered protection.

I must, of course, take full responsibility for the ideas that I have advanced in this paper – it would be unfair to try to blame anybody else. But it is obvious to me, as it must be to everybody else here, how much they owe to Professor Jagdish Bhagwati. For over thirty years he has set standards of analysis, ingenuity and originality that few of us can hope to match. Thus if I have shown one thing, it is that it is impossible to think sensibly about international trade and trade policy without repeatedly coming back to feed at Jagdish's table. For the pleasure and intellectual nourishment that that has provided me, I should like to record my deepest thanks.

NOTES

1 I am grateful to Jagdish Bhagwati, Paul Brenton, Carl Hamilton, Brian Hindley, André Sapir, the editors of this volume and the participants of the symposium for comments on an earlier draft of this chapter, and to Sue James for typing. I claim the usual proprietory rights to the remaining infelicities.
2 Martin Wolf offers an excellent discussion of the issue in Chapter 5 of this volume.
3 It is much less clear, however, that such sanguinity extends to discriminatory liberalization, such as in customs unions.
4 This is for me the strongest practical argument for free trade as a universal policy rule. If governments cannot resist the lobbyists, better lose a few opportunities for profitable intervention than surrender the policy-making process to the lobby barons.
5 There may, of course, be external costs to undermining the integrity of the bureaucracy, in which case the complacency of the text would not be justified.
6 Bhagwati and Brecher also note that it is important whether VERs are set and manipulated to fix the level of imports *per se* or to maintain a domestic relative price ratio for importables. They opt for the latter interpretation, which turns out to be rather important analytically.
7 Bhagwati (this volume, ch. 2) notes that making welfare judgements is a treacherous business in the presence of downstream DUPs. Essentially nothing guarantees that P* is attainable, because someone – maybe the lobbyists – has to write the rule book. My point is that events which make the rule-book more liberal and more difficult to capture will be beneficial. We should perhaps be thankful for the wave of goodwill, optimism and internationalism that fostered the establishment of international restrictions on policy discretion just after the Second World War.
8 One also hears talk of certain import-competing sectors volunteering – from

the best of motives, of course – to be the sector on which tariffs should be raised in retaliation for foreigners' allegedly illegal actions in quite different sectors.

REFERENCES

Baldwin, R.E. (1982) *The Inefficacy of Trade Policy*, Essays in International Finance 150, Princeton University.

Barker, T.S. (1977) 'International trade and economic growth: an alternative to the neo-classical approach'' *Cambridge Journal of Economics* 1: 153–72.

Bhagwati, J.N. (1958) 'Immiserizing growth: a geometrical note', *Review of Economic Studies* 25: 201–5.

—— (1968) 'Distortions and immiserizing growth: a generalisation', *Review of Economic Studies* 35: 481–5.

—— (1987) 'VERs, *quid pro quo* DFI and VIEs: political economy theoretic analyses', *International Economic Journal* 1: 1–12.

—— (1988) *Protectionism*, Cambridge, MA: MIT Press.

—— and Brecher, R.A. (1987) 'Voluntary export restrictions versus import restrictions: a welfare-theoretic comparison', in H. Kierzkowski (ed.) *Protectionism Competition in International Trade, Essays in Honor of W.M. Corden*, Oxford: Basil Blackwell.

—— and Irwin, D. (1987) 'The return of the reciprocitarians: US trade policy today', *World Economy* 10: 109–30.

—— and Ramaswami, V.K. (1963) 'Domestic distortions, tariffs, and the theory of optimum subsidy', *Journal of Political Economy* 71: 44–50.

—— Brecher, R.A. and Srinivasan, T.N. (1984) 'DUP activities and economic theory', *European Economic Review* 24: 291–307.

Body, R. (1984) *Farming in the Clouds*, London: Temple Smith.

Chappell, H.W. Jr (1982) 'Campaign contributions and congressional voting: a simultaneous probit–tobit model', *Review of Economics and Statistics* 64: 77–83.

De Melo, J. and Winters, L.A. (1990) 'Do exporters gain from VERs', Centre for Economic Policy Research Discussion Paper 383, London: CEPR.

Esty, D.C. and Caves, R.E. (1983) 'Market structure and political influence: new data on political expenditures, activity, and success', *Economic Inquiry* 21: 24–38.

Finger, J.M. (1987) 'Ideas count, words inform', in R.H. Snape (ed.) *Issues in World Trade Policy: GATT at the Crossroads*, London: MacMillan, pp. 257–80.

—— Hall, K. and Nelson, D.R. (1982) 'The political economy of administered protection', *American Economic Review* 72: 452–66.

Goldstein, J. (1986) 'The political economy of trade: institutions of protection', *American Political Science Review* 80: 161 –84.

Grinols, E. (1989) 'Procedural protectionism: the American Trade Bill and the new interventionist mode', *Weltwirtschaftliches Archiv* 125: 501–21.

Guither, H.D. (1980) *The Food Lobbyists*, Lexington, MA: Lexington Books.

Hamilton, C.B. (1989) 'The political economy of transient ''new'' protectionism', *Weltwirtschaftliches Archiv* 125: 522–46.

Helpman, E. and Krugman P.R. (1985) *Market Structure and Foreign Trade: Increasing Returns, Imperfect Competition and the International Economy*, Cambridge MA: MIT Press.

Hindley, B. (1987) 'GATT safeguards and voluntary export restraints: what are the interests of developing countries?' *World Bank Economic Review* 1: 689–706.

—— (1988) 'Dumping and the Far East trade of the European Community', *World Economy* 11: 445–64.

Hughes, G. and Newbery, D. (1986) 'Protection and developing countries' exports of manufactures', *Economic Policy* 2: 409–40.

Krueger, A.O. (1974) 'The political economy of the rent-seeking society', *American Economic Review* 64: 291–303.

Maizels, A. (1965) *Industrial Growth and World Trade*, London: Cambridge University Press.

Messerlin, P.A. (1989) 'The EC anti-dumping regulations: a first economic appraisal, 1980–85'. *Weltwirtschaftliches Archiv* 125: 563–87.

Nogues, J.J., Olechowski, A. and Winters, L.A. (1986) 'The extent of industrial countries' non-tariff barriers to trade', *World Bank Economic Review* 1: 181–99.

Norall, C. (1986) 'New trends in anti-dumping practice in Brussels', *World Economy* 9: 97–110.

OECD (1988) *The Newly Industrialising Countries: Challenge and Opportunity for OECD Industries*, Paris: OECD.

Otsuka, K. and Hayami, Y. (1985) 'Goals and consequences of rice policy in Japan, 1965–80', *American Journal of Agricultural Economics* 67: 529–38.

Petit, M., de Benedictis, M., Brittan, D., de Groot, M., Henricksmeyer, W. and Lechi, F. (eds) (1987) *Agricultural Policy Formation in the European Community: The Birth of Milk Quotas and CAP Reform*, Amsterdam: Elsevier.

Thurow, L.C. (1980) *The Zero-Sum Society*, New York: Basic Books.

Varian, H.R. (1989) 'Measuring the deadweight costs of DUP and rent-seeking activity', *Economics and Politics* 1: 81–95.

Winters, L.A. (1989) 'Patterns of world trade in manufactures: does trade policy matter?', in J. Black and A. MacBean (eds) *Causes of Changes in the Structure of International Trade*, London, Macmillan, ch. 3, pp. 24–59.

World Bank (1987) *World Development Report*, New York: Oxford University Press.

Yoffie, D. (1983) *Power and Protectionism*, New York: Columbia University Press.

4 Strategy wars: the state of debate on trade and industrialization in developing countries

James Riedel

INTRODUCTION

For over two decades a great debate was waged between the proponents of the inward-oriented and the outward-oriented industrialization strategies. Although no formal armistice has been signed, and skirmishes continue to break out, one side in this debate can claim a clear and decisive victory. It is time therefore to honour those who led the battle, and no one is more deserving than Professor Bhagwati. His historical contributions were important in clarifying the issues and giving direction to the academic foot soldiers who carried out countless field studies of the relative success and failure of the competing strategies in developing countries. But, like every great general, Bhagwati also spent a lot of time at the front, dirtying his hands with data and tackling mundane methodological problems. The project he directed (with Anne Krueger) on *Foreign Trade Regimes and Economic Development* (1978), his work on Indian trade and industry (separately with Padma Desai, 1970, and T.N. Srinivasan, 1975) and his many other contributions in the field (e.g. 1985a, b) were decisive to the outcome of the debate.

At the end of a successful campaign it is rewarding to look back and be reminded of how victory was won. I shall indulge in some of that, reviewing briefly the theoretical and empirical arguments used to demonstrate the superiority of what has become known as the export promotion (EP) strategy over its arch rival the import substitution (IS) strategy. But that will not be the main purpose of the paper, since it has already been done by many of those who led the battle, including Bhagwati himself. (Bhagwati 1987, 1988; Little 1982; Lal 1983; Krueger 1984; Lal and Rajapatirana 1987). Instead, this paper's main purpose will be to explain what victory for the EP strategy means: what issues were won, what issues were conceded and what issues are still being contested. Do the on-going skirmishes over as yet unresolved issues pose a threat to the hegemonic position the EP strategy currently enjoys within the economics profession, if not among policymakers in developing countries?

WHAT VICTORY MEANS

The ascendancy of the EP strategy was a victory for 'markets over mandarins', to use Deepak Lal's vivid phrase, but only to a limited extent. The case for EP does not argue for *laissez faire*, or even for free trade. It does not even rule out import substitution, which most of the leading proponents of EP, including Bhagwati, Balassa and Krueger, concede is an appropriate *strategy* in the early phase of industrialization and, if practised selectively, is not precluded in later stages of industrialization when EP becomes the appropriate strategy.

What is required of an EP strategy, according to Bhagwati (1988), is simply the equality of the *average* effective exchange rate for exports (EER$_X$) and the *average* effective exchange rate for imports (EER$_M$). This is what Bhagwati (1988) calls the trade-neutral or bias-free strategy. In contrast, the IS strategy is defined by a system of incentives in which EER$_X$ < EER$_M$, while EER$_X$ > EER$_M$ is termed the ultra-export promotion (UEP) strategy.

It is important to recognize that the EP strategy, as defined, is consistent with a substantial amount of policy-induced price distortion within the framework of an articulated programme of *selective* import substitution. As Bhagwati argues:

> We also need to remember that the average EER$_X$ and EER$_M$ can and do conceal very substantial variations among different exports and among different imports. . . . Thus, within the broad aggregates of an EP country case, there may well be activities that are being import substituted (i.e. their EER$_M$ exceeds the average EER$_X$). Indeed, there often are.
>
> (Bhagwati 1988: 93)

Given that the EP strategy is consistent with substantial policy-induced price distortion, the notion that the EP strategy is necessarily 'trade-neutral or bias-free' is valid only in a limited sense. If, within a neutral trade regime, policy-induced distortions reduce the set of production possibilities, for example by introducing intersectoral differences in marginal factor productivities or by causing a diversion of resources to rent-seeking or other 'directly unproductive' activities, there may remain a substantial bias against exports, either in terms of the absolute level of export production or in terms of the export sector's relative claim on resources.

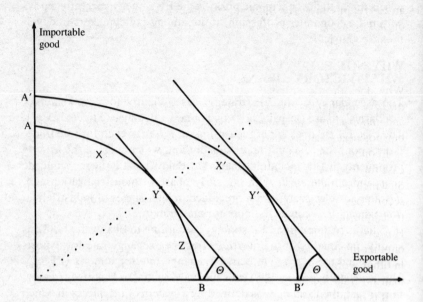

Figure 4.1

The point is illustrated in Figure 4.1, which is an adaption of the diagram Bhagwati (1988) uses to distinguish between the IS, EP and UEP strategies. The condition that the *average* EER_X equal the *average* EER_M is equivalent to the condition that the average domestic opportunity cost of producing exports in terms of forgone production of import-competing goods is equal to the average relative price of exports to import-competing goods in world markets, which in Figure 4.1 is shown by tan θ. This condition is satisfied at point Y on AB, which let us assume is the frontier of a distortion-ridden production possibility set. The same condition holds Y' on A'B', which represents the frontier of a distortion-free production possibility set. The EP equilibrium at Y is clearly superior to either the IS equilibrium at X or the UEP equilibrium at Z, but it cannot be considered 'trade-neutral or bias-free' over all possible outcomes, only relative to alternative outcomes for a given set of production possibilities. Indeed, an IS policy whose only instrument were the exchange rate or equivalently a uniform tariff-cum-export tax, creating thereby a divergence between a *uniform* EER_M and a *uniform* EER_X (e.g. X' on A'B'), could be associated with a greater level of exports and a larger share of domestic output than would obtain under an EP regime in which there were substantial price distortion (e.g. Y on AB).

WHY NOT FREE TRADE?

Why does the EP strategy recommend only that $EER_X = EER_M$ *on average* and not that the EERs be uniform across all export-competing and import-competing sectors? In other words, why a neutral trade regime but not necessarily a liberal or free trade regime?

Economic theory is not very generous in providing exceptions to the case for free trade. According to the conventional theory of trade, much of which is due to Bhagwati, restrictions on trade are no better than second-best policy instruments, except in circumstances where a country can influence world prices of the goods it either exports or imports. However, when domestic markets are imperfect, because of externalities or other imperfections, restrictions on trade may be superior to free trade; in other words, a second best trade policy may (or may not) be better than no trade policy at all.

It is on this fragile foundation that the oldest and most enduring argument for protection in developing countries, the infant-industry argument, rests. The case for infant-industry protection requires a series of conditions: first, that there are 'economies of time' which make new firms or industries in less developed countries (LDCs) uncompetitive with established foreign firms or industries; second, that it is not profitable for firms to enter an infant industry under free trade conditions, either because the long-run benefits are external to the firms or because the short-run losses cannot be financed against long-run profits; third, that if protected from foreign competition, domestic firms in infant industries would eventually be profitable under free trade conditions; fourth, that the near-term social opportunity costs of protecting an infant industry are outweighed by the long-term social benefits of having the industry established; and, finally, that measures superior to trade policy are not available to promote infant industries.

Before examining whether the practice of infant-industry protection in developing countries generally meets these conditions, it is useful to consider whether the so-called 'new theory of trade' which emphasizes the implications of scale economies, imperfect competition and product differentiation offers any convincing arguments for protection.

Perhaps the most interesting and controversial proposal to be derived from the new trade theory is the idea of using trade restrictions to give domestic firms a strategic advantage in world markets. A role for strategic trade policy *à la* Brander and Spencer requires at a minimum that domestic firms in developing countries have the potential to establish a substantial position in world markets and that LDC governments can make a credible impression on foreign competitors by announcing trade policy initiatives (Krugman 1986). Since there are few firms in LDCs with a commanding presence in world markets and few governments that are sufficiently well financed to make an aggressive strategic trade policy credible to foreign competitors, the potential for this kind of policy would seem to be extremely limited for developing countries.

There are other applications of the new theory, however, that may be more relevant. One is where oligopolistic foreign firms use their market power in small LDCs to extract rent. Srinivasan (1986b) shows how an optimal lump sum tax on the foreign firm combined with an optimal import subsidy can capture the oligopolist's rent for the host country. He concludes, however, that 'while the logic of this argument is impeccable, whether many developing countries are capable of designing or credibly implementing such a two-part tariff is open to doubt' (Srinivasan 1986b: 19).

Another recent argument for restricting trade is the idea of import protection as export promotion, a version of the old infant-industry argument, but one which supposedly avoids the pitfalls of the original. It is suggested that protecting infant export industries is superior to protecting import-competing industries because export activities stimulate greater efficiency and productivity growth through direct competition in foreign markets and because expanding market opportunities abroad allow scale economies to be realized more quickly, reducing the cost and shortening the duration of infant-industry protection (Westphal 1982; Pack and Westphal 1986). Srinivasan (1986a: 19) remains sceptical, however, arguing that 'except perhaps a few large developing economies that are at the same time sufficiently advanced technologically, developing countries by and large are unlikely to have domestic markets for high technology products, large enough for this argument for protection to be of any significance'. Thus, Srinivasan concludes, 'the exercise of an interventionist trade policy by developing countries, based on recent theories of oligopolistic competition and increasing returns, is unlikely to be beneficial'. These sentiments are echoed by Paul Krugman (1986) who argues that 'there is nothing in the theory so far that would restore intellectual respectability to the strategy of import substitution. Import substituting industrialization looks even worse in the new theory than it does in the standard theory.'

THE EVIDENCE ON INFANT-INDUSTRY PROTECTION

While import-substitution may have lost intellectual respectability as a strategy, it still does have its advocates when it is applied selectively. Moreover, the theoretical justification for selective import substitution rests, as did the case for import substitution as a strategy, on one version or another of the old infant-industry argument. And yet, Krueger and Tuncer (1982: 1142) claim that 'there has been virtually no systematic examination of the empirical relevance of the infant industry argument'. As they correctly argue:

> Even if there are conditions under which dynamic factors and exter-
> nalities in an infant industry might warrant intervention, that does
> not prove that those conditions are in fact met. In the last analysis,
> defense of infant industry protection must rest on empirical grounds:
> do the long-run benefits justify the short-run costs of starting up an
> initially high-cost infant?

What evidence is there? Certainly there is ample evidence that beyond some point import substitution as a strategy encounters rapidly diminishing returns, and that trade policy reforms which neutralize the disincentive to export, but do not necessarily eliminate all trade restrictions, improve economic performance. This evidence is in fact the heart of the case for the EP strategy (which will be reviewed in the next section). It does not, however, provide much basis for judging the validity of the infant-industry argument. The failure of the IS strategy as it has been practised, spreading the net of protection ever wider, from consumer goods to intermediates and eventually to heavy capital-intensive investment goods industries, cannot easily be interpreted as a refutation of the underlying premises of the infant-industry argument since such an all-encompassing system of protection is essentially inconsistent with the infant-industry argument. It is inconsistent because one sector can be favoured only at the expense of other sectors. To protect all is to protect none, and thus to deny support to worthy infants which may deserve it.

If failure of the IS strategy is only a qualified indictment of the infant-industry argument, what conclusions can be drawn from the relative success of the EP strategy? Ironically, the argument is commonplace that the EP strategy has been successful only because infant-industry protection provided an industrial foundation on which it could build. This claim, however, is virtually impossible to substantiate, or refute, since every country save one, Hong Kong, started off with the IS strategy. Whether the EP strategy succeeded in East Asia and elsewhere because of, or in spite of, the earlier experience with the IS strategy is a moot issue, at least as far as those countries are concerned. However, since there are some countries, mainly in Africa, which may not have yet completed the 'easy phase' of import substitution the issue is not entirely moot. It may be asked whether such countries are ripe yet for the EP strategy, or whether they should press on with the IS strategy until such time as they achieve a level of industrialization comparable with that which Taiwan and South Korea achieved when they first launched the EP strategy.

If the success or failure of the IS strategy is not a fair test of the infant-industry argument, what is? Krueger and Tuncer suggest the following:

> the important aspect of the infant industry case seems summarizable in the proposition that, in order for it to be empirically valid, a necessary (but not sufficient) condition is that costs in (temporarily) assisted or protected industries should have fallen over time more rapidly than costs in non-protected or less protected countries.
>
> (Krueger and Tuncer 1982: 1143)

There are two reasons why one industry's unit costs could change relative to another's: either unit input requirements fall more (or rise less) than the other's, or the relative reward to the factor it uses relatively intensively falls. Krueger and Tuncer dismiss the latter as irrelevant to the infant-industry argument, and focus on the former. Should industry i have been protected on infant industry grounds and its costs have fallen relative to k, it will be judged that there were some dynamic factors in industry i that *may* have warranted intervention (although there is no presumption whatsoever that intervention was optimal); (1982: 1145).

In the case of Turkey in the 1960s and 1970s, a country as committed as any, Krueger and Tuncer found no systematic tendency for more protected firms or industries to have had higher total factor productivity growth than less protected firms and industries. This, they suggest, is sufficient to prove that protection was not warranted.

Aside from the Krueger and Tuncer study there is scant evidence relating directly to the infant industry argument. In a recent paper Pack (1986), a leading advocate of selective infant-industry protection, surveyed the literature thoroughly and found little evidence of a difference in total factor productivity growth between relatively open and closed developing countries. The more rapid gross domestic product (GDP) growth observed in more open economies must therefore be attributable to more rapid growth of resource endowment. Pack and Westphal (1986) imply that the lack of any significant difference in total factor productivity growth is a shortcoming of the EP strategy and undermines the validity of the underlying neo-classical theory. But of course it is the infant-industry argument rather than any known theorem of neo-classical theory which suggests differences in productivity growth among sectors. Since the link between infant-industry protection and intersectoral productivity growth differentials has yet to be established empirically, the argument remains, after all these years, a theoretical possibility without much to substantiate it.

THE CASE FOR THE EXPORT PROMOTION STRATEGY

Since so little empirical support can be found for the infant-industry argument, one might reasonably ask why conventional wisdom stops short at a neutral trade regime rather than going all out for a free and neutral trade strategy in developing countries. The answer is simple. The case for the EP strategy was built on real world experience rather than on pure theoretical reasoning. That is why the case is so powerful and appealing, even to 'practical men' who, as Keynes noted, 'believe themselves to be quite exempt from intellectual influences'. Taiwan, South Korea and thereafter a number of countries showed that removing some, but not necessarily all, trade restrictions (especially the quantitative variety) and offsetting the bias against exports inherent in the import substitution regime, led almost invariably to improved economic performance. Bhagwati and others documented and painstakingly analysed the successes and failures under the competing strategies, and then like good economists everywhere set about to answer the question: 'does what works in practice also work in theory?'

A free trade strategy works best of all in theory, but alas has rarely been tried in practice. The single case of it in recent times, Hong Kong, is a phenomenal success, but is routinely dismissed as irrelevant because of the peculiarities of Hong Kong (not the least of which is success itself). The case for the EP strategy is therefore a practical compromise between a free trade strategy, which looks good in theory but has not been practised, and the IS strategy, which looks bad in theory and worse in practice.

The gains from (partial) trade liberalization, which is what implementation of the EP strategy requires, are well documented. There are two kinds of studies which purport to show the superiority of the EP strategy: country case studies of industrialization under different trade policy regimes (Little *et al.* 1970; Balassa 1971; Donges and Riedel 1977; Bhagwati 1978; Krueger 1978) and cross-country studies of the relationship between export expansion and economic growth (Michalopoulos and Jay 1973; Michaely 1977; Balassa 1978; Krueger 1978; Tyler 1981;

Feder 1983). The former, as Bhagwati (1988) correctly notes, are the more compelling. The latter, however, are easier to summarize and better highlight the stylized facts of the case. Indeed, since the cross-country studies invariably rely on data from the World Bank's *World Development Report*, it is easier to replicate their results than to summarize them.

The simple relationships between real GDP growth and industrial growth, on the one hand, and export growth, on the other, are shown in Figures 4.2 and 4.3, which contain observations for every developing country for which there are data in the *World Development Report*,

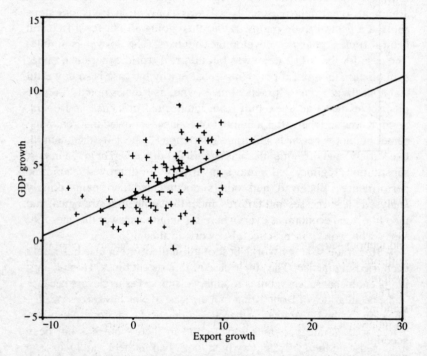

Figure 4.2 Real GDP and export growth rates, 1965–86 (percentages)

1988. The observed positive association between export growth and either GDP growth or industrial growth is suggestive, but can never be more than that without a theory. A primal question is whether this association indicates that export expansion causes GDP growth, or the reverse, or the more likely and more theoretically appealing case that output growth and export growth are determined simultaneously and, as two

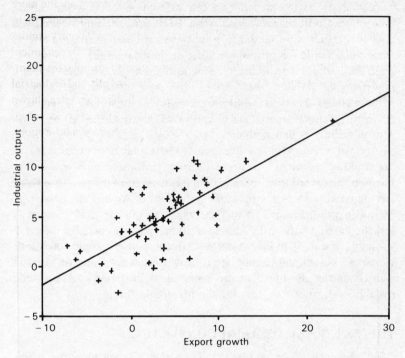

Figure 4.3 Industrial output and export growth rates, 1965–86 (percentages)

endogenous variables, may be either positively or negatively correlated with one another depending on the sources of economic change in the system.

There is some evidence, however, to suggest that export growth, standing as a proxy for openness, or as a force in its own right, exerts an independent positive influence on real output growth. That is, after account is taken for the effect of capital accumulation and labour force growth, export growth is found to have a strong and statistically significant positive effect on GDP growth (Balassa 1978; Feder, 1983). This result is easily replicated using *World Development Report* data for all developing countries for which there are data (t-statistics in parentheses): where $\hat{Y}$ is real GDP growth, I/Y is the average ratio of gross domestic investment to GDP, $\hat{L}$ is the labour force growth rate and $\hat{X}$ is the real export growth rate, all defined for the period 1965–86.

$$\hat{Y} = \begin{array}{cccc} -1.20 & + & 0.13(I/Y) & + & 0.81\hat{L} & + & 0.22\hat{X} \\ (-1.80) & & (4.63) & & (3.81) & & (6.52) \end{array} \qquad \begin{array}{l} R^2 = 0.61 \\ n = 75 \end{array}$$

Numerous hypotheses have been offered to explain the strong independent influence of exports on GDP growth: improvement in allocative efficiency due to trade policy reform; demonstration effects from contact with foreign competitors; increased domestic competition; realization of scale economies; reduction in rent-seeking and 'directly unproductive' activities; and various forms of X-efficiency gains. None of these effects is easy to identify empirically, but the weight of evidence, albeit some circumstantial, in favour of an outward-oriented or trade-neutral regime is undeniable.

And yet, many countries strenuously resist trade liberalization, often undertaking it only as a last resort during periods of economic crisis. It cannot be denied that liberalization has worked in the past, but there are many who doubt it can work in the future. Among the concerns, the most prominent are (i) that external demand for LDC exports is insufficient to justify an EP strategy; (ii) that past successes of the GDP strategy, especially in East Asia, were due to non-economic conditions which are absent and cannot be replicated elsewhere; and (iii) that in many countries short-term macro-economic stabilization goals preclude trade liberalization, at least for the forseeable future.

THE EXTERNAL DEMAND CONSTRAINT

Of all the excuses for erecting trade barriers, or not lowering them, export demand pessimism is by far the favourite. In the 1950s, when intellectual justification was sought for the IS strategy that most developing countries had already adopted, export demand pessimism was called into service by many of the pioneers of development economics, including Nurkse, Prebisch, Myrdal and Chenery. Two decades later, in laying out the argument for a development strategy of collective self-reliance through the substitution of South–South trade for North–South trade, Lewis (1980) again called up export demand pessimism to provide justification. More recently, economists at the International Food Policy Research Institute have advocated an 'agriculture-based development strategy', and not surprisingly they justify their otherwise sensible recommendations on grounds of weak demand for LDC manufactured exports (Bautista 1988).

There are two sources of pessimism about demand for LDC exports of manufactures: (i) price inelastic demand, and (ii) protectionism in developed countries. The fact is that most econometric estimates of LDC export demand functions do indicate price inelasticity. Goldstein and Khan's (1985) thorough review of the literature found a 'consensus view' that the price elasticity of demand for LDC exports (either in aggregate or for individual countries or commodity groups) is in the range of -0.5 to -1.0, with the income elasticity of demand between 2.0 and 4.0.

The problem with these estimates is that often they are not consistent with the way that LDC exports behave. For example, following trade liberalization, some countries (e.g. Sri Lanka in the late 1970s and Turkey in the early 1980s) have experienced export growth rates as high as 50–100 per cent per annum. For these to occur, if the consensus view of demand elasticities is correct, the relative price of their exports in world markets would have had to have declined precipitously. But that never occurred. Furthermore, if the price elasticity of demand were as low as is commonly believed, a fairly stable relationship should be observed between LDC export growth and income growth in developed countries, their major export markets. But that also is not observed (Riedel 1984).

What then explains the inconsistency between the observed behaviour of LDC exports and what econometric estimates of demand parameters imply about their behaviour? Perhaps the answer is that most econometric estimates are misleading because they almost invariably ignore the supply of exports by conveniently assuming it to be infinitely elastic. As shown elsewhere (Riedel 1988a), if one estimates Hong Kong's export demand function with the usual assumption of infinitely elastic supply, one gets the usual elasticity results. If, however, one estimates the Hong Kong export demand function as part of a simultaneous system of supply and demand equations, one gets very different results; namely, that Hong Kong is a price-taker in world markets. To suggest that Hong Kong is a 'small country', albeit the developing world's leading exporter of manufactures, does not seem very remarkable, and it is not, except in relation to the consensus view about demand parameters for LDC manufactured exports.

The threat of protection in developed countries, as a deterrent to LDC export expansion, is also somewhat more apparent than real. The divergence between perception and reality has two sources: confusion between the rhetoric of protectionism and the actual implementation of protectionist measures; and confusion between the enactment of protectionist measures and their impact.

It is difficult not to be alarmed about a 'rising tide of protection', given the prominence of xenophobia in the politics of the Western democracies. And yet, the bite of protectionism is clearly less than its bark, as numerous studies have shown. (Gard and Riedel 1980; Balassa and Balassa 1984; Hughes and Krueger 1984; Hughes and Newbery 1986; Noguès *et al* 1986; Balassa 1988a). Tariff barriers to LDC exports have steadily fallen, but non-tariff barriers (NTBs) have gone up.

However, as of 1985, only 12.9 per cent of LDC exports to the USA, 21.8 per cent to the European Economic Community and 10.5 per cent to Japan were subject to NTBs (Balassa 1988a). It is of course difficult to interpret these measures since they are subject to bias in both directions. On the one hand, if NTBs are effective in limiting imports, weighting their incidence by the volume of imports involved understates their restrictiveness. At the same time, if the measures are non-binding, the weighting procedure overstats their restrictiveness.

Measuring the impact of NTBs is as problematic as measuring their incidence. Developing countries have found many ingenious ways of getting around them, especially the most common form of NTB, the voluntary export restraint (VER). By upgrading quality, altering product specifications and transhipping through third countries and through direct investment in countries with unused quotas, many of the leading LDC exporters have made VERS a very porous form of protection (Baldwin 1982; Pearson 1983).

Because of the intractable problem of measuring either the incidence or the effect of NTBs *ex ante*, most analysts have had to assess their impact on the basis of LDC export performance *ex post*. The following quote from Hughes and Krueger (1984) is representative of the conclusion reached by those who have examined the issue:

> Based on the export performance of the developing countries in manufactured goods during the 1970s, it is difficult to infer that increasing protection was the dominant factor at work. . . . The rate of increase of LDC market shares was sufficiently great that it is difficult to imagine that rates would have been significantly higher in the absence of any protectionist measures.
>
> (Hughes and Krueger 1984: 413)

If the developed countries' threshold for tolerance of LDC imports has not yet been crossed, would it be if the EP strategy were adopted worldwide? One who believes it would is Cline (1982), who bases his conclusion on a (statistically insignificant) regression model for predicting the incidence of protection against LDC exports. The weakness of his case in favour of the 'fallacy of composition' argument lies not so much in his poor econometric results as in his underlying assumption that all things (including the commodity composition of LDC exports and the level and composition of LDC imports) remain equal as all LDCs emulate the Hong Kong experience. Even though this argument is patently absurd and has been thoroughly demolished in the literature (Riedel 1987; Balassa 1988b), it retains currency among those who view the world economy as a zero-sum game and are prepared to see protectionist measures undertaken which make their prophecy self-fulfilling. Therefore, as Bhagwati (1988: 42) reminds us, 'in assessing the extent to which the protectionist threat must be taken seriously, one may first make the prudential statement that it should never be regarded lightly'.

NON-ECONOMIC DETERMINANTS OF EXPORT PROMOTION

There is a saying: 'success has many fathers, failure has none'. Neo-classical economics may claim the paternity of success in East Asia, but so do others and in doing so deny the importance of 'getting prices right' as a lesson for other countries. Some claim that the East Asian success is due to culture, while others attribute it to the kind of government those countries have rather than the policies they pursued.

Many argue that what distinguishes the East Asian newly industrialized countries (NICs) and makes replication of their experience impossible, is a culture which favours diligence, loyalty, hard work and a strong appreciation of education. It is true that these attributes appear to be more abundant in the East Asian NICs than elsewhere. Since these countries share a common Confucian heritage, it may be natural to look for the explanation in culture, a factor relegated to the dustbin of development economics for more than three decades, but currently enjoying an appeal broad enough to embrace the likes of futurologist Kahn (1979) and mathematical economist Morishima (1982).

There are at least two crucial weaknesses, however, in the cultural explanation for Asian diligence and hard work. First, Confucianism is cited as the reason for economic stagnation in Asia before the 1960s as frequently as it is for economic dynamism thereafter (Needham 1954; Baum 1982; Han 1984). Second attributes of diligence and hard work depend as much on the availability of jobs and the reward given for effort, both of which are generally greater in East Asia than elsewhere in the developing world, thanks, some would say, to their being more open economies and putting more reliance on the market incentives.

The importance of political organization and the administrative competence of government, on the other hand, cannot be overstated. After sifting through the accumulated historical evidence on 100 years of development in forty-two contemporary developing countries, Reynolds (1983: 976) concluded that this is 'the single most important explanatory variable [of successful economic development]'. An examination of the post-war development of the Asian NICs reached the same conclusion (Riedel 1988b). There is little room for debate about this, but there is wide disagreement about what it means. Some (eg. Pack and Westphal 1986; Wade 1988) interpret this as a refutation of neo-classical economic doctrine, on the mistaken premise that the latter is equivalent to *laissez faire*. Nothing could be further from the truth, as Keynes (1926: 20) made clear: 'the phrase *laissez faire* is not to be found in the works of Adam Smith, of Ricardo or of Malthus. Even the idea is not present in a dogmatic form in any of the authors'.[1] As Smith explains:

> the sovereign has only three duties to attend to: three duties of great importance, indeed, but plain and intelligible to common understandings: first the duty of protecting society from the violence and invasion of other independent societies; secondly, the duty of establishing an exact administration of justice; and thirdly, the duty of erecting and maintaining certain public works and certain public institutions, which it can never be in the interest of any individual, or small number of individuals, to erect and maintain.
>
> (Smith 1776: 651)

To this list, Adam Smith might add, were he writing about contemporary developing countries, the duty of the sovereign to maintain a stable macro-economic environment.

These four duties the governments of the East Asian NICs have fulfilled reasonably well, and probably better than most other developing countries. They have also gone beyond these duties, establishing public enterprises to produce private goods and intervening in markets to influence incentives, but whether they have succeeded because of, or in spite of, these activities is by no means clear. It is more apparent, from their experience and from that of other countries where efforts at trade liberalization failed (eg. Chile and Sri Lanka in the 1970s), that the East Asian countries would not have been nearly as successful had they not adequately fulfilled the minimal functions of government, especially that of maintaining macro-economic stability.

Debating whether the key to success in Asia or elsewhere is culture, politics or economics is fruitless, for, as Jones (1981) suggests, growth and development work more like a giant combination lock for which there is no one key. A number of tumblers must fall into place to unlock growth, and one of them perhaps is a minimally rational economic system. The point is sharply put in Timmer's (1973: 76) famous quip: 'Getting relative prices right is not the end of development. But getting prices wrong often is'.

THE TIMING OF LIBERALIZATION

Few economists would dispute that countries should 'get prices right', but some argue that it should not be done while a macro-economic stabilization programme is in progress. As Sachs (1987: 293) states: 'The success stories of East Asia, so frequently pointed to as illustrations of the benefits of export led growth, do not demonstrate the utility of trade liberalization in the midst of a macroeconomic crisis'. As he correctly points out, in Japan, South Korea and Taiwan, liberalization, such as it was, occurred only after macro-economic stability was achieved. Furthermore, Sachs suggests that 'the attempt to stimulate exports at all costs through trade liberalization or aggressive depreciation of the exchange rate can often undermine a stabilization program and thus postpone a resolution of debt crisis' (p. 294). The reason he gives is that 'The current focus on liberalization is distracting attention from the more urgent needs of the debtor countries by overloading the political circuits in those countries and by misdirecting the energies and attention of the international community' (p. 294).

To present trade liberalization as an alternative to fiscal and monetary control, or even as a necessary ingredient of a stabilization package, is to set up a straw man. The record is clear that macro-economic stability is more a requirement for succesful liberalization than the reverse. Macro stability and a very illiberal trade regime are perfectly compatible, as the Indian experience clearly demonstrates. What is not so obvious is that trade liberalization necessarily undermines rather than enhances an otherwise sound stabilization programme.

The Turkish experience after 1980 is instructive. At the height of a debt crisis (1978–1980) every bit as severe as that experienced by the Latin American debtors, Turkey implemented a stabilization programme incorporating all the orthodox prescriptions, including the elimination of quantitative restrictions on imports, a massive real depreciation of the currency and unification of the exchange rate. The results in terms of lowering inflation, restoring growth and expanding exports, which in only five years went from 2 per cent to 15 per cent of gross national product were astounding. It is premature to declare the Turkish experiment a complete success since inflation has accelerated in recent years and threatens to undo the progress that has been made. However, there is no question that rapid expansion of both exports and imports allowed Turkey to adjust with more growth and less austerity than has been possible in Latin America.[2] Furthermore, there is no evidence that the recent resurgence of inflation is in any way due to trade liberalization; it is earned the old fashioned way, by monetizing fiscal deficits (Riedel 1988c).

Another important lesson from the Turkish experience is that, while trade liberalization may not be a necessary part of solving a macro-economic crisis, a macro-economic crisis may be, if not necessary, at least highly conducive to the undertaking of trade liberalization. It is hard to imagine that Turkish leaders would have been willing to break with fifty years of *étatism*, which carried the all-important imprimatur of the great Atatürk, had they not found themselves, as they did in 1980, in a near-catastrophic state of economic and political chaos. The need for shock treatment to break down political resistance to trade liberaliza-tion is apparently widespread. A series of case studies of the timing and sequencing of trade liberalization carried out under the auspices of the World Bank found that 'Liberalizations implemented under ex-treme duress are more likely to succeed than those starting from a "normal" economic performance' (Michaely 1988: 6). By this criterion, the opportunities for successful liberalization and export promotion should abound.

CONSOLIDATING VICTORY

To conclude, the debate between proponents of the IS and EP strategies has been decided, although not on the basis of the relative strength of their theoretical arguments, but rather on the basis of what has been found to work in the real world. The debate has therefore left open the question of whether there are alternative strategies which may be superior to those that have been tried, such as that special case of the EP strategy, free trade. Also left open is the question of whether the IS strategy is necessary in the first stage of industrialization, since in practice it was invariably the initial strategy adopted. This issue is not only of historical interest however, but is also of practical significance to those countries which may not yet have completed the 'easy phase' of import substitution.

Skirmishes will no doubt continue over the issue of whether external demand is a binding constraint on growth in developing countries. Past experience suggests that believing demand to be a binding constraint, and acting on that belief by adopting inward-looking trade policies, makes it a self-fulfilling prophesy. In order to put this issue to rest, however much more careful empirical analysis of supply and demand parameters for LDC exports is required.

The protectionist threat to LDC exports will always be an elusive issue. But, for developing countries, perhaps the more important question is what they themselves can do to restore faith in the liberal trading system. In the past, developing countries insisted that the rules of the international trading system should not apply to themselves and took advantage of this freedom to construct complex systems of protection with the aim, in part, of breaking the supposed external constraint on their development. However, to the extent that their demand for exemption from the rules has given reason or excuse to the developed countries to break the rules, the constraint has only resurfaced in another form.

Finally, it should be acknowledged that there remains at least one vast area of the globe over which the EP strategy does not hold sway, even in the minds of many professional economists. That is of course Africa. The contest between the IS strategy and the EP strategy was fought elsewhere, mainly in the NICs where the contrasting experiences of industrialization under each strategy offered relatively clear, unambiguous lessons. But are those lessons relevant to Africa, where industrialization has barely begun and where the obstacles to progress seem so overwhelming and largely unrelated to the issues at stake in the IS–EP debate?

Even if the lessons are relevant, it does not mean that they will necessarily work the same magic in Africa that they have elsewhere. However, one should not confuse a policy with its outcome. The EP strategy is defined by a certain structure of relative incentives, not by any given rate of export growth. The incentive structure associated with the EP strategy may be (and probably is) as appropriate in Africa as it is elsewhere, even though it may not (and probably would not) yield results that are at all comparable with those obtained elsewhere. Unfortunately this point is often lost in the vain search for the 'key' to progress in Africa and other regions that lag behind, which more often than not seems to lie in the realms of culture and politics rather than in economics. Trade policy will therefore remain a contentious issue, and many battles will be waged before the victory of the EP strategy is consolidated.

NOTES

1 Lal (1983), in his brilliant exposé of the 'poverty of development economics', makes this point and gives this quote from Keynes.
2 True to Bhagwati's Law, Sachs (1985) dismisses the role of export growth in allowing Turkey to achieve adjustment with growth, attributing it instead to official capital inflows from NATO countries worried about Middle East stability. It is doubtful, however, that those inflows would have been forthcoming had Turkey not raised its capacity to manage debt by expanding the share of exports in GNP. *Bhagwati's Law*: 'economic miracles are a public good; each economist sees in them a vindication of his pet theories' (1987: 285).

REFERENCES

Balassa, B. (1971) *The Structure of Protection in Developing Countries,* Baltimore, MD: Johns Hopkins Press.
—— (1978) 'Exports and economic growth: further evidence', *Journal of Development Economics* (June): 181–9.
—— (1988a) 'US trade policy towards developing countries', Symposium on New Directions in Trade Policy, Johns Hopkins University School of Advanced International Studies, 21 October 1988.
—— (1988b) 'The adding up problem', World Bank PPR Working Paper 30.
—— and Balassa, C. (1984) 'Industrial protection in the developed countries', *World Economy* (June): 179–96.
Baldwin, R. (1982) *The Inefficacy of Trade Policy,* Essays in International Finance 150, Princeton University.
Baum, R. (1982) 'Science and culture in contemporary China: the roots of retarded modernization', *Asian Survey* 1 (12): 1166–86.
Bautista, R.M. (1988) 'Agriculture-based development strategy: issues and policy framework', Washington DC: International Food Policy Research Institute, unpublished mimeo.
Bhagwati, J.N. (1978) *Anatomy and Consequences of Exchange Control Regimes,* Cambridge MA: Ballinger for the National Bureau of Economic Research.
—— (1985a) *Wealth and Poverty: Essays in Development Economics,* vol. I, Oxford: Basil Blackwell.
—— (1985b) *Dependence and Interdependence: Essays in Development Economics,* vol. II, Oxford: Basil Blackwell.
—— (1987) 'Outward orientation: trade issues', in V. Corbo, M. Goldstein and M. Khan (eds) *Growth-Oriented Adjustment Programs,* Washington, DC: the International Monetary Fund and International Bank for Research and Development.
—— (1988) 'Export-promoting trade strategy: issues and evidence', *World Bank Research Observer* (January): 27–57.
—— and Desai, P. (1970) *India: Planning for Industrialization,* London: Oxford University Press.
—— and Srinivasan, T.N. (1975) *Foreign Trade Regimes and Development: India,* New York: Columbia University Press for the National Bureau of Economic Research.
Cline, W. (1982) 'Can the East Asian model be generalized?', *World Development 10* (2): 81–90.
Donges, J. and Riedel, J. (1977) 'Expansion of manufactured exports in developing countries: An empirical assessment of supply and demand issues', *Weltwirtschaftliches Archiv* (May): 58–87.
Feder, G. (1983) 'On exports and economic growth', *Journal of Development Economics* (February–April): 59–74.
Gard, L. and Riedel, J. (1980) 'Safeguard protection of industry in developed countries: assessment of the implications for developing countries', *Weltwirtschaftliches Archiv* 3: 471–92.
Goldstein, M. and Khan, M. (1985) 'Income and price effects in foreign trade', in R.W. Jones and P. Kenen (eds) *Handbook of International Economics,* vol. 2, Amsterdam: Elsevier.

Han, S.S. (1984) 'Of economic success and Confucianism', *Far Eastern Economic Review,*126 (51): 104–6

Hughes, H. and Krueger, A. (1984) 'Effects of protection in developed countries on developing countries', in R. Baldwin and A. Krueger (eds) *The Structure and Evolution of Recent U.S. Trade Policy,* Chicago, IL: Chicago University Press for the National Bureau of Economic Research.

Hughes, G.H. and Newbery, D.M.G. (1986) 'Protection and developing countries' exports of manufactures', *Economic Policy* 1: 409–41.

Jones, E.L. (1981) *The European Miracle: Environment, Economics and Geopolitics in the History of Europe and Asia,* Cambridge: Cambridge University Press.

Kahn, H. (1979) *World Economic Development,* Boulder, CO: Westview Press.

Keynes, J.M. (1926) *The End of Laissez Faire,* London: Hogarth Press.

Krueger, A.O. (1978) *Foreign Trade Regimes and Economic Development Liberalization Attempts and Consequences,* Cambridge, MA: Ballinger for the National Bureau of Economic Research.

—— (1984) 'Trade policies in developing countries', in R. Jones and P.B. Kenen (eds) *Handbook of International Economics,* New York: North Holland.

—— and Tuncer, B. (1982) 'An empirical test of the infant industry argument', *American Economic Review* (June): 1142–52.

Krugman, P. (1986) 'New trade theory and the less developed countries', paper presented at the Carlos Diaz-Alejandro Memorial Conference, World Institute for Development Economics Research, Helsinki.

Lal, D. (1983) *The Poverty of Development Economics,* London: Institute of International Affairs.

—— (1988) 'Markets, mandarins and mathematicians', *Cato Journal,* forthcoming.

—— and Rajapatirana, S. (1987) 'Trade regimes and economic growth in developing countries', *World Bank Research Observer* (July): 189–217.

Lewis, W.A. (1980) 'The slowing down of the engine of growth', *American Economic Review* (September): 555–64.

Little, I.M.D. (1982) *Economic Development: Theory, Policy and International Relations,* New York: Basic Books.

—— Scitovsky, T. and Scott, M. (1970) *Industry and Trade in Some Developing Countries,* London: Oxford University Press.

Michaely, M. (1977) 'Exports and growth: an empirical investigation', *Journal of Development Economics* (March): 49–53

—— (1988) 'Trade liberalization policies: lessons of experience', World Bank, unpublished mimeo.

Michalopoulos, C. and Jay, K. (1973) 'Growth of exports and income in the developing world: a neo-classical view', Agency of International Development Discussion Paper 28, Washington DC.

Morishima, M. (1982) *Why has Japan Succeeded? Western Technology and the Japanese Ethos,* Cambridge: Cambridge University Press.

Needham, J. (1954) *Science and Civilization in China,* Cambridge: Cambridge University Press.

Noguès, J.J., Olechowski, A. and Winters, L.A. (1986) 'The extent of non-tariff barriers to industrial countries' imports', *World Bank Economic Review* (September): 181–98.

Pack, H. (1986) 'The links between development strategies and industrial growth', World Bank, unpublished mimeo.

—— and Westphal, L.E. (1986) 'Industrial strategy and technological change: theory and evidence', *Journal of Development Economics*, 22: 87–128.

Pearson, C. (1983) *Emergency Protection in the Footwear Industry*, Thames Essay 36, London: Trade Policy Research Centre.

Reynolds, L.G. (1983) 'The spread of economic growth to the third world: 1850–1980', *Journal of Economic Literature*, 21 (3): 941–80.

Riedel, J. (1984) 'Trade as an engine of growth, revisited', *Economic Journal*, (March): 56–73.

—— (1987) *Myths and Realities of External Constraints on Development*, London: Gower for the Trade Policy Research Centre.

—— (1988a) 'The demand for LDC exports of manufactures: estimates from Hong Kong', *Economic Journal*, (March): 138–48.

—— (1988b) 'Economic development in East Asia: doing what comes naturally?' in H. Hughes (ed.) *Achieving Industrialization in East Asia*, London: Cambridge University Press

—— (1988c) 'Macroeconomic crises and long-term economic growth in developing countries: a case study of Turkey, part II', Johns Hopkins University, School of Advanced International Studies, unpublished mimeo, May.

Sachs, J. (1985) 'External debt and macroeconomic performance in Latin America and East Asia', *Brookings Papers on Economic Activity*, 2: 523–64.

—— (1987) 'Trade and exchange rate policies in growth-oriented adjustment programs', in V. Corbo, M. Goldstein and M. Khan (eds,) *Growth-Oriented Adjustment Programs*, Washington, DC: International Monetary Fund, 291–325.

Smith, A. (1776) *The Wealth of Nations*

Srinivasan, T.N. (1986a) 'Development strategy: is the success of outward orientation at an end?, in S. Guhan and M. Schroff (eds) *Essays on Economic Progress and Welfare*, New Delhi: Oxford University Press.

—— (1986b) 'Recent theories of imperfect competition and international trade: any implications for development strategy?', World Bank, unpublished mimeo.

Timmer, C.P. (1973) 'Choice of technique in rice milling in Java', *Bulletin of Indonesian Studies*, 9 (2): 57–76.

Tyler, W. (1981) 'Growth and export expansion in developing countries: some empirical evidence', *Journal of Development Economics*, 9 (1): 121–30.

Wade, R. (1988) 'The role of government in overcoming market failure: Taiwan, South Korea and Japan', in H. Hughes, (ed) *Achieving Industrialization in East Asia*, Cambridge: Cambridge University Press.

Westphal, L.E. (1982) 'Fostering technological mastery by means of selective infant industry protection', in M. Syrquin and S. Teitel, (eds) *Trade, Stability Technology and Equity in Latin America*, New York: Academic Press.

5 Why voluntary export restraints? A historical analysis

Martin Wolf

INTRODUCTION

The new protectionism . . . has been growing gradually. Industries have used intelligent, long-term planning in creating an expanded system of protection. The expansion proceeds sectorally; instead of an effort to reduce all imports as much as possible, we are witnessing the construction of industrial protection systems, each tailored to the special needs of the industry in question, each administered by a highly specialized bureaucracy, often co-opted into public service from the respective industry associations. The system coordinates several instruments – trade restrictions, subsidies, explicit or tacit exemptions from competition or anti-trust laws and elements of direct government regulation. The protectionism of the 1930s was openly adversary; the new . . . is in a perverse way the result of international cooperation.

(Tumlir 1951: 38)

If a country's executive branch is characterized by the pro-trade bias I sketched above whereas its legislators must respond to protectionist pressure from various constituency groups, then it can be argued that a smart executive branch will prefer to use a porous form of protection that, while ensuring freer market access, will nonetheless appear to be a concession to political demands for protection from the legislators or from their constituencies. . . . The non-transparency of VERs then is an advantage, not a hindrance, to the continuation of relatively free . . . trade as long as the obfuscation does not become apparent before the industry has adjusted to the fact of effective foreign rivalry.

(Bhagwati 1988: 58)

Two excellent books, by two distinguished authors, both with the same main title, come to opposite conclusions on the reasons for, and seriousness of, the phenomenon of voluntary export restraints (VERs).[1] It is clear that the analysis of VERs is like the blind man's description of an elephant: it depends on what part he is holding. VERs have a good side and a dark side. A temperamentally optimistic author, like the Indian economist Jagdish Bhagwati, sees the former, while the more pessimistically inclined Jan Tumlir, who was for years the 'conscience' of the General Agreement on Tariffs and Trade (GATT), focused on the latter. The author of the present article sees both. That VERs are a phenomenon of deceit, not to say skulduggery, is evident. Whether the deceit is ultimately for good or not depends not only on the facts of each case but on the longer-term implications of the phenomenon.

By now VERs are familiar. They are found everywhere, along with their twin sisters, price undertakings. Familiarity may not breed contempt, but it does breed familiarity. The shock has gone. But there should be shock, for VERs are shocking things.

Why should governments – notably those of the USA and the European Community (both as a whole and its individual members) – think VERs are a good idea? Why – to put the matter more bluntly – should they actively promote, indeed force, the creation of export cartels against their own citizens? It is as if the Organization of Petroleum Exporting Countries (OPEC) has been created by the consumers. One of the ironies of history is that the great success of OPEC and the negotiation of the Multi-Fibre Arrangement (MFA), the apotheosis of VERs, were achieved at the same time, the end of 1973.[2] The MFA has proved the more robust cartel, thanks to the involvement of the governments of consuming countries.

It is this enthusiasm that is puzzling. It forces reconsideration of the standard assumptions of economists about what governments are trying to maximize. It cannot be the economic welfare of their citizens. For this reason VERs should be of interest not merely to economists working on trade but to all who are interested in public policy.

WHAT VERs ARE

Economically, VERs are quite a simple phenomenon. They are an arrangement by particular groups of exporters to limit the quantity or hold up the price of exports to particular markets. But legally they are more complex, as is made clear by John Jackson, one of the leading authorities on the GATT and other trade law.

The principle classification of importance is the distinction between those measures imposed by the *government* of the exporting country and those imposed or effected totally by an *industry* through an industry association or some other non-government entity.

Non-government measures could include agreements, whether explicit or implicit (tacit), between industry groups in the exporting and importing countries. Various subtle approaches have also been observed, such as 'predictions' of export trends.

Government measures can include explicit government-to-government agreements (usually, technically, in treaty form) in which the exporting government agrees to limit exports to the other country in certain ways. In the law of the United States, and in some other countries, these are termed 'orderly marketing arrangements'. In some cases, a government on one side may explicitly agree with a non-government group on the other side . . . that exports should be restrained. The government might be that of the exporting country or it might be that of the importing country. In such cases the agreement is usually deemed 'informal' and not legally binding.

With government measures that are informal or tacit, the usual pattern is for the government of the exporting country to make some sort of 'statement', or explanation of intent, by which it will seek to ensure that exports of a particular product to another country will be kept below certain limits. The Japanese restraints on automobile exports to the American market are a prime example.

(Jackson 1988: 586–7)

Proposition One: *All VERS are voluntary, but some are more voluntary than others.*

Some VERS are so voluntary that nobody outside the exporters' association knows they exist. So there are VERS and voluntary VERS. How then is one to distinguish between a VER and a purely private, old-fashioned export cartel?

Proposition Two: *An agreement to restrict exports to a particular market is a VER and not an export cartel when the government of the importing country approves of the arrangement, if it knows about it, or would approve of it if it were to know about it, even though it does now know about it, or pretends that it does not know about it, or would like to pretend that it does not know about it.*

If the above formulation reminds the reader of the celebrated British television programme, *Yes Minister*, this is no accident.

WHERE VERs COME FROM

To whom do we owe VERS? The idea of a gentleman's agreement in trade seems to begin with relations between the USA on the one hand and Far Eastern suppliers (principally Japan) on the other. There were a number of VERs on Japanese exports in the 1930s but the most important were on textiles, the longest lasting and most painful headache afflicting the trade in manufactures of industrial countries.[3]

In 1934 the UK had already imposed discriminatory quotas against Japanese exports of textiles to India. Meanwhile, in the USA in 1930, an average tariff of 46 per cent on cotton goods and 60 per cent on wool and woollen manufactures exceeded those for metals and metal manufactures (35 per cent) and chemicals (31 per cent). Furthermore, in spite of these high levels of tariff protection, the threat of a low-wage supplier – in this case Japan – was seen as needing a more decisive riposte even in 1935 when, at the suggestion of a Cabinet Committee (Keesing and Wolf 1980: 11), it was agreed that a voluntary export quota should be negotiated.

It was in Osaka in 1937 that the first 'gentlemen's agreement' between the American and Japanese trade associations was negotiated.

> The US Government clearly favoured the unofficial approach, *else anti-trust law would have been used to prevent it*. . . . It is particularly significant that at the very beginning of the modern era of American trade policy the two prime movers in its development – Roosevelt and Hull – recognized the uniqueness of the textile import problem and arranged to handle it separately from their general trade program [as embodied in the Reciprocal Trade Agreements Act of 1934] (emphasis added).
>
> (Brandis 1982: 7–8)

The explanation for these governmental nods and winks to an informal, probably illegal, agreement was that the USA possessed no legal authority for the introduction of import quotas, let alone discriminatory quotas. On the contrary, both were precluded not merely by existing law but by the fundamental policy of the Administration. The political itch created by 'disruptive' imports from Japan could only be scratched in an extra-legal way. Nor was it an accident that the Japanese were on the other end. By virtue of their status as outsiders, they were resigned to special treatment; by virtue of their exceptional competitiveness, they were a prime focus for resentment; and, by virtue of their culture, they were inclined towards informal solutions to conflict.

In the history of the VERs, textiles appear to have been the leading sector, even though those restraints were to experience an apotheosis onto a higher plane, where they lost the informal dross of mere VERs. A special international arrangement was created to organize these restraints, one that grew into the MFA of today. None the less, it was the treatment of textiles that made export restraints legitimate. 'Although never intended to be a precedent, although explicitly stated to be addressed to a unique problem, and to be exceptional and temporary in character, the textile arrangements have acted as precedents all the same' (Dunkel 1984: 363).

Proposition Three: *All industries are equal, but textiles and clothing are more equal than others.*

For what had happened before the Second World War happened again soon after, but at a time when the USA was strongly committed to non-discrimination – the most-favoured-nation (MFN) principle – within the GATT, a treaty made in the image of its own pre-war legislation.

> Towards the end of 1955, Japan began to impose internal restrictions on some of her cotton textile exports to the United States. . . . In January 1957, Japan gave American officials details of a five-year programme of 'voluntary' export controls. . . . American pressure contributed to this outcome, particularly a provision in a new law, the Agricultural Act of 1956, which empowered the President, 'whenever he determines such action appropriate', to negotiate agreements limiting exports from other countries or imports into the United States of textiles or textile products and also giving him some emergency power to restrict these imports unilaterally.
>
> (Keesing and Wolf 1980: 15)

The battle to coerce the Japanese was not an easy one, largely because of the resistance of the exporting industry itself. So 'in order to induce the Japanese Government to try to coerce its textile industry to use self-restraint, the conditions on which Okinawa would revert to Japanese sovereignty had to be brought into the negotiation' (Tumlir 1985: 41). What was it that persuaded the US Administration, averse to such intervention as it appeared to be, to put the required pressure on Japan?

Pressure from the US Congress is the answer, pressure orchestrated by the American Textile Manufacturers Institute. In 1956 the Senate only narrowly defeated an amendment to a pending foreign aid bill that would have mandated import quotas on cotton textiles based on the preceding 3-year average import level. One reason for the defeat was that several senators were persuaded that other action would be taken to deal with the problem, as was indeed to be the case (Brandis 1982: 10). As the Senate Finance Committee commented, 'the Senate may not wish to continue past support of international programs which contribute to widespread unemployment or serious injury to domestic producers' (Brandis 1982: 11).

Proposition Four: *Congress plays 'bad cop', the Administration plays 'good cop' and out pops a VER.*

The VER with Japan might have been the end of the matter. But the textile industry spread like a plague. Exports expanded rapidly from Hong Kong, Portugal, Spain, Egypt and India. Worse, Hong Kong refused to accept a VER with the USA, although it, along with India and Pakistan, did accept VERs on exports to the UK (but then, being a colony, it could hardly do otherwise (Keesing and Wolf 1980: 15–16)).

Within the US the political pressure grew so great that John F. Kennedy committed himself to support of the textile industry during the Presidential election campaign of 1960. Thereupon, the search was on for an internationally respectable figleaf to cover the abandonment of the GATT's first article. That figleaf was found in 'the question of the avoidance of market disruption', already placed on the GATT agenda by the USA in 1959. For, to the horror of the developed countries, the GATT appeared to commit them to trading over 'bound' tariffs with countries that had a decisively different pattern of comparative advantage from themselves. Of no country was this more true than Japan and of no industry was this more true than textiles and clothing (Dam 1970: ch. 17, esp. pp. 297–300).

In the end, 'market disruption' was incorporated into a new international agreement, an anti-GATT specially for textiles: the Short Term Arrangement Regarding International Trade in Cotton Textiles of 1961, which begat the Long Term Arrangement of 1962, which begat the MFA of 1974 and so on to the present day. With an international agreement behind it that contained an explicit clause for unilateral safeguard action in Article 3, it was no longer particularly difficult for the USA to persuade the exporters to sign up for 'voluntary' bilateral agreements under Article 4. It merely required plenty of action under Article 3 (Dam 1970: 308). For, although not usually considered in this light, bilateral agreements under Article 4 of the textile arrangements are VERs. They are merely less 'voluntary' than others because the legal alternative to a voluntary agreement is more unfavourable to the exporting countries than in other cases.

Proposition Five: *The bigger the stick, the more restrictive the restraint.*[4]

HOW VERs SPREAD

Textiles are special in one important sense. Only textiles and clothing have a formal international arrangement authorizing a network of export-restraint arrangements. In most cases this proved unnecessary. Production of other goods is neither so widespread nor so swift to jump from one country to another. In most industries, it is easier to reach agreement directly with industry associations, without a complex web of governmental controls. Unavoidably, therefore, any system of VERs to deal with textiles and clothing has to be more complex and comprehensive, with its thousands of individual export quotas by product, by source and by destination out-numbering those in all other industries put together.

Most other domestic industries are also not as politically effective. The textile arrangements are irritating and complex to manage. They served as a precedent for the use of VERs, but also as a warning of what undue legalism might lead to. So in other industries it was informal VERs that grew more plentiful as time went by, although many of the *leitmotifs* of the textile saga were to be repeated: 'market disruption' by overly competitive suppliers, often Japanese and almost always from the Far East; intensive political pressure when there was no acceptable alternative to a VER; the US Congress playing the role of 'bad cop' and the US Administration that of a 'good cop'.

One area in which VERs spread with great rapidity was textiles and clothing itself, to cover new exporters, new products and new fibres. Meanwhile, they also spread to new industries. Discussion of three examples is all that space permits. But these examples do at least cover the three most important sectors affected by VERs after textiles and clothing, namely automobiles, steel and consumer electronics. They also cover the principal routes to VERs. Finally, they cover the three main players – the USA and the European Community (EC), at one end, and Japan at the other.

Automobiles

'In most instances', wrote Destler in his study of American trade politics, 'the aim of particular quota bills was still not to get them enacted into law. Rather, it was to demonstrate the sponsor's allegiance to a particular industry, or to pressure the executive branch, the appropriate foreign government, or both. . . . In the early 1980s, the most dramatic and visible example of this phenomenon was the struggle over trade in automobiles' (Destler 1986: 69).

With the second oil shock and the shift in demand towards smaller cars, the American automobile industry found itself in dire straits, with unemployment in the industry soaring above 300,000 out of a total of almost one million directly employed in the industry. As Dr Destler (1986: 70) explains, the Congressional response to the crisis went through three stages.

First, they hoped that the established escape-clause procedures would resolve the problem. But the United States International Trade Commission (USITC) let them down, deciding by a three-to-two vote 'that it could not recommend relief because the major cause of the industry's woes were other than imports' (Destler 1986: 70). Charles Vanik, as Chairman of the House Trade Subcommittee, 'had frequently urged that import issues be handled by "economic law", not politics' and was therefore naturally prepared to accept the outcome of the USITC's objective procedure (Destler 1986: 71). The moon is made of green cheese, too.

Proposition Six: *The fight between overwhelming political pressure, on the one hand, and objective trade law, on the other, is no contest.*

In the second stage of the crisis, Representative Vanik moved quickly with a special resolution asking the President to negotiate an orderly marketing agreement with Japan. Then, in the new Congress, Senator John Danforth of Missouri introduced a bill that would have imposed statutory quotas on automobile imports for three years, the aim not being to pass the bill but to pressure the Administration to pressure the Japanese to agree to a VER. Tokyo was willing, but the smaller automobile companies – particularly Honda, which looked to the American market as the best way to improve its position *vis-à-vis* Toyota and Nissan – were not. So the Ministry of International Trade and Industry (MITI) needed a great deal of 'foreign sovereign compulsion' to justify the restraints, precisely what Ronald Reagan's Administration wished to avoid. 'The result was a "look-no-hands" approach that confused Tokyo and increased the need for congressional threats' (Destler 1986: 71). In the end, the threats were sufficient to obtain a 2–3 year VER that has endured in a still more informal manner ever since.

Proposition Seven: *A VER is a way of getting another dog to scratch your fleas, when you lack the legs.*

Proposition Eight: *VERs also keep MITI (and Japan Inc.) in business.*

Proposition Nine: *VERs are how established Japanese firms deal with their most fearsome competitors – other Japanese firms.*

In the third stage of the crisis the United Auto Workers made a great effort to pass a domestic-content bill. But this was unsuccessful. The agreement to the VER combined with the recovery of the industry was sufficient to defuse the pressure. The bill never even reached the floor of the Senate.

But VERs on automobiles from Japan are not just an American story. European countries also have such VERs, all far more restrictive. The case of the UK's restraint agreement is of interest for the differences from, and similarities to, the American approach.[5]

'In 1967', wrote Brian Hindley in *What Britain Pays for Voluntary Export Restraints*, 'the Japanese share of the British market for motor cars was 0.2 percent. By 1972, the figure had risen to 3.1 percent and by 1976 to 9.4 percent. In 1977, an Anglo-Japanese agreement effectively froze the Japanese market share of the British market at 11 percent [where it has been ever since]' (Hindley 1985a: 64). The most interesting feature of the British agreement is that it has no official status whatsoever. It is in the form of a market-sharing agreement between the Society of Motor Manufacturers and Traders and the Japanese Automobile Manufacturers Association. This does not mean, of course, that the Government of the UK was not firmly behind the negotiations. On the contrary, embassy officials have been present in meetings in Japan. What it does mean is that the British Government is able to parade its clean hands.

Why the elaborate charade? The most important reason is that, under the common commercial policy of the EC, the UK should not have national restraints which are unauthorized by the EC. But there is little likelihood of agreeing on such a Community-wide policy in the case of automobiles. Accordingly, the UK had to promote the policy informally, with the Commission in Brussels showing a Nelsonian blind eye to the consequent violations of Community trade and competition policies.

Proposition Ten: *When it comes to 'look-no-hands' VERs, anything the USA can do, the EC can do better.*

Steel

After textiles, steel is the industry that has the most complete network of export-restraint arrangements, covering imports by the USA and the EC. There have even been times when a 'multi-steel agreement' appeared to be in the offing. More interesting still, the VERs have usually been presented as a way of resolving or anticipating particular 'fair trade' remedies, namely anti-dumping or subsidy-countervailing duties.[6]

In the case of the EC, a web of export-restraint arrangements was imposed in 1977 at the time of the first emergency plan for dealing with the post-1973 crisis of the steel industry that also incorporated – initially voluntary, subsequently mandatory – production quotas on Community steel companies. The VERs were (and still are) justified as an alternative to anti-dumping measures.

But perhaps the clearest example of the general theme is the events that led up to the VER on exports of steel products from the EC to the USA in 1982. American firms have recognized the potency of anti-dumping and countervailing duty action since 1977 (that *annus horribilis* in the history of trade policy). They know that

> foreign interests are dismayed because the trade-remedy procedures seem arbitrary and unfair to them. . . . They (Europeans above all) are anxious about the real trade effects of US legal decisions. . . . They are unwilling to let their fates be determined by procedures that might seem objective and fair and non-political to Americans, but which to foreign eyes appear either unpredictable or skewed in favor of the import-affected petitioner.
>
> (Destler 1986: 126)

The cases brought by the American steel industry in 1982 were entirely justified. There was no doubt that some European governments were pouring money down the insatiable maws of their steel industry. But the 150 petitions brought forward in 1982 were too much for the Europeans to cope with. They wanted to settle out of court.

> The end result was a political solution entirely outside established procedures. The EC 'voluntarily' restricted carbon steel exports to the United States to 5.44 percent of the US market. And while this overall limit corresponded roughly to what the outcome of enforcing our law would have been the Europeans distributed the pain among

themselves so that the efficient Germans ended up worse off than they would have been, and the inefficient British and French better off.
(Destler 1986: 129)

This was not the end of the steel saga. Comprehensive VERs were still to come. The USITC ruled in 1984 by three to two in favour of an escape-clause petition brought by Bethlehem Steel and the United Steel workers. It recommended a mixture of tariffs, quotas and tariff-quotas for 5 years, a recommendation that President Reagan proudly rejected in what Dr Destler calls 'a political master stroke and a trade policy disaster' (Destler 1986: 134). 'The President', asserted William Brock, as the US Trade Representative, 'has clearly determined that protectionism is not in the national interest. It costs jobs, raises prices and undermines our ability to compete here and abroad' (Destler 1986: 134).

So what did President Reagan prefer to protectionism? VERs, of course, with a target for the market share of imports of 18.5 per cent. In the event, VERs were negotiated with every significant supplier. So the President's national policy for the steel industry ended up, 'if anything, more protectionist than the USITC program he rejected' (Destler 1986: 135). Dr Destler further commented: 'In the months that followed, agreements were negotiated or reaffirmed with every major foreign seller, whether or not they subsidized sales, whether or not the USITC had found injury from imports of the specific products. What it amounted to was systematic circumvention of the rules for enforcing fair trade' (1986: 135).

Proposition Eleven: *When you want protection without being a protectionist, thank the Lord for VERs. Or, you can fool all of the people some of the time and some of the people all of the time – and that's enough.*

Consumer electronics

Perhaps it appears that the discussion focuses unduly on the USA. This is not entirely unfair because VERs probably play a more central role in the trade policy of the USA that in that of the EC, but as the various constraints imposed by membership of the Community became more binding, the use of VERs grew more frequent, too. As already discussed, they are a way for national governments to evade Community scrutiny. But in 1983 they also became a way for the Commission to evade scrutiny by the Community's member countries. This was the year of the first VER between Japan and the Community as a whole, the most important affected prcduct being video cassette recorders (VCRs).[7]

The trigger for this agreement was an anti-dumping suit brought in December 1982 by the Association of Firms with a Common Interest in Video 2000. This followed a decision by France in October of that year to require customs clearance of all VCRs through a small post in the inland town of Poitiers (a town chosen perhaps because it was where Charles Martel had turned back the Arabs early in the eighth century). Subject to these pressures and fearful that it would have to defend these indefensible French measures in the GATT, even though it had no responsibility for introducing them, the Commission was keen to exert its authority. 'I am your leader', the Commission said to itself, 'so I must follow you' and follow it did – all the way to Tokyo, where it announced the new VER on St Valentine's Day 1983 (sweetheart deal or massacre?). The anti-dumping case was then dropped.

The negotiators, Commissioners Etienne Davignon and Wilhelm Haferkamp, hailed the deal as a turning point. 'The turning point referred to is relevant to the contest for control of trade policy between the Commission of the European Community and the governments of the member countries.'[8]

WHERE VERs ARE NOW

It is impossible to deal in a similarly detailed way with all VERs, even if we knew about them, which by their very nature we do not. What is clear, however, is that VERs have grown like Topsy. The four industries discussed above – textiles and clothing, steel, automobiles and electronics – are the most significant. Dr Destler notes that, in the first three sectors alone (i.e. excluding electronics) and under a President supposedly inclined to free trade, one-quarter of American manufactured imports were subject either to VERs or to export restraints under the MFA. 'When the special cases in trade policy reach this magnitude, they begin to look less like the exception and more like the emerging rule' (Destler 1986: 168).

The position of the EC is similar, with coverage of the same major industries. The proportion of imports affected might be smaller, largely because restraints are generally tighter than those of the USA, notably in automobiles. The proportion of output distorted by VERs is almost certainly larger in the Community than in the USA (at least until the semiconductor agreement between the USA and Japan) because the textiles and clothing, steel and automobile industries are somewhat more important to the Community's economy than to that of the USA.

Michael Kostecki, of the GATT Secretariat, provides an analysis for 1986–7 that excludes textiles and clothing restraints under the MFA and even so is far from exhaustive, as the author himself admits (Kostecki 1987). He reports 137 arrangements, of which sixty-eight cover the EC, forty-five cover the USA and ten cover Canada. In addition, 'Thirty-two cases cover exports originating in high-income countries other than Japan, while 26 cases cover exports originating in Japan. Eighteen cases cover exports originating in Eastern Europe. Forty-four cases cover exports originating in developing countries other than the Republic of Korea and in Eastern Europe, wile seventeen cases cover exports originating in the Republic of Korea' (Kostecki 1987: 428). Dr Kostecki added:

> Product categories most heavily affected by export-restraint arrangements include steel and steel products (44 arrangements), textile and clothing . . . machine tools (six arrangements), automobiles and transport equipment (fifteen arrangements of which thirteen are with Japan), electronic products (ten arrangements of which seven are with Japan), foot wear (eight arrangements) and agricultural products (25 arrangements) . . . .
>
> Moreover, the 1986 arrangement between the United States and Japan on trade in semi-conductors firmly established managed trade in the electronics industry, for the United States and Japan accounted then for about 90 percent of the $30 billion worth of world production of semi-conductors from which derives an electronics industry with sales of $300 billion. . . .
>
> The import-weighted coverage of 'grey area' measures [using 1984 trade data] was about 38 percent for the European Community's imports from Japan and not less than 33 percent for the United States imports from Japan. . . .
>
> [O]verall, in the mid-1980s, not less than 10 percent of world trade, and about 12 percent of world non-fuel trade, is covered by export-restraint arrangements [including here those under the MFA].
>
> (Kostecki 1987: 428–9)

On Dr Kostecki's analysis, the coverage of world trade in manufactures would be about 15 per cent. The proportion of trade directly covered by export restraints, however, is far below the share of world trade *distorted* by those restraints. Trade in motor vehicles, iron and steel and textiles and clothing amounts to 28 per cent of world trade in manufactures. All this trade must have been altered, much of it radically, by the existence of a pervasive web of restraints on exports from the most competitive producers.

Proposition Twelve: *A VER here and a VER there and pretty soon you have real protection.*

WHY VERs MATTER

That VERs are costly in relation to any explicit objective is well established. What is more controversial is the costliness of the whole array of VERs when set against any likely alternative. It is on the latter point that a conflict of view apparently emerges between the late Jan Tumlir, on the one hand, and Professor Bhagwati and the American economist Robert Baldwin, on the other (Tumlir 1985; Bhagwati 1988; Baldwin 1988).

As Table 5.1 indicates, VERs impose large economic costs for any success they may have in achieving their ostensible purposes, particularly if one of those purposes is the preservation of employment. The main reason is that, over and above all the normal costs of quantitative restrictions (which are large enough), the quota rent (the vergeld, a relative of the Anglo-Saxon wergeld)[9] is transferred to the exporting country

Table 5.1 The Hierarchy of Policies for the problem of unemployment caused by labour-market distortions

Remedies	Adverse side effects
1 Remove distortion directly	None
2 Subsidize labour	Cost of raising revenue and subsidy administration
3 Subsidize production	As in (2) *plus* labour intensity too low
4 Tariff plus export subsidy	As in (3) *minus* cost of raising revenue and subsidy administration plus consumption distortion
5 Tariff	As in (4) *plus* home-market bias
6 Import quota	As in (5) *plus* loss of government revenue to licensees administrative complexity
7 Discriminatory export restraints	As in (6) *plus* export of quota rent to foreign licence holders diversion to higher-cost imports still further administrative complexity

Source: Wolf *et al.* 1984: Table 2.1

and usually to the exporters themselves. For example, one study has suggested that in American textiles and clothing the ratio of the present value of the cost of export restraints to the value of the job 'saved' was of the order of one hundred to one.[10]

It is also well substantiated that VERs are poor at achieving their ostensible objectives. This is so for two reasons. First, as Professor Baldwin points out, VERs are porous. Products can be trans-shipped, upgraded, exported in a less processed form or fraudulently exported and there can be shifts to substitute commodities or to different countries of origin. Second, even if they do achieve the desired increase in prices, this is unlikely to have some of the supposed effects: improved long-term competitiveness, for example, or even preservation of employment (Baldwin 1988: *passim*).

Proposition Thirteen: *VERs are economically ineffective and cheap or economically effective and expensive. There is no such thing as an economically effective and cheap VER.*

What must be true is that if a considerable degree of protection is ultimately to be given by a system of export restraints, its long-term costs must be both large and pervasive, as argued by Tumlir in his last published work (Tumlir 1985: ch. 3). The existence of such a system *fragments* the world market, *encourages* cartelization in import-competing industry, *forces* the creation of cartels in the most competitive exporting countries, *makes* intimate details of production and investment the subject of international negotiations, *creates* a complex web of vested producer interests in protection, *warns* newcomers to an industry, both companies and countries, of the perilous consequences of successful entry and *leads* the governments of both the importing and exporting country to connive at violations of both the letter and the spirit of their domestic and international legal obligations.

If all this is true, VERs can only be benign if they are, indeed, contained at the chrysalis stage of ineffectiveness before they turn into a dark moth like the MFA. When one considers the historical examples discussed above, it seems unlikely that they are, or can be, contained in this way. The question is which sort of VER is the more common: the ineffective and cheap or the effective and expensive. This, in turn, depends on why there are VERs in the first place. Are they there because protection is really required or because what is needed is window-dressing for liberalism?

WHY THERE ARE VERs

What needs to be explained is why our lords and masters have chosen the VER as a preferred instrument of trade policy. The spread of export restraints is remarkable. It does need an explanation, at least where the governments of the importing countries are concerned. In searching through the literature, one can identify the following hypotheses (which are not mutually exclusive): stupidity, benevolence, bribery, governmental schizophrenia, bureaucratic and corporate self-interest, deceit (malign or benign) and political or legal inhibitions.

Stupidity

Economists are very uncomfortable with explanations founded on stupidity. It violates their fundamental assumption of intelligent self-interestedness. But anyone with even a small knowledge of history will realize that the assumption of intelligent self-interestedness is quite difficult to apply to the behaviour of states (as Machiavelli discovered to his despair). It is possible that one reason why President Reagan said of his steel VERs that they were an alternative to protection is that the dear old buffer actually believed it. After all, the great majority of practical men do not recognize the very concept of 'costs of protection'. Costs of free trade, yes; costs of protection, no.[11]

A particular stupidity undoubtedly underlies the whole business of VERs: the idea that trade would be fine if only some countries were not so competitive. What is wanted is trade without comparative advantage. That idea appeared in the so-called 'scientific tariff'. Then it appeared in 'market disruption' and subsequently in the demand, particularly from the EC, for 'selectivity' in safeguard action.

Proposition Fourteen: *VERs are an attempt to have trade without comparative advantage.*

Benevolence

If one were to take the assumption of intelligent action seriously, one might hypothesize that governments choose VERs precisely because it is their special economic characteristic that appeals to them: the transfer of income to exporters. A benevolent US Administration might, for example, be concerned that Hong Kong clothing exporters are not yet rich enough and wish to make them a little richer. Alternatively, it may fear that the Japanese automobile or semiconductor industries have been struggling to make ends meet in a fierce battle with their own industries, just as the EC is concerned about the fate of the Japanese consumer electronics industry. By forcing these industries to upgrade while giving them the resources with which to do this, they can achieve their generous objective.

Bribery

Perhaps the above suggestion stretches credulity just a little far. Governments may well be stupid, but benevolence on this scale is another matter. It is possible, however, to put another gloss on the idea of benevolence, since the vergeld is a direct way of compensating exporters for accepting a quota restraint. Professor Jackson notes that arranging compensation within the framework of the GATT's Article XIX is quite difficult. VERs obviate the need since the compensation is neatly wrapped up along with the restriction in an all-in-one package (Jackson 1988: 495–6). While the need for a bribe does, indeed, provide a better explanation for the apparent benevolence, it is not entirely convincing on its own. Why, after all, should governments want to compensate foreigners for doing to them what is usually so popular at home? The explanation, one might suggest, is that countries wish to co-operate with their 'trading partners'. They do not want hostile international relations and prefer appeasement.

Schizophrenia

An alternative approach is simply to reject the concept of a unitary government pursuing coherent objectives. The 'good cop, bad cop' routine might not just be a device to trick exporters into accepting restraints; perhaps there really is a good cop and a bad cop. Under this explanation, the Administration in the USA is convinced of the merit of liberal trade and wishes to preserve it. Under irresistible pressure from Congress, the Administration looks for porous protection and finds it in VERs. One might envisage a similar schizophrenia in the EC, but the idea of a Commission secretly devoted to liberal trade is not quite so convincing.

The problem with the theory of schizophrenic government is that it is not obvious that an Administration in the USA which wishes to preserve liberal trade needs to go along with the rigmarole at all. As Tumlir pointed out, often (although perhaps not always) the Administration would have a good change of upholding a veto of the sort of protectionist bill that Congress discusses in order to put pressure upon it. 'The bluff is a thin one and an insufficient explanation of what follows' (Tumlir 1985: 39–40). It is easier to believe that the Administration wants to introduce some protection, but through an administrative device that gives it control over the process.

Bureaucratic and corporate self-interest

The key characteristic of VERs is that they are administrative devices. One might hypothesize that the US Trade Representative and the Commission of the EC on one end and MITI on the other share an interest in internationally-negotiated arrangements, which have the additional merit of excluding outsiders from discussion of the details, by virtue of their complexity. Their self-interest is to be added to that of the firms involved, above all the large and well-established exporters, for whom a VER can clearly be a valuable element in corporate strategy.

There is, undoubtedly. a great deal in this, but what needs to be explained then is why the government of the importing country should be concerned about the welfare of either the exporters or their government. Furthermore, while it seems quite likely that bureaucratic and commercial self-interest can sustain a given protectionist regime once established (governments being conservative institutions), it seems less likely that it can bring them into being in the first place, unaided.

Deceit

An explanation for some of the puzzles is that VERs have the merit of allowing deceit. A more opaque and confusing method of protection would be difficult to find. If a government wishes to provide protection without letting the public know how much it costs, an arrangement that keeps the exporters happy and is non-transparent in virtually all its details would seem ideal (this being an alternative explanation for President Reagan's preference for the steel VERs). Conversely, if a government does not wish to provide protection but wants to convince the import-competing industry that it does, then a VER might again seem just the right instrument.

Proposition Fifteen: *VERs are either the homage vice pays to virtue or vice versa.*

It is in the interest of politicians to offer protection to affected interest groups, whatever remarks they may feel obliged to make in favour of liberal apple pie. Similarly, it is in the interest of individual consumers to purchase imports, whatever they may say about preserving jobs. Hypocrisy is rife in trade policy. But politicians may double-cross the public, being well aware of the costs of granting too much protection. So Congress pretends to be protectionist and the Administration pretends to protect.

The question is who is ultimately successful in this game of bluff and double bluff. Professor Baldwin's analysis suggests that the liberals may come out on top in the end, however indirect their strategy. Tumlir suggested the opposite. Given the way VERs have spread, the latter view looks increasingly persuasive. Initially, a government may, indeed, wish to grant the appearance of protection without the substance. But, having granted the precedent, it may be driven by unassuaged pressures and the logic of events to extend protection to new suppliers and new supplies. In that case, VERs in major industries will remain limited in coverage and scope only if the industry itself does not spread. The VERs on Japanese textiles of the 1950s have become the MFA and the VERs on Japanese steel of the 1960s have become the present web of steel restrictions. Who, then, can doubt what lies in store for Korean automobiles?

Proposition Sixteen: *Even if VERs start as an attempt to do good by doing bad, the perpetrator is likely to be out-smarted in the end.*

Inhibitions

Perhaps the most persuasive reason for choosing a method of protection that benefits foreigners and involves a mountain of deceit, too, is that a government feels constrained from more direct alternatives. It is important to be careful in applying this hypothesis. Professor Jackson notes that the GATT illegality of VERs is a little uncertain (Jackson 1988: 497). What is less uncertain is that they are a violation of GATT principles. VERs also raise serious questions in relation to anti-trust policy in both the USA and the EC and are probably illegal in Japan, too, by virtue of being inconsistent with GATT obligations (Tumlir 1985: 52). Furthermore, VERs on exports to individual members of the Community appear to be a violation of the commitment to a common commercial policy.

The question is what would persuade all these major governments to sail so close to the wind of their domestic and international obligations. One clings to nurse for fear of something worse. That something worse is, first, the international and domestic ructions that would follow from non-discriminatory protection, second the visibility of such protection and, finally, the possibility of a spiral of retaliation.

Governments feel obliged to offer somewhat porous (and probably illegal) forms of protection because legal protection is like a nuclear bomb. Small wars have multiplied under the umbrella of the bomb and VERs have multiplied under the umbrella of reciprocally bound MFN tariffs.

> These special deals circumvented both national and international rules. Typically, they involved pressuring foreign governments . . . to enforce 'voluntary' export restraints. This device got around the domestic rules for providing injury and limiting the duration of protection. For the United States, VERs had the international benefit that, unlike measures taken directly against imports, they were not subject to the GATT proviso allowing other nations to impose equivalent trade restrictions, unless the United States offered 'compensation' in the form of offsetting tariff reductions. In both of these ways, they undercut the American trade policy-making system.
>
> (Destler 1986: 25)

Proposition Seventeen: *If illegal measures are thought preferable to legal ones, a great deal of bribery and deceit will be needed.*

CONCLUSION

It is difficult to be convincingly complacent about VERs. It is also difficult to be certain why they exist. All of the above hypotheses seem to have merit. Governments are schizophrenic. From time to time the more intelligent and liberal part finds itself under great pressure to do something about 'disruptive' imports and so looks around for something that will cause the least domestic and international fuss. What is needed, therefore, is something porous, something that keeps the exporters quiet, something non-transparent, something that minimizes international conflict. What is needed, in fact, is a VER. Then bureaucratic and corporate self-interest takes over, economic logic unfolds and the government finds itself increasingly entangled in its self-made web of deceit and illegality.

Conclusion: *The road to hell is paved with good intentions.*

NOTES

1   This article was prepared as part of the Trade Policy Research Centre's programmme of studies on the political economy of export-restraints arrangements and was presented at a conference in Washington convened by

the Centre on 6–8 June 1989 to review the papers arising from the programme. The project has been funded by grants from the Ford Foundation and the Rockefeller Foundation, in New York, and the Sasakawa Peace Foundation, in Tokyo (Hindley, forthcoming).

2 OPEC really made its mark on the world scene with the price increases that dated from the Yom Kippur War of October 1973. The first MFA, formally the Arrangement Regarding International Trade in Textiles, was negotiated in the final months of 1973 and entered into force on 1 January 1974.

3 The precise origin of VERs seems to be still unknown. See Bhagwati (1987: 2).

4 This is one of the main points in Hindley (1987).

5 See Hindley (1985a). The two most restrictive agreements in the EC are those with Italy (2,200 units per annum both ways) and France (3 per cent of the market), but neither is really a VER. The Italian agreement is even bound within the GATT.

6 Tumlir (1985: 44–8) elaborates the increasingly close relationship between 'fair-trade' law and VERs. VERs have, in fact, been one way of settling such cases 'out of court', although sometimes they have been resolved by price undertakings instead.

7 Hindley (1985b) provides a discussion of these complex events. In addition to VCRs the agreement also covered colour television tubes of above 52 cm. A number of other products were to be 'monitored'.

8 See Hindley (1985b: 34). Viscount Davignon was the EC's Commissioner for Industry; Mr. Haferkamp, the Commissioner for External Affairs.

9 Wergeld is 'the price set upon a man . . . paid by way of compensation or fine in cases of homicide and certain other crimes to free the offender from further obligation or punishment' (*Shorter Oxford English Dictionary*). Vergeld is the price set upon an importing country by way of compensation in cases of protection to free the offender from further obligation under the GATT or any other law.

10 Wolf *et al.* Pelzman (1984: 126). The literature on the costs of VERs has become substantial. See *inter alia* Kostecki (1987: Table 1) who reports a large number of estimates of the tariff equivalent of VERs; Greenaway and Hindley (1985: Table 1.1); Tarr and Morkre (1984), ch. 3 (automobiles), ch. 4 (textiles) and ch. 6 (steel); and Hufbauer and Rosen (1986: Table 2.2).

11 This was the principle of David Henderson's little masterpiece (Henderson 1986) in which he referred to the dominant school as 'do-it-yourself economics'.

REFERENCES

Baldwin, R.E. (1988) *Trade Policy in a Changing World Economy*, London: Harvester Wheatsheaf, ch. 9.

Bhagwati, J.N. (1987) 'VERs, *quid pro quo* FDI and VIEs: political-economy-theoretic analyses', *International Economic Journal*, Seoul, (Spring).

—— (1988) *Protectionism*, Cambridge, MA, and London: MIT Press.

Brandis, R.B. (1982) *The Making of Textile Trade Policy 1935–1981*,

Washington, DC: American Textile Manufacturers Association.

Dam, K.W. 1970) *The GATT: Law and International Economic Organization*, Chicago, IL, and London: University of Chicago Press, ch. 17.

Destler, I.M. (1986) *American Trade Politics: System under Stress*, Washington, DC, and New York: Institute for International Economics and the Twentieth Century Fund.

Dunkel, A.(1984) 'Lessons from textile experience for general trade policy', *World Economy* (December).

Greenaway, D. and Hindley, B. (1985) *What Britain Pays for Voluntary Export Restraints*, Thames Essay 43, London: Trade Policy Research Centre.

Henderson, D. (1986) *Innocence and Design: the Influence of Economic Ideas on Policy*, 1985 BBC Reith Lectures, Oxford: Basil Blackwell.

Hindley, B. (1985a) 'Motor cars from Japan', in D. Greenaway and B. Hindley (eds) *What Britain Pays for Voluntary Export Restraints*, Thames Essay 43, London: Trade Policy Research Centre.

—— (1985b) 'European venture: VCRs from Japan', in D. Greenaway and B. Hindley (eds) *What Britain Pays for Voluntary Export Restraints*, Thames Essay 43, London: Trade Policy Research Centre.

—— (1987) 'GATT safeguards and voluntary export restraints', *World Bank Economic Review* (September): 689–705.

—— (ed.) (forthcoming) *The Political Economy of Export Restraints*, London: Macmillan for the Trade Policy Research Centre.

Hufbauer, G.C. and Rosen, H.F. (1986) 'Trade policy for troubled industries', Policy Analyses in International Economics No. 15, Washington, DC: Institute for International Economics.

Jackson, J.H. (1988) 'Consistency of export-restraint arrangements with the GATT', *World Economy* (December).

Keesing, D.B. and Wolf, M. (1980) *Textile Quotas Against Developing Countries*, Thames Essay 23, London: Trade Policy Research Centre.

Kostecki, M. (1987) 'Export-restraint arrangements and trade liberalization', *World Economy* (December): 428–9.

Tarr, D.G. and Morkre, M.E. (1984) *Aggregate Costs to the United States of Tariffs and Quotas on Imports: General Tariff Cuts and Removal of Quotas on Automobiles, Steel, Sugar and Textiles*, Washington, DC: Federal Trade Commission.

Tumlir, J. (1985) *Protectionism: Trade Policy in Democratic Societies*, AEI Study No. 436, Washington, DC: American Enterprise Institute.

Wolf, M., Glissmann, H.H., Pelzman, J. and Spinanger, D. (1984) *Costs of Protecting Jobs in Textiles and Clothing*, Thames Essay 37, London: Trade Policy Research Centre.

6 Quota auctions and adjustment assistance: an international perspective

Robert C. Feenstra

INTRODUCTION

It is indeed a pleasure to contribute to this volume honouring the many contributions of Jagdish Bhagwati to international trade, commercial policy and economic development. As a colleague, editor and former student of his, I am familiar with well over a hundred of his writings in these areas. His contribution to this volume – Is free trade passé after all? – captures both his newest work on political economy and its relation to his earlier influential work on trade policy under domestic distortions. This piece also illustrates two important qualities which typify his writings: using theory to understand the policy dimension of each problem: and taking a world perspective of welfare, rather than the national view of a single country.

I intend to apply these two qualities to a problem which Jagdish and I jointly studied some years ago: tariff seeking and the efficient tariff. In that paper (Feenstra and Bhagwati 1982) we explained the presence of tariffs by the lobbying activities of an industry, and then introduced a government instrument which could be used to *offset* this lobbying. In particular, we allowed the government to commit the revenue raised from the tariff for direct compensation to the industry, as a means of reducing the lobbying activity. In most cases compensating the industry with the available revenue, and thus reducing lobbying, would indeed raise welfare. It was paradoxically possible, however, that the government would choose not to do this if the initial tariff so distorted the allocation of resources that the lobbying activity itself was welfare improving; a necessary case for this to occur was that the shadow price of resources in the lobbying activity was negative.

The policy relevance of our analysis was demonstrated by subsequent writings in the USA: Hufbauer and Rosen (1986) and Lawrence and Litan (1986) proposed that revenue from temporary tariffs be used for adjustment assistance, as part of their overall plans to liberalize trade. Subsequent work by Bergsten *et al*. (1987) examined more closely the revenue which would be available to finance the adjustment, and proposed *auctioning* US import quotas.[1] They estimated that auctioning existing US quotas on steel, textiles and apparel, machine tools, sugar and dairy imports could raise as much as $5.15 billion. Lower estimates of $3.7–4.7 billion for 1987–9 were provided by Parker (1987). At a time of high budget deficits, this potential source of revenue has attracted both Congressional and media attention in the USA.

The proposals to auction US import quotas as a source of revenue go well beyond the 'efficient tariff' which Bhagwati and I originally had in mind, and raise the issue of the reaction of US trading partners. It is very likely that US trading partners would view the auction of existing quotas as a serious violation of implicit or explicit trade agreements in each industry. It is often argued that the transfer of quota rents to the supplying country – as occurs when 'voluntary' export restrictions (VERs) are used – acts as compensation for the restriction itself. If this compensation were removed, we should not expect US trading partners to remain passive. Moreover, it seems plausible that, if the USA were to collect all the revenue/rents from trade restrictions, then this could create an incentive to preserve rather than to reduce the trade barriers, so as to maintain this source of funds.

From an international perspective, then, it seems desirable to have an instrument which allows a country to use tariff revenues to finance adjustment assistance, but *removes* the incentive to apply tariffs just to improve its terms of trade and obtain revenue. In addition, the instrument should compensate trading partners for any drop in their welfare. We shall argue that these goals are achieved by applying *tariff-rate quotas* to industries which are injured by imports. This instrument allows duty-free imports up to some quota level, and then levies a tariff on imports in excess of the quota. The supplying country therefore earns rents on the duty-free imports, while the demanding country earns tariff revenue on the additional imports. Thus, by varying the duty-free quota level, any allocation of the revenue/rents across the two countries can be achieved. We shall argue that if the foreign country is allocated just enough rents to keep its welfare equal to that in free trade, then the incentive for the home country to restrict imports and obtain a terms of trade gain is eliminated.

In the following section we outline our model, which is drawn from Feenstra and Lewis (1989). As in Feenstra and Bhagwati (1982), we suppose that policy choices are influenced by political pressures. In addition, we shall assume that the political pressure is *private information* to the home government, and cannot be directly observed abroad. In this setting, the home government may seek high trade barriers claiming political pressure as a reason, when in fact the barriers serve only to promote the interests of the home country at the expense of foreigners. To resolve this problem we shall determine 'incentive-compatible' trade policies, in which the home government has no incentive to overstate (or understate) the political pressures for protection.[2] We show in the section entitled 'Incentive-compatible policies' that incentive compatibility is maintained by the use of tariff-quotas, which keep foreign welfare at its free trade level. In addition to ensuring that the home country does not exaggerate the need for protection, the tariff-quotas are optimal from a global point of view.

In the section entitled 'Committing the revenue' we extend the analysis and suppose that the revenue from the tariff-quota is committed to the domestic industry. This changes the objective function of the home government, since now the same political pressures which lead to protection could be applied to the acquisition of revenue: a form of 'revenue-seeking' occurs, to use the phrase coined by Bhagwati and Srinivasan (1980). We again derive the incentive-compatible policy for the home government, and compare the tariff levels which are obtained with those when the revenue is *not* committed. It turns out that committing the revenue to the domestic industry can either *raise* or *lower* the incentive-compatible tariff which is applied, depending on whether imports are high or low respectively. Thus, there is an interesting parallel to Feenstra and Bhagwati (1982), who found that the optimal government policy could involve either an increase or a decrease in the tariff.

In the penultimate section we show how our results can be applied to the recent policy debate over auctioning US import quotas. As an alternative to quota auctions, we consider the system of tariff-rate quotas which would compensate exporters for the trade restriction. We calculate that tariff-quotas could raise $0.67–1.55 billion in revenue for the USA, while keeping imports at their current level and foreign welfare equal to that in free trade. While this revenue is much less than is available through quota auctions, it could still fund a significant programme of worker adjustment and assistance in the USA. Our theoretical results indicate that this policy is much preferred to quota auctions, since it removes the incentive to restrict imports to obtain the terms of trade gain. Conclusions are given in the final section.

THE MODEL

Suppose that consumers in the home country are all alike, with the utility function $\varphi(c_1) + c_2$, $\varphi' > 0$, $\varphi'' < 0$, where good 1 is imported and good 2 is the numeraire. Supply from industry 1 is given by $y_1(p)$, $y_1' > 0$, where p is the domestic price. Letting z denote imports of good 1 consumption is $c_1 = y_1 + z$, and utility maximization requires that

$$\varphi'[y_1(p) + z] = p \Rightarrow p = \pi(z). \tag{6.1}$$

where

$$\pi' = \varphi''/(1 - \varphi'' y_1') < 0.$$

Consumer surplus is obtained as the difference between utility and expenditure on good 1, so

$$CS \equiv \varphi\{y_1[\pi(z)] + z\} - p\{y_1[\pi(z)] + z\}$$

Producer surplus is defined as

$$r(z) \equiv \int_0^{\pi(z)} y_1(p) dp \text{ with } r' = y_1 \pi' < 0.$$

Denoting exports by x, the terms of trade are x/z and so tariff revenue is

$$TR \equiv (p - x/z)z = \pi(z)z - x.$$

We then form social welfare as the sum of consumer surplus, tariff revenue and producer surplus, giving a weight of $\alpha > 1$ to the latter:

$$U(z,x,\alpha) = CS + TR + \alpha r(z) = u(z) - x + (\alpha - 1)r(z) \tag{6.2}$$

where

$$u(z) \equiv \varphi\{y_1[\pi(z)] + z\} - \pi(z)y_1[\pi(z)] + r(z)$$

The extra weight given to producers reflects their lobbying pressure. It is assumed that consumers do not lobby as effectively, because of the diffuse nature of their losses from protection and the free-rider problem. Feenstra and Bhagwati (1982) make the extra weight given to producer surplus *endogenous*, depending on the extent of lobbying, but here we shall simply treat it as exogenous.[3] We shall assume that the political pressure is *private information* to the home government: the trading partner realizes that political pressure is present but cannot directly verify its level.

In (6.2), $u(z) - x$ can be interpreted as a trade utility function, i.e. social welfare as a function of imports and exports. The term $(\alpha - 1)r(z)$ reflects the extra weight given to producer surplus. Its derivative $(\alpha - 1)r'(z) < 0$ is interpreted as the marginal political cost of importing, which is increasing in absolute value with α.

We shall let the foreign country's utility function be

$$V(z,x) = x - v(z) \tag{6.3}$$

where v represents the cost of supplying z, with $v' >, 0$, $v'' \geqslant 0$. Since we have assumed that the utility function for each country has an additively separable numeraire good (x), it makes sense to sum these utility functions to obtain world welfare:

$$W(z,\alpha) \equiv (u(z) + (\alpha - 1)r(z) - v(z) \tag{6.4}$$

Note that this measure of global welfare is *inclusive* of the political costs of imports in the home country. In this sense, we are not passing judgement on whether the political pressure at home is 'justified' by distress in the industry, but simply accept this pressure as a fact of life. We shall be interested in deriving policies which maximize world welfare, recognizing that only the home government knows the true value of α.

INCENTIVE-COMPATIBLE POLICIES

Global welfare is maximized by imports $z^*(\alpha)$ which satisfy the first-order condition

$$W_z = u'[z^*(\alpha)] + (\alpha - 1)r'[z^*(\alpha)] - v'[z^*(\alpha)] = 0 \quad (6.5)$$

We shall refer to z^* as the *politically optimal* level of trade. It provides for efficient trade subject to political constraints at home. Note that $z^{*\prime} = r'/(v'' - U_{zz}) < 0$, since higher values of α raise the political cost of imports and reduce their optimal level.

Since $u' - v'$ in (6.5) is the difference between the domestic and foreign prices, it appears that $z^*(\alpha)$ could be achieved with a specific tariff of

$$\tau(\alpha) \equiv u' - v' = -(\alpha - 1)r'[z^*(\alpha)] \tag{6.6}$$

The difficulty with using this tariff, however, is that it depends on the level of political pressure α, which is only known by the home government. This could create an incentive for the home government to exaggerate the level of political pressure, thereby obtaining a higher tariff. Whether or not the government would want to do so depends on how the tariff revenues are to be distributed, as we now examine.

As a first example, suppose that the tariff schedule (6.6) is applied and the home economy collects all the tariff revenue. Then foreigners are paid their marginal cost so that $x(\alpha) = v'[z^*(\alpha)]z^*(\alpha)$. In this case utility at home is

$$U(\alpha'|\alpha) = u[z^*(\alpha')] - v'[z^*(\alpha')]z^*(\alpha') + (\alpha - 1)r[z^*(\alpha')] \qquad (6.7)$$

In this notation, α' denotes the level of political pressure announced by the home government, while α is the true value. An *incentive-compatible* policy is one in which the government would always find it in its own interest to announce the true value of α.

Differentiating (6.7) with respect to the announcement α', and evaluating it at $\alpha' = \alpha$, we obtain

$$U_1(\alpha|\alpha) = - v''z^*(\alpha)z^{*'}(\alpha) \, ' \, 0$$

using (6.5). Thus, the home country has an incentive to announce a higher value of α than actually occurred, or to *overstate* the pressure for protection. The reason is that the tariff in (6.6) is less than the 'nationally optimal' tariff for the home country, which would take into account both the political costs of importing and the ability to lower foreign prices. Computing the maximum of (6.7) over all z^*, the nationally optimal tariff is obtained as $u' - v' = -(\alpha - 1)r' + v'z^*$, which exceeds (6.6). Thus, the exaggeration of political pressure which occurs under the tariff in (6.6) is used to improve the home terms of trade. The only exception to this occurs when $v'' = 0$, meaning that the home country faces fixed international prices, in which case a tariff is incentive compatible.

As a second example, suppose that the foreign country were to collect all the tariff revenues, as would occur under VERs. Then foreigners would receive the full domestic prices of imports so that $x(\alpha) = u'[z^*(\alpha)]z^*(\alpha)$. It follows that domestic welfare is

$$U(\alpha'|\alpha) = u[z^*(\alpha')] - u'[z^*(\alpha')]z^*(\alpha') + (\alpha - 1)r[z^*(\alpha')] \quad (6.8)$$

Differentiating (6.8) with respect to the announcement α', and evaluating at $\alpha' = \alpha$, yields

$$U_I(\alpha|\alpha) = - [u''z^*(\alpha) - (\alpha - 1)r']z^{*'}(\alpha)$$

This expression is of ambiguous sign, so there may be incentive to overstate or to understate the value of α. This is because all consumers would experience a decline in utility due to the higher import price, but producer surplus would rise, and the relative magnitude of these effects on domestic welfare is ambiguous.

We are now in a position to determine the incentive-compatible policy. Drawing on the results of Feenstra and Lewis (1989), let us consider a policy which would just keep foreign welfare *constant*, say at its free trade level V^0. Then payments to foreigners are $(x\alpha) = V^0 + v[z^*(\alpha)]$, from (6.3). Substituting this into (6.2), we obtain utility depending on the actual (α) and announced (α') political pressure:

$$U(\alpha'|\alpha) = u[z^*(\alpha)] - V^0 - v[z^*(\alpha)] + (\alpha - 1)r[z^*(\alpha)] \quad (6.9)$$

Differentiating (6.9) with respect to α', and evaluating at α, we obtain

$$U_1(\alpha)|\alpha) = [u' - v' + (\alpha - 1)r']z^*(\alpha) = 0$$

using (6.5). Thus, a policy of compensating the foreign country to keep its welfare equal to that in free trade means that the home government has no incentive to overstate (or understate) the political pressure for protection: this policy is incentive compatible. In addition, we see that by using the tariffs in (6.6), while compensating the foreign country in this manner, the global optimum is achieved.

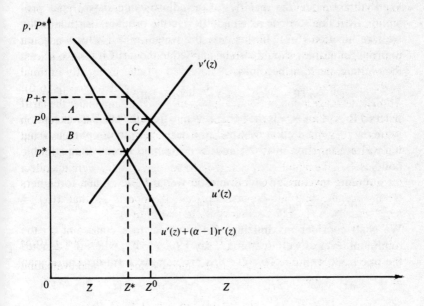

Figure 6.1

This policy is illustrated in Figure 6.1, where p^0 and z^0 denote the free trade equilibrium. Applying the tariff in (6.6), z^* is the politically optimal trade level (for a given α). p^* is the foreign price and $p^* + \tau$ is the domestic price. The area $A + B$ could be collected as tariff revenue, while $B + C$ must be transferred back to foreigners to compensate for their drop in producer surplus. If $B + C < A + B$, then this transfer can be achieved by applying the tariff τ only to imports exceeding the quota limit $\tilde{z} \equiv z^*(B + C)/(A + B)$.[4] Then the foreign country obtains quota rents of $\tau\tilde{z} = \tau z^*(B + C)/(A + B) = B + C$, compensating for its drop in producer surplus, while the home country collects tariff revenue of $\tau(z^* - \tilde{z}) = (A + B) - (B + C)$. Thus, the tariff-quota policy can ensure that the foreign country obtains the same welfare as under free trade while the domestic country truthfully reports the political pressure for protection. In this way, a global optimum (subject to the political constraints at home) is achieved.

COMMITTING THE REVENUE

We next examine the case where the domestic revenue from the tariff-quota policy is committed for adjustment assistance in the local industry. We shall not model the specifics of the adjustment assistance but shall simply treat this revenue as an addition to the producer surplus in the welfare function (6.2). In this case the weight $\alpha > 1$ which is given to producer surplus should also be applied to the tariff revenue, so that the welfare function becomes

$$\tilde{U}(z,x,\alpha) = \text{CS} + \alpha\text{TR} + \alpha r(z) = u(z) - x + (\alpha - 1)[(r(z) + \pi(z)z - x] \quad (6.2')$$

where $\text{TR} = \pi(z)z - x$ is the home revenue from the tariff-quota policy. As in the previous section, we shall first derive the global optimum using the welfare function in (6.2′) and then examine incentive-compatible policies.

Summing the foreign and domestic welfare, we obtain

$$\tilde{W}(z,\alpha) = u(z) + (\alpha - 1)[r(z) + \pi(z)z - x] - v(z) \quad (6.4')$$

We shall consider maximizing (6.4′) subject to a constraint on the minimum level of welfare abroad, say $V(z,x) > V^0$, where V^0 denotes the free trade welfare. To solve this problem we form the Lagrangian

$$L = u(z) + (\alpha - 1)[r(z) + \pi(z)z - x] - v(z) + \lambda[x - v(z) - V^0]$$

Computing the first-order conditions with respect to z and x, we obtain

$$u' - v' + (\alpha - 1)[r' + \pi'\tilde{z}^*(\alpha) + \pi] - \lambda v' \ = 0 \quad (6.10a)$$
$$- (\alpha - 1) + \lambda = 0 \quad (6.10b)$$

where all the functions in (6.10) are evaluated at the optimum $\tilde{z}^*(\alpha$ and $\tilde{x}^*(\alpha)$.

Substituting (6.10b) into (6.10a) and simplifying, we obtain an expression for the politically optimal tariff, which can be compared with (6.6):

$$\tilde{\tau}(\alpha) \equiv u' - v' = - \frac{\alpha - 1}{\alpha} r'[\tilde{z}^*(\alpha)] - \frac{\alpha - 1}{\alpha} \pi'[\tilde{z}^*(\alpha]\tilde{z}^*(\alpha) \quad (6.11)$$

where we have used the fact that the marginal utility of imports at home equals their price, $u' = \pi$. Note that both the terms on the right of (6.11) are negative, since $r' < 0$ and $\pi' < 0$, and so the entire expression is positive. In addition, since $\alpha > 1$ the *first* term on the right of (6.11) is *less* than the globally optimal tariff in (6.6). However, since the second term on the right increases the tariff in (6.11), we see that the tariffs obtained with and without committing the revenue cannot be ranked in general.

Suppose now that the tariff in (6.11) is applied and that the foreign country is compensated with enough of the revenue to keep its welfare equal to that in free trade, $V[\tilde{z}^*(\alpha), \tilde{x}^*(\alpha)] = V^0$. As before, this compensation can be achieved with a tariff-quota policy, under which the foreign country earns rents on the duty-free imports. We shall now demonstrate that this tariff-quota policy again preserves incentive compatibility at home, and so the domestic government finds it in its own interest to report the true value of α.

To demonstrate this, let the payments to foreigners be $\tilde{x}^*(\alpha) = V^0 + v[\tilde{z}^*(\alpha)]$ and evaluate domestic welfare as

$$\tilde{U}(\alpha'|\alpha) = u[\tilde{z}^*(\alpha)] - V^0 - v[\tilde{z}^*(\alpha)]$$
$$+ (\alpha - 1)\{r[\tilde{z}^*(\alpha)] + \pi[\tilde{z}^*(\alpha)]\tilde{z}^*(\alpha) - \tilde{x}^*(\alpha)\} \quad (6.12)$$

Differentiating (6.12) with respect to the announced political pressure α' and evaluating at $\alpha' = \alpha$ we obtain

$$\tilde{U}_1(\alpha|\alpha) = \{u' - v' + (\alpha - 1)[r' + \pi'\tilde{z}^*(\alpha) + \pi - v']\}\tilde{z}^{*'}(\alpha) = 0$$

using (6.10). Thus, as we found in the previous section, the home government would choose to report α truthfully, and there is no incentive to exaggerate political pressure to improve the terms of trade and obtain revenue.

The expression for the politically optimal tariff in (6.11) can be simplified by noting that $r' = \pi'y_1$ as mentioned in the second section. Substituting this into (6.11) and noting that $y_1 + \tilde{z}^* = c_1$, we can express the tariff as

$$\tilde{\tau}(\alpha) = -\frac{\alpha - 1}{\alpha}\pi'[\tilde{z}^*(\alpha)]c_1 \quad (6.13)$$

Similarly, the politically optimal tariff if the revenue is not committed can be expressed as $\tau(\alpha) = -(\alpha - 1)\pi'[z^*(\alpha)]y_1$, using (6.6). Comparing this with (6.13) we see that committing the revenue for the domestic industry will increase (decrease) the politically optimal tariff as $c_1/\alpha > (<) y_1$, or as $c_1/y_1 > (<) \alpha$.[5] Since $\alpha > 1$ and consumption c_1 equals production y_1 plus imports, we see that the optimal tariff will *increase* with the committing of revenues if imports are *high* but *decrease* if imports are *low*. The latter case is more likely when the political pressure α, and the level of protection, is high so that imports are low because of the restriction.

The intuition for these results seems to be that if imports are initially high (political pressure is low) and the revenue becomes committed, the government will find it desirable to increase the tariff so as to raise producer surplus: this action will raise domestic welfare $\tilde{U}(z,x,\alpha)$ since the gain to producers more than offsets the loss to consumers. However, if imports are initially low (political pressure is high) and the revenue becomes committed, then raising the tariff would further distort prices for consumers and lead to a drop in domestic welfare. Instead, the government now finds it optimal to lower the tariff, leading to a gain for consumers which exceeds the loss to producers. The fact that we have found that *either* case can arise has an interesting parallel to Feenstra and Bhagwati (1982), who also found that the optimal government policy could involve either an increase or a decrease in the tariff. The reasoning behind the result in that case was different, however, from what we have discussed here.

AUCTIONING IMPORT QUOTAS

As an application of our theoretical results, we consider the recent proposals to auction US import quotas, allowing the US government to obtain the revenues. Bergsten *et al.* (1987) estimate potential auction revenues from US quotas on textiles and apparel, steel, machine tools, sugar and dairy products as $5.15 billion, while lower estimates of $3.7–4.7 billion are provided by Parker (1987) for 1987–9. The detailed industry estimates are shown in columns 1 and 2 of Table 6.1. These figures differ slightly owing to varying treatment of exchange rates and estimates of the tariff-equivalent to quotas (see Bergsten *et al.* 1987: 49–50).

From our discussion in the section on incentive-compatible policies, we know that the quota auctions or tariffs would not be incentive compatible. As long as the USA is large enough to affect world prices, it will have an incentive to overstate the political pressure for protection, thereby obtaining a terms of trade gain. A preferable policy from an international perspective would be a system of tariff-rate quotas, designed to keep foreign welfare constant at its free trade level. In Figure 6.1, imports are allowed duty free up to the quota level of $\bar{z} = z^*(B + C)/(A + B)$, after which a tariff of τ is applied by the USA. This policy

Table 6.1 Revenue available from US quota auction or tariff-quota ($ million)

Industry	1 Auction revenue (IIE) [a]	2 Auction revenue (CBO) [b]	3 Loss/ rent [c]	4 Tariff-quota revenue [d]
Steel	1,330	700	0.2	560–1,060
Textiles and apparel	3,000	2,400	1.8	0
Machine tools [e]	320	100	n.a.	0–320
Sugar	300	300	0.8–1.1	0–60
Dairy	200	200	0.45	110
Total	5,150	3,700		670–1,550

Notes:
n.a., not available.
[a] From Bergsten *et al.* (1987, Table 4.1), estimates for 1986 or 1987.
[b] From Parker (1987, Table 1), estimates for 1987.
[c] Estimates from computable partial or general equilibrium models, as reported in Feenstra (1989).
[d] Is equal to columns 1 or 2 multiplied by (1-loss/rent). A lower bound of zero is imposed.
[e] A range of 0–1 is used in column 3 when calculating column 4.

would be acceptable to trading partners compared with free trade, since their welfare is constant, and is incentive compatible at home.

In the remainder of Table 6.1, we show how the tariff-quota policy could be applied to existing US quota restrictions. In column 3 we show loss/rent, which is the ratio of the loss in foreign producer surplus (below its free trade value) to the quota rents in each industry. The estimates we report are obtained from various computable partial or general equilibrium models, as discussed by Feenstra (1989). Letting z^* denote current US imports and τ the tariff-equivalent to existing quotas, then loss/rent $= (B + C)/(A + B)$ in Figure 6.1. For example, in steel we calculate that existing US quotas lead to a fall in foreign producer surplus ($B + C$ in Figure 6.1) which is 20 per cent of the quota rents ($A + B$). In sugar and textiles and apparel, the fall in foreign producer surplus is equal to or even greater than the quota rents. Under the tariff-quota plan the amount $\bar{z}$ is imported duty free, and so supplying countries collect the rents $\tau z = \tau z^*(B + C)/(A + B) = B + C$. This leaves them in the same welfare position as free trade.[6]

For imports exceeding the quota limit, the US then collects tariff revenue of $\tau(z^* - \bar{z}) = (A + B) - (B + C)$. The estimated tariff revenue is shown in the last column of Table 6.1. Note that in textiles and apparel the required compensation to foreigners exceeds the total quota rents, since loss/rent > 1. Since it is unlikely that such compensation would be politically feasible, we assume that the total quota rents are given to foreigners (as under the VER) and tariff revenue collected by the USA is zero. Totalling the estimates in column 4, we see that $0.67–1.55 billion would be available to the USA as tariff revenue.

While the revenue available from the tariff-quota plan is much less than with quota auctions, this plan has several desirable features. By lowering foreign welfare below its free trade level, the quota auctions would invite retaliation. In contrast, the tariff-quotas are designed to be neutral to foreigners compared with free trade, and can be viewed as optimal from an international perspective. Of course, this policy still has a number of limitations: determining the critical quota level $\bar{z}$ would itself be subject to political manipulation; and the participation of trading partners may require that they receive more than their free trade level of welfare.[7] However, we feel that the tariff-quotas are a viable alternative to quota auctions, and illustrate how our theoretical results can be applied to a policy situation.

CONCLUSIONS

From an international perspective, it seems desirable to have an instrument which allows a country to use tariff revenue to finance adjustment assistance but removes the incentive to apply tariffs just to improve its terms of trade. In addition, the instrument could compensate trading partners for any drop in their welfare. In this paper, we have argued that these goals are achieved by applying tariff-rate quotas to industries which are injured by imports. This instrument allows duty-free imports up to some quota level, and then levies a tariff on imports in excess of the quota. The supplying country therefore earns rents on the duty-free imports, while the demanding country earns revenue on the additional imports. We have found that if the foreign country is allocated just enough rents to keep its welfare equal to that in free trade, then the incentive for the home country to restrict imports for a terms of trade gain is eliminated.

We have applied our results to the recent policy debate over auctioning US import quotas. As an alternative to quota auctions, we consider the system of tariff-rate quotas which would compensate exporters for the trade restriction. We calculate that tariff-quotas could raise $0.67–1.55 billion in revenue for the USA while keeping imports at their current level and foreign welfare equal to that in free trade. While this revenue is much less than is available through quota auctions, it could still fund a significant programme of worker adjustment and assistance in the USA. Our theoretical results indicate that this policy is much preferred to quota auctions, since it removes the incentive to apply a trade restriction to obtain the terms of trade gain. In addition, the preference of trading partners for tariff-quotas over quota auctions would make it easier to conclude multilateral trade agreements, allowing trade liberalization to proceed.

NOTES

1 Of course, the idea of auctioning import quotas is not new, and was discussed in the Indian context by Bhagwati (1962).
2 Incentive-compatible trade policies were introduced by Feenstra (1987).
3 Baldwin (1987) argues that an objective function such as (6.2), with producer surplus weighted more heavily than consumer surplus, can be viewed as a reduced form for a model where lobbying is explicitly introduced.
4 If $B + C$ exceeds $A + B$, then foreigners would have to be compensated with more than the total tariff revenue. This amount of compensation may not be politically feasible, as we shall discuss in the penultimate section.
5 From our derivation of this condition, it is evident that c_1 is evaluated with the tariffs $\bar{\tau}(\alpha)$ while y_1 is evaluated with the tariffs $\tau(\alpha)$. We do not make these arguments explicit.
6 To be precise, this would leave supplying countries in the same welfare position as without the quotas. However, existing US tariffs would still be in place.
7 If the foreign welfare must be raised above its free trade level to ensure their participation, then the incentive compatible policy becomes more complicated than the tariff-quotas we have discussed. This case is analysed by Feenstra and Lewis (1989).

REFERENCES

Baldwin, R. (1987) 'Politically realistic objective functions and trade policy', *Economics Letters* 24: 287–90.
Bergsten, C.F., Elliot, K.A., Schott, J.J. and Takacs, W.E. (1987) *Auction Quotas and United States Trade Policy*, Washington, DC: Institute for International Economics.
Bhagwati, J.N. (1962) 'Indian balance of payments policy and exchange auctions', *Oxford Economic Papers* 14: 51–68. Reprinted in J.N. Bhagwati (1985) *Essays in Development Economics*, edited by Gene Grossman, Oxford: Basil Blackwell, vol. 2, ch. 9.
—— and Srinivasan, T.N. (1980) 'Revenue seeking: a generalization of the theory of tariffs', *Journal of Political Economy* 88: 1069–87.
Feenstra, R.C. (1987) 'Incentive compatible trade policies', *Scandinavian Journal of Economics* 89: 373–87.
—— (1989) 'Auctioning U.S. import quotas, foreign response, and alternative policies', *International Trade Journal* 3: 239–60.
—— and Bhagwati, J.N. (1982) 'Tariff seeking and the efficient tariff', in J.N. Bhagwati (ed.) *Import Competition and Response*, Chicago, IL: University of Chicago Press and National Bureau of Economic Research, ch. 9.

—— and Lewis, T.R. (1989) 'Negotiated trade restrictions with private political pressure', University of California, Davis, mimeo.

Hufbauer, G.C. and Rosen, H.F. (1986) *Trade Policy for Troubled Industries*, Washington, DC: Institute for International Economics.

Lawrence, R.Z. and Titan, R.E. (1986) *Saving Free Trade: A Pragmatic Approach*, Washington, DC: The Brookings Institution.

Parker, S. (1987) 'Revenue estimate for auctioning existing import quotas', Congressional Budget Office, Washington, DC, 27 February.

7 International transactions in services and developing countries

Brian Hindley[1]

INTRODUCTION

Jagdish Bhagwati's economics is characterized by the co-existence of abstract theory and practical concern. In Jagdish's work, concern about policy motivates theory and theory illuminates issues of policy in a way that few economists can emulate, and with an effectiveness that is unique to Jagdish.

These characteristics of Jagdish's work have been well displayed in the debate of the past few years about international transactions in services. The 'services issue' arrived on the world stage as a result of purely practical concerns and interests, having been largely ignored by economists.[2] But good policy cannot be shaped without theory. 'Practical men' make policy proposals all the time. An essential part of the job of a policy*maker* is to assess the weight of the conflicting interests that will be engaged by putting into effect any particular proposal. That requires some ability to foresee, even if only in a hazy way, the consequences of the proposed policy. It requires, in short, theory.

The essence of the services issue, in terms of international economic policy, is whether, and under what conditions, national policy towards international transactions in services should be subject to the discipline of the General Agreement on Tariffs and Trade (GATT). In what follows, I present a view of the development of that issue as it applies to developing countries. It is not a story that can be told without reference to Jagdish's contributions.

WHAT IS A SERVICE

Before thinking about policy towards services, it is useful to have some notion of what a 'service' is. One way of conveying a preliminary idea is through a list. A typical list of services might include the transport of goods and persons by land, sea or air; banking, insurance and other financial services; communications; wholesaling and retailing; franchising; education; health care; engineering, architecture and construction; consultancy; accounting; advertising; legal services; recreation and entertainment; and tourism.

The provision of services accounts for a very large part of economic activity. The United Nations Commission on Trade and Development (UNCTAD) Secretariat 1985: 13) comments that: 'In terms of its contribution to gross domestic product, the service sector is the largest in the world economy. . . . [S]ervices comprised 64 per cent of world GDP, 67 per cent of the GDP of developed market economies and 51 per cent of the GDP of developing countries in 1979.' These fractions will evidently vary with what is counted as a service.[3] A more immediately relevant point is that there is no definition on which services are trivial.

Even apart from their sheer bulk, the activities included in the list above give a basis for supposing that services are an important and even crucial element in economic development.[4] Economic development is often discussed in terms of expanding industrial or agricultural output, i.e. in terms of increasing the output of goods. Yet lumps of output at the end of a production line or in a field do not have much value to anyone. And all the activities involved in transportation, marketing, communications, design, financial arrangements and risk-sharing and in improving techniques of production (e.g. technology transfer) are services.

Services are essential inputs into the production of other goods and services. Roughly half of the output of the service sector becomes an input into other production processes. The price and quality of the services available within an economy are therefore likely to have a major impact on all other sectors of the economy. Unreliable transportation, poor communications, poor product or production design, or bad financial or legal advice can diminish or destroy the otherwise favourable prospects of industries of all kinds.

However, these are generalities. They may be a useful introduction to the issues that cluster under the heading of 'the economics of services', but on the basis merely of a list, it is difficult to move far beyond them. To go further, a definition of services is needed.

Probably the most useful – and certainly the most intellectually stimulating – effort to define services is that of Hill (1977). In Hill's basic definition, a service is:

a change in the condition of a person, or of a good belonging to some economic unit, which is brought about as a result of the activity of some other economic unit, with the prior agreement of the former person or economic unit.

(Hill 1977: 318)

Two elements in this definition are crucial in the present context. The first is that a service brings about a *change* in condition. This carries the implication that services are not, as is sometimes asserted, like goods that perish especially quickly. Rather, services are in a different logical category from goods.

The second important element of Hill's definition is that services are created *between* economic units. Among other things, that condition prevents the expansion of 'services' to include the entire economic universe. The difficulty can be seen in a statement such as 'the production processes of all goods consist of services (such as the services of labour and capital), and goods are purchased for the services that they provide (e.g. transport, appeasing hunger . . .)'.

There is a sense in which such statements are true. Nevertheless, to analyse the service sector, e.g. the activities of people who provide taxi rides as opposed to those who produce taxis, a boundary line between services and other activities is necessary. Hill's boundary line is the form of the transaction.[5]

DOES THE THEORY OF COMPARATIVE ADVANTAGE APPLY TO SERVICES?

When discussion turns to policy towards the service sector, an economist is likely to wonder how much of what he knows – or thinks he knows – about goods can be applied to services. A natural way of formulating the query, as far as international transactions in the service sector are concerned, is to ask whether the theory of comparative advantage, as developed over the past 200 years for trade in goods, applies to international transactions in the service sector.

I think the answer to this question is 'yes'. The arguments lying behind this belief are given in greater detail in Hindley and Smith (1984) and so I shall only summarize them here.

The basic Ricardian proposition about comparative advantage, stated baldly, is that the residents of a country will in aggregate be better off if they buy where the cost, in terms of forgone goods and services, is lowest – regardless of whether that is at home or abroad. That is not an easy proposition to dispute – one might wonder where the material for the 200 year (and still fiercely continuing) debate about it comes from.

One answer, of course, is that the content of the debate lies in the difficulties of defining the circumstances in which the real costs of buying at home *are* greater or less than those of buying elsewhere. Broadly speaking, there are four classes of argument that say that the relative costs of buying at home or abroad, as they appear to individuals in a free market, are in some way distorted. These four classes are as follows.

1 Terms of trade arguments: arguments in this class derive from the proposition that in a free and competitive market individuals will base their choices on average costs, although when the marginal and average costs of buying diverge it is marginal cost that is relevant to the aggregate welfare of the country. This proposition is, of course, the basis for optimal tariff arguments. Theories of trade under monopolistic competition have recently given rise to a variant of these arguments.

2 Exchange rate/balance of payments arguments: these are based on the proposition that the exchange rate between currencies is 'wrong', so that individuals comparing the money prices of domestic and foreign goods at that exchange rate get a distorted picture of their true comparative cost. Similar arguments appear as wage rate/unemployment issues.

3 Externality and inappropriability arguments: the most interesting and important member of this group is the infant-industry argument. Arguments in this group are based on the proposition that prices in a free and competitive market leave out of account some benefit or cost to members of the economy, e.g. the benefit that will come through 'learning by doing'.

4 National culture and sovereignty arguments: these are essentially arguments about public goods. They are probably of greater importance in discussion of international transactions in services than in discussion of trade in goods.

This is not the place to expand upon these different types of argument. Two other points are of greater importance in the present context. The first is to caution against a false interpretation of comparative cost theory. To believe that comparative cost theory as developed for goods applies to services is not, *ipso facto*, to believe in free trade in services. Some of the arguments noted above are quite feeble in intellectual terms (though they nevertheless seem to have substantial political appeal). Others, however, cannot easily be disposed of. But, before arriving at a prescription of free trade, they must be disposed of.

The more important and useful point is that all the classes of argument noted above have counterparts in debates about the costs and benefits of liberalizing international transactions in services – while, so far as I know, no new argument, applicable only to services, has appeared. Thus, all the arguments of the past two hundred years about liberalization of international trade in *goods* seem applicable with only minor modification to international transactions in *services*.

That is a great benefit. Two hundred years of debate has not resolved the issues between free trade and protection. But, after that amount of time, the arguments one way or the other are quite well understood. It is a bonus not to have to go through another two hundred years of issue-clarifying debate just because the world is now contemplating liberalization of services!

DIFFERENCES BETWEEN GOODS AND SERVICES

To assert that the theory of comparative advantage applies to services as well as to goods obviously is not to say that goods and services are the same in all respects. At least three differences are relevant to multilateral trade negotiations (MTN):[6]

1 the 'invisible' properties of services mean that domestic service suppliers are not normally protected – and in the case of many services *cannot* be protected – by border measures such as tariffs and quotas;
2 efficient delivery of many services requires the service provider to have a presence in the market of the service receiver, so that international service transactions often entail some form of international factor movement;
3 service industries are often regulated by governments, but different jurisdictions have different forms and stringency of regulation.

Each of these is crucial to understanding the problems of the Uruguay Round negotiation on services, and I shall discuss each one in turn.

Tariff and non-tariff protection

The 'invisible' properties of services mean that domestic service suppliers cannot usually be protected against foreign competition by means of tariffs. Service industries typically are protected by means which are analogous to 'grey area measures' or non-tariff barriers (NTBs) to trade in goods.

Thus, domestic providers of services are protected by methods such as outright prohibitions on foreign suppliers or by laws, regulations or administrative actions which bear with particularly heavy weight on foreign suppliers. Bans on, or barriers to, the establishment of foreign suppliers are prominent among these measures.

This characteristic of protection in service industries goes some way to explaining both the past neglect of services in the GATT and the current interest in them. When the GATT was formed, in the aftermath of the Second World War, border measures affecting trade in goods – tariffs and quotas for example – were a severe and evident problem, whose solution took a natural priority. But since trade in services typically is not controlled by those means, the focus on border measures had the effect of excluding trade in services from attention.

As border measures affecting goods trade were reduced through successive GATT negotiations, however, an array of NTBs appeared, some of which held (and hold) the potential to neutralize or reverse the effects of negotiated declines in tariffs. An attempt to come to grips with this problem was a major part of the business of the last MTN (the Tokyo Round). But if efforts were to be made in the GATT to deal with this kind of problem for *goods* trade, there seemed no good reason (especially to service suppliers in the USA) to ignore the same kind of problem in *services* trade.

A sad fact, however, is that the GATT process has so far been much more successful in reducing tariffs than in controlling NTBs.

Several problems that have become important in the negotiation, or that are likely to become important, flow from the inapplicability of tariffs to (most) services. The concept of national treatment, for example, has played a central role in the negotiation, and is likely to continue in that position.

In the GATT (Article III) 'national treatment' means that a government uses *no means other than those authorized by the GATT* (normally only a tariff) to discriminate between foreign and domestic suppliers.[7] Since tariffs cannot be used to protect domestic service suppliers, however, the proposition that national treatment ought to apply to trade in services can become the proposition that there should be no protection of domestic service suppliers against foreign competitors. That is a very much stronger conclusion than the GATT has traditionally arrived at.

The negotiation must also deal with the issues of whether there will be a services equivalent of emergency protection (GATT Article XIX) and of subsidy and dumping actions (Articles VI and XVI). The difficulties of using tariffs to protect domestic service suppliers add very substantially to the difficulty of those discussions.

International service transactions and establishment

Goods are tangible and, with more or less trouble or cost, they can be shifted from place to place. Hill's definition of a service as a *change* in the condition of a thing or a person, however, implies that services are not tangible, and so cannot be shifted from place to place.

The outcome of a service – the person or thing changed by the service –can be transported. So can the signifiers of property rights generated by a service, e.g. a bank statement or an insurance policy. And, of central importance, the means of providing a service – people or goods – can be moved.

In many service industries, transactions require geographical proximity of the service provider and the service receiver. International transactions in services are much more likely to require some form of international factor movement than international transactions in goods.

This does not necessarily mean that the factors of production needed to provide the service will have to move to the country of the receiver of the service (Sampson and Snape 1985). That is what it will often mean in practice,[8] however, and many of the most effective barriers to international transactions and competition in the service sector take the form of restrictions on establishment.

In the GATT, the issue was first raised by developing countries. They perceived that genuine liberalization in the service sector requires a right of service providers to locate in the proximity of service receivers. Many developing countries are suspicious of direct foreign investment, however, and many of them are hostile to the notion of introducing a GATT *right* of foreign service suppliers to locate in their territory (a point on which some developed countries are also likely to have doubts).

That the issue appeared as a problem of foreign investment, however, is a consequence of the way in which it was posed. From an analytical point of view, the need of service industries that are intensive in capital or skilled labour to locate those factors in potential markets in order to sell their products is symmetrical with the need of producers of labour-intensive services to locate that factor in potential markets in order to sell their services.

In an effort to avoid the difficult and contentious issues raised by direct foreign investment and by any claim of a 'right of establishment' in a foreign market (and also, perhaps, to avoid the at least equally contentious issues that would be raised by a counter-claim by developing countries for a right of labour to temporary residence abroad for the purpose of supplying services), the USA initially suggested that negotiations should be restricted to non-factor services. Thus, the USA proposed that the focus should be on services that can be traded in the conventional sense of a person or firm in one country selling something to a person or firm located in another country without relocation of either buyer or seller.

This attempt to avoid one problem, however, created others. One of these appeared in the form of a conflict within the USA on its negotiating position. Whatever the tactical advantage of an approach to a GATT negotiation that focused on traded non-factor services, many US service suppliers perceived their major international problem to be a lack of a right of establishment in foreign markets. They were therefore sceptical of the value of a negotiation that did not include discussion of rights of establishment.

The focus on tradable services raised a different problem when viewed from the standpoint of developing countries. Although it may be true that service suppliers based in developed countries would find it easier to sell services from local establishments, it is also true that almost all the services for which trade without establishment is possible are services in which developed countries currently appear to possess a comparative advantage (e.g. banking and financial services and informatics). Any successful measure of liberalization in this restricted range of services therefore would probably mean that developing countries increased their imports of services from developed countries without any compensating increase in their exports of services (Hindley (1982) discusses balance of payments problems and a variety of other developing country concerns regarding the services sector).

In GATT terms, this is a major problem. A GATT negotiation centres upon an exchange of 'concessions', where a concession is defined as a reduction in restrictions on imports and where concessions from other countries are won at the 'cost' of relaxations in one's own import regime.

Economists tend to scoff at the language of GATT negotiations. Ricardo's demonstration of the principle of comparative advantage, they say, destroyed once and for all the possibility of regarding increased openness to imports as a cost. That is correct. Economic analysis, however, offers no solution to the *political* problem that is addressed by concessions in the GATT process.

The structure of protection in a particular country at a particular time must be taken to be the outcome of a process of *political* equilibration. To change the protective structure, therefore, the factors that support the political equilibrium must be changed.

Exchanges of concessions offer a means of achieving such change. By altering the opportunities available to actors in the domestic political process – by providing exporters with a direct connection between the barriers they face in foreign markets and the level of their own country's protection against imports – the offer of concessions alters their economic interests and makes possible new domestic coalitions. Hence, the offer of an exchange of concessions is likely to help a government that would like to liberalize but that faces domestic opposition to such a policy. It may also serve to put pressure on a government that is not persuaded of the case for liberalization.

The USA's suggestion that the GATT negotiation be restricted to tradable non-factor services, however, defined services in such a way that comparative advantage lies predominantly with developed countries. Hence, the great bulk of potential GATT concessions in services lay in the gift of the developing countries, and this seems to preclude an *equal* exchange of concessions between developed and developing countries – at least *within* the service sector.

One response to this problem has been to point to the economic gains available to developing countries as a result of liberalization in their service sectors. That such gains exist seems very likely (Hindley 1988). Their existence, however, does not solve the dilemma for the MTN. The economic gains that developing countries can obtain through liberalization of their service sectors can for the most part be obtained through *unilateral* action; and gains that can be obtained through unilateral action are unlikely to be enough to persuade a country to join a *multilateral* liberalization (though if the tactic *were* successful, it could be applied to many aspects of developed country trade policy, e.g. to protection of agriculture by Japan or the European Economic Community (EC) or to protection of textiles and clothing by the EC and the USA).

These two problems – the wish of US service suppliers to obtain rights of establishment and the lack of 'concessions' for developing countries – have a single potential solution. It is to introduce rights of establishment into the GATT talks but with rights of establishment defined to include a right to locate labour in a country temporarily for the purpose of supplying a service.

What has actually happened in the negotiation is that the USA has abandoned its insistence that the subject of the negotiation is tradable services and has started to talk in terms of rights of establishment, rights of presence and so on. Its first submission to the Group on Negotiations on Services (GNS),[9] for example, said that 'The framework should apply to cross-border movement of services *as well as to the establishment of foreign branches and subsidiaries for the purposes of producing and delivering the service within the host country*' (emphasis addded).

The *Statement of the Trade Negotiating Committee Meeting at Ministerial Level* issued after the mid-term review held in Montreal in December 1988 deals with the issue in terms of definition:

Work on definition [of services] should proceed on the basis that the multilateral framework may include trade in services involving cross-border movement of services, cross-border movement of consumers, and cross-border movement of factors of production where such movement is essential to suppliers.

(GATT 1989)

A later paragraph, under the heading of market access, states that:

When market access is made available to signatories it should be on the basis that consistent with the other provisions of the multilateral framework and in accordance with the definition of trade in services, foreign services may be supplied according to the preferred mode of delivery.

These words clearly do not commit anybody to anything very much. Nevertheless, the possibility that the negotiation will attempt to liberalize international factor movements for the purpose of supplying services is open.

To introduce for labour from developing countries a temporary right of abode to provide services is widely regarded as politically infeasible. That judgement may be correct.[10] Nevertheless, the analytical basis for the suggestion that developing countries will gain from a relaxation on the control of factor movements into heavily protected service sectors equally suggests that developed countries will gain from the same process.

The idea of permitting such flows, however, is not popular anywhere.

Why this should be so is an interesting question. Suppose that a Korean construction firm, allowed to temporarily locate Korean labour in Europe, can construct a road or an airport in Europe more cheaply than any European firm supplying a similar quality of output.

If the output was manufactured in Korea and sent to Europe, like motor cars or television sets, most economists would reject the notion that the relative cheapness of Korean labour is a valid reason for resisting the import of those goods. But airports cannot be built in Korea and shipped to Europe. European airports have to be built in Europe.

Despite that difference, the logic of comparative cost that applies to cars and television sets seems to apply to airports. And that logic implies that if an airport can be built at a lower cost by Koreans, then they should build it. In turn, that implies that they should be allowed to locate in Europe temporarily for that purpose.

That trade is consistent with the logic of comparative advantage is not at all the same thing as saying that it is politically feasible. It is as well to understand, however, that the fundamental difficulty with the idea of shifting factors of production to a location when the ouput of the factors cannot be shifted is political rather than economic.

Developing countries, symmetrically, often reject the notion that foreign service providers should be able to set up local establishments, even when their services can only be provided through such establishments. This is in spite of the fact that the terms of the rejection often concede, implicitly or explicitly, that foreign providers of the service are more efficient than local providers.

Even if something like a temporary right of abode to provide services were offered, developing countries might not regard it as a satisfactory *quid pro quo* for rights of establishment or commercial presence in their markets. But, unless the negotiation proceeds on the basis of threat, either a *quid pro quo* must be found or the possibility must be faced that the bulk of the developing countries will not join any eventual agreement.

Regulation

The third relevant characteristic of services is that the industries providing them are often subject to regulation. Services are typically customized to a much greater extent than goods. A lawyer or a doctor advises one person on one problem and one set of circumstances, and another person on another problem and another set of circumstances.

For this reason, regulation of the *output* of service industries is difficult. It is less costly for governments to regulate the quality of *inputs* into the provision of services. Regulation of inputs, however, can easily become a control on the entry into the industry of new competitors.

In particular, regulatory powers can be used to create barriers to the entry of foreign competitors – a barrier to trade or inward investment. From that point of view, regulation is a particular form of NTB, and its use for protective purposes is analogous to the use of health and safety regulations to impede trade in goods.[11] As with health and safety regulation, regulation of service industries is widely regarded as a justified measure of public policy and as essential to the efficient supply of the regulated service. As when health and safety regulations are used to impede trade in goods, therefore, identification of the point at which legitimate action ends and protection against foreign competition begins is not easy. Nevertheless, the nature of the problem is clear.

That the nature of the problem is understood, however, does not mean that the problem itself is tractable. If domestic service industries are to be protected against foreign competition, they typically must be protected by NTBs, and hence to a large extent by regulation. This means that the problem bulks larger in service trade than in goods trade. It probably also means that it is even less tractable in services than in goods – where it is nevertheless a source of major difficulty.

The difficulty of dealing with regulation in service sectors, moreover, is likely to be further increased by the broad discretionary power given to many regulatory authorities. Regulations on paper might appear to apply equally to foreign and domestic suppliers, but action by a regulatory authority might produce a quite different outcome.

The issues in dealing with regulatory NTBs are well understood, even though they are still difficult to deal with. Another problem raised by regulation, on the other hand, is less well understood. That problem is created by the mere fact of regulation. It stems from differences in the form and/or the level of regulation between national jurisdictions.

Regulation is likely to affect the costs of producers of the service. Hence, when producers subject to the regulations of country A are free to sell services in country B without being subject to the B regulatory system, there is not only competition between A and B producers but also competition between the national regulatory systems of A and B.

The experience of the EC illustrates the problem. The Treaty of Rome (Articles 59–66) says that there shall be free trade in services within the EC. Nevertheless, until the 1992 initiative, there had effectively been no movement towards actually freeing trade in most of the service sector of the EC. The basic reason for this failure was the prior existence of different national levels of regulation.

To take a specific and, in the EC context, important case, consider British and German regulation of the insurance industry. German regulation of insurance tends to be heavy and detailed. British regulation is much lighter.

Suppose the Germans said 'Fine we've signed the Treaty of Rome and the Treaty requires free trade in services. So let's go ahead. Let British insurers operating from a London base, which in this context means operating under the looser regulation of the British authorities, come here and sell insurance. Let there be cross-border trade.'

What will be the consequences for Germany? One possible consequence is that the Germans will not be able to maintain their more stringent regulatory system. If they do maintain those more stringent regulations (which are expensive for German-based insurers) then German insurers are likely to lose in unrestricted competition with insurers operating under the looser (conformity with which, therefore, is less expensive) British regulations.

Free cross-border trade in insurance therefore is likely to seem to the Germans to imply either that they lose their insurance industry or that they lose their more stringent regulatory system. And since they do not want to lose either, the Germans, and other European Community (EC) member states, have been unenthusiastic about implementing free intra-EC trade in services, so unenthusiastic that they have until recently been unwilling to allow it to happen – hence, in large part, the past failure to liberalize intra-EC trade in services.[12]

Several points about this EC experience are relevant to the broader horizons of the Uruguay Round. The first refers to the idea of legitimate and illegitimate regulation. As noted earlier, to define a boundary line between the two is very important. But it is not the only problem, nor even the most important problem, raised by regulation. The British and German regulatory systems, for example, both have advantages. German insurance companies do not become bankrupt. British ones sometimes do. A given policy typically seems to be cheaper in Britain than in Germany, but the different trade-offs between stability and cost of different regulatory authorities cannot easily be translated into an issue of legitimate and illegitimate regulation.

The difficulty between Britain and Germany is not one, or is not primarily one, of legitimate or illegitimate regulation. It is better viewed as an issue of competition between regulatory systems. Free cross-border trade in a regulated service implies not only competition between providers of insurance, but competition between systems. The survival of at least one regulatory system – or of one regulated industry – is likely to be at risk in such competition. Cross-border trade threatens the ability of a national regulatory system to apply what it regards as proper and legitimate regulation when that regulation is more costly to comply with than the regulations of another national regulatory authority. When that happens, there is likely to be strong opposition to cross-border trade. Mere differences in regulation, in other words, can be a major barrier to the negotiation of free trade in services.

An obvious solution to this problem, in principle, is to harmonize regulations between countries. The difficulty is to choose the harmonized regulations. To return to the EC context, if Britain and Germany have different regulatory structures, which each regards as the best way to do the job, how can a compromise be struck between them?

That may not sound a very difficult problem. Nevertheless, the Commission of the European Communities, backed up by the Treaty of Rome, spent years trying to do it and finally gave up. If the Commission, with substantial legal powers, could not negotiate harmonized regulations within a group of countries that are very much more homogeneous than the members of the GATT, a reasonable guess is that that is not a useful route for GATT negotiators to contemplate.

Another solution to the problem raised between regulatory systems is to combine a right of establishment with an agreement that the national regulations of the host country apply to establishments. That solution avoids, or begs, the question of appropriate regulatory structure and it runs into the hostility to rights of establishment noted above.

Such a solution would, however, allow competition between service providers of different nationalities within given regulatory structures. That is likely to be a considerable advance on the current situation, in which, in many services and countries, there is neither competition between regulatory systems nor competition between domestic and foreign suppliers (and sometimes little competition between domestic suppliers!)

A final point that is relevant to the Uruguay Round – and that adds to the difficulties regarding solution – is that the term 'regulatory system' should be interpreted broadly. A national regulatory system is usually taken to consist of rules for specific service industries, such as requirements for minimum levels of reserves or for minimum numbers of years of training at approved institutions.

But a liberalized world market for a service is likely to entail international factor flows. Hence, to talk seriously about liberalization, the term 'national regulatory system' must be interpreted to include, for example, immigration laws and laws regarding the establishment of foreign firms or subsidiaries or branches of foreign firms. Furthermore, it must cover conditions imposed on employment generally, such as minimum-wage laws and contributions to social security.

A construction company from a developing country, using labour from that country and paid on that country's terms, may be capable of constructing a highway or an airport of a given quality in Europe more cheaply than could a European company using European labour. But a company from a developing country will have great legal difficulty in getting labour from the developing country into Europe. Even if it could do so, it might not be able to produce more cheaply were that labour, once in Europe, subject to European employment laws.

THE MULTILATERAL TRADE NEGOTIATIONS AND THE DEVELOPING COUNTRIES

That some form of services agreement will emerge from the Uruguay Round now seems quite likely. But there is still a question of whether the agreement will be one of substance, one that has real impact on the policies of governments towards international trade in services, or whether it will be empty and lacking in any real effects. That an 'agreement' containing few hard commitments will emerge is a very real possibility.

An empty agreement, of course, could be signed by all or most of the participants in the negotiation. That might be presented as a diplomatic feat. But the number of signatures on the agreement will be a very poor indicator of whether the negotiation has been successful. Genuine success depends not only on the number of adherents, but on the content of what they are adhering to.

In order to arrive at an agreement of substance, the negotiation must solve the two major and very difficult problems that I have just been discussing (and, of course, a much larger number of smaller ones). There may be services in which international transactions are not heavily affected by national regulation. There are certainly services that can be cross-border traded without establishment. But there are very few services that are neither regulated nor require establishment. If neither the regulatory nor the establishment problem is solved, it is difficult to see that a worthwhile agreement could emerge although a solution to one of them could open a route to worthwhile results.

'Solved' does not necessarily mean that a cut-and-dried solution emerges from the Uruguay Round itself. 'Solved' might mean – and probably will mean – the acceptance of some set of principles, and some legal or political process for implementing them, that continues well beyond the end of the Uruguay Round, but that nevertheless holds the promise of expanding rights of establishment and presence and/or of reducing the restrictive effects on international transactions of regulation.

There is a third problem, however. That is the 'concession' problem, the problem of the developed countries finding sufficient concessions to match those that a substantial agreement would require developing countries to make in favour of developed countries.

This only becomes a problem of course, if solutions to the regulation and establishment problems emerge. It is only if the proposed agreement has substance that the 'concession problem' becomes an issue.

But does it even become an issue then? A major possibility, of course, would be to structure the agreement so that it has little or no substance for developing countries. That after all is the basic structure of GATT itself – 'special and differential' treatment eliminates for developing country contracting parties much of the content of the GATT as it applies to developed countries. If all that was wanted for a services agreement was the *accession* of developing countries, for purely decorative or diplomatic purposes, this would be a way to do it.

That would be a pity. The liberalization of international transactions in services holds the promise of real gains for many developing countries.

But more to the point, is it what the major developed country participants want? At least some evidence suggests that neither the USA nor the EC seeks an outcome which excludes developing countries. They may settle for such a solution, but they do not appear to want it.

The developed countries have been attentive to the views of developing countries in this negotiation. Yet why should they have been?

Legal opinion appears to support the view that developed countries can conclude a legally valid argument to insert a code on services into the GATT without the adherence of any developing country. Moreover, the obligations to one another of signatories to such an agreement apparently do not have to be extended to non-signatories, as would be the case with an agreement elaborating some existing part of the GATT.

Even if the developed countries did run into difficulties in inserting into the GATT an agreement on services arrived at among themselves, they have the option of forming a new organization to administer a services agreement. Such an organization could copy the GATT whenever that suited the purposes of developed countries.[13] The developed countries therefore appear to be in a very strong position: the developing countries have no means of preventing the emergence of a services agreement.

At least two hypotheses are available to explain a genuine concern on the part of developed countries for the willing assent to a services agreement of developing countries. One is contained in the assertion that GATT agreements do not work very well if they have the adherence of only a small proportion of the total membership. This statement is popular with delegations in Geneva, but the evidence for it seems to be based on the Tokyo Round codes, which might function poorly for reasons other than small membership. Moreover, if the assertion is true, it is not clear why it is true. A code has the same legal force whether it has ten members or ninety-six. It does not seem implausible to suppose that a strong code with ten members might be more successful than a weak code with 102 members.

A second hypothesis is that the greatest opportunities for developed country providers of services lie in the heavily protected markets of developing countries, and that to gain access to those markets is a major point – perhaps *the* point – of the negotiation. The recent Section 301 actions of the USA over the insurance market of the Republic of Korea and the Brazilian informatics market might be taken to lend substance to this view, at least as far as the USA is concerned. The comments of the Chairman of Citicorp, noted above (note 10), are also consistent with it.[14]

Mention of the Section 301 actions must bring to mind – especially in the Republic of Korea – the possibility that an attempt will be made to drive the Uruguay Round negotiation to a conclusion through threat: to solve the 'concession problem' by threatening to withdraw market access already granted – not necessarily in services – rather than offering new opportunities of access. Perhaps that will happen, but I do not think so.

Were the negotiation about a simple yes–no issue, threat might be effective and threat might be used. But the subject matter of the services negotiation is not simple – to put into effect the outcome of any agreement satisfactorily demands some degree of willingness on the part of participants. Threat alone cannot achieve that willingness. In this context, threat is unlikely to be effective and I therefore do not think that it will play a major role in this part of the Uruguay Round.

So, *if* an agreement with substance appears to be on the cards at the close of the negotiation – and that is a very large if – real concessions for developing countries may become available. If that happens, what should developing countries ask for?

Developing countries might, of course, ask for concessions outside the services sector; though the attitudes of the developed country participants do not suggest that such concessions will be generously given. *Within* the service sector, the obvious exchange to be made between developed and developing countries is of rights of establishment – or some variant or modification of such a right – for a temporary right of abode for persons to provide services.

That suggestion was forcefully made by Bhagwati in 1985 and Bhagwati (1986) gives a more complete analysis. It is likely to be a good exchange from an economic standpoint, whatever its political difficulties. It would be good to see the developing countries ask for that, and better to see them get it.

WHAT ARE THE INTERESTS OF DEVELOPING COUNTRIES?

Still, what are the economic interests of developing countries in the services issue? There is a danger that too single-minded a focus on the MTN, and what might be obtained from it, will distract attention from another issue, one that is more important for most developing countries.

At the start of this paper, I stated the basic Ricardian proposition about comparative advantage and suggested that the principle applies to services as well as to goods. That principle can now be restated as saying that the residents of a country will in aggregate be better off if they buy goods and services where the cost is lowest, regardless of whether that is at home or abroad, or from domestically owned or foreign-owned establishments. That proposition and its implications for policy are likely to be very much more important to developing countries (and indeed developed countries) than anything that emerges from the MTN.

The arguments for protecting the service sector are much less solid than the structures of protection that some countries have built upon them (Hindley 1988). But neither that conclusion nor the principle of comparative advantage implies that developing countries should abandon all restrictions on trade and establishment, or that they should give up regulations merely because the regulations are disliked by foreign service providers.

The point is rather a different one. It is that the primary objective of policy towards the service sector should be to secure for residents of the economy the best available combinations of price and quality of a service. If that objective is accepted, it then follows that participation in the domestic market by foreign service providers, whether by trade or establishment, should be determined on the basis of the effect on the price and quality of the service available to domestic users of the service.

I acknowledge that these are trite statements. There can only be one excuse for making them. It is that, however trite they are, these principles clearly have not guided the policies towards the service sector of most countries. In many countries – developed and developing – things seem to go the other way round. The high price and low quality of the service available to members of the economy is determined by restrictions on foreign service providers. And those restrictions have much to do with the interests of domestic service suppliers in restricting competition, and nothing to do with obtaining the best price–quality combinations for domestic users of services.

The economic interest of countries with heavy restrictions upon international transactions (or, indeed, upon domestic transactions) in services lie in making sure that those restrictions have a genuine economic justification – and, if they do not, in getting rid of them.

Of course, it is also in the interests of developing countries to get the best possible 'price' for such actions through the MTN. I hope that developing countries can extract a high price.

But there may not be such a price. The negotiation may fail to solve its broader problems, so that developing country participation in an effective services agreement does not become a live issue. The worst thing that could then happen is that developing countries decide that, if there is no price to be obtained for liberalizing heavily restricted service sectors through the MTN, there is no economic benefit to liberalization in the service sector.

That is wrong. The economic benefits that will derive from the unilateral liberalization of a highly protected service sector are likely to outweigh by a large amount any gain that arrives through an MTN settlement. That the debate about services in the MTN has this proposition as its most important conclusion may be ironic. Nevertheless, it is a conclusion that it will be costly to ignore.

NOTES

1 An earlier version of this paper was presented as a lecture at the Korea Development Institute (KDI), Seoul, in September 1989, where I had the good fortune to be a KDI Distinguished Lecturer. I am grateful to KDI for permission to use that material here.
2 Bhagwati (1984 a,b) was one of the first contributions to the new wave of literature dealing with trade and services.
3 UNCTAD Secretariat (1985): ch. III) discusses definitions and their effects on statistics such as those cited above.
4 Bhagwati (1987) analyses the role of services in economic development.
5 This same boundary is used in national income accounting and it can give rise to substantial problems of measurement. The same *activity* is sometimes classified as a service and sometimes as something else. If households do their own laundry, for example, rather than taking it to a commercial laundry, the activity will vanish from the national accounts. Painting a car might sometimes be part of a manufacturing process, sometimes a service and sometimes nothing (so far as the accounts are concerned).

   More generally, if a firm primarily engaged in manufacturing supplies its own advertising, accounting or window-cleaning, the persons engaged in these activities will typically be classified as employed in manufacturing. If these activities are spun off into new companies, however, and the manufacturing firm purchases from those companies on an out-of-house basis, the activities will then be classified as services. The statistical measure of the share of services in gross domestic product and the recorded share of services in employment will rise, even though there has been no change in the activity of any person.

   Statistics about the service sector need to be handled with especial care (though the known biases are likely to create *under*estimates of the importance of services in production and trade).
6 Bhagwati (1985) gives an insightful account of the services issue in the context of the MTN.
7 In general, 'national treatment' means that a government treats foreign nationals in the same way as it treats its own nationals. National treatment in the OECD sense, for example, implies that laws and regulations do not discriminate between foreign-owned subsidiaries and firms owned by nationals of that country.

8 Not all international transactions in services call for proximity in the immediate geographical sense. One exception is the class of 'tradable services' – that can be provided by a supplier in country A to a user in country B without relocation by either of them. Such services (long-distance services in the terminology of Bhagwati, 1984a) do exist. If I can conduct business with my bank by computer terminal, so can a person in another country. Any service transaction that takes place within a country entirely by mail, fax or phone, without direct personal contact, can also, in principle, be traded internationally.

   The scope of tradable services can be extended somewhat by adding to that category services whose provision requires only brief periods of relocation, rather than permanent or semi-permanent residence. An architect or consulting engineer, for example, may be able to function effectively with a few brief visits to the site of a project. A bank, on the other hand, is likely to need a permanent presence in a country if it is to provide a full range of banking services successfully.

9 GATT document, *Concepts for a Framework Agreement on Services* (MTN.GNS /W/24) of 27 October 1987 (p. 3).

10 However, the *Financial Times* of 12 July 1988 reports Mr John Reed, (Chairman of Citicorp and of the Services Policy Advisory Committee, which advises the US Administration) as saying that 'US business wanted a global agreement on services with as broad a participation as possible by developing countries. The Reagan Administration should be prepared to trade off freer movement of Third World labour to US projects in return for greater access for US service companies to developing markets'. Mr Reed's remarks were made as he arrived in Geneva with the then Special Trade Representative of the USA, Clayton Yeutter, and fourteen members of the Committee 'to push for swifter progress on services in GATT's trade liberalizing Uruguay Round'.

11 Of course, direct regulation of inputs also occurs in goods trade – as when a government, on health grounds, insists that food-processing or pharmaceutical plants must be inspected before their output can be sold in its territory. Restrictions of this type are more prevalent in service industries than in goods industries, however. Moreover, such restrictions in goods industries provide classic examples of high protection, amounting to bans on importation. An example is British behaviour towards UHT milk imports, in which inspection was required by local authorities but no funds were available for the inspectors to travel abroad.

12 The economics of regulation and the consequent problems of liberalization in the EC service sector are discussed in more detail by Hindley (1987).

13 It could, for example, copy GATT dispute-settlement procedures. That a GATT agreement is legally binding, whereas OECD ones are not, was the primary reason given by the USA before the Uruguay Round for preferring GATT to OECD as a forum for the services negotiation.

14 Of course, not all developed countries are likely to have the same interest in, for example, negotiating rights of establishment. The interest of a country in the issue will depend, among other things, on its perception

of the comparative advantage of its own service suppliers. A country that believes that it has a comparative advantage in supplying financial services, as the USA appears to do, will be concerned about rights of establishment. The EC, which seems to believe that its advantage lies in the provision of management services, which can be supplied without establishment, is likely to be less concerned about establishment.

Moreover, the position is complicated by current positions in protected markets. Some EC service suppliers, for example, are already established in the markets of former colonial possessions. Such EC establishments may well be earning high profits as a result of the heavy protection against new suppliers from abroad of the host country. Service suppliers in that position may be cool to the idea that protected markets should be open to new establishments of efficient suppliers. Such considerations may go some way to explaining the ambivalent attitude of EC service suppliers to US proposals on services.

In addition, the 1992 initiative of the EC may complicate matters from the standpoint of the EC. Removing protection by one member state against the service providers of another is difficult, and a major potential bargaining chip in its hands is the possibility of increasing protection against suppliers from outside the EC. Whether the chip will be used or not is still an open question. The Commission will not be eager to give it away in a GATT negotiation, however.

REFERENCES

Bhagwati, J.N. (1984a) 'Splintering and disembodiment of services and developing countries', *World Economy* (June).
—— (1984b) 'Why are services cheaper in the poor countries?', *Economic Journal*, (June).
—— (1985) 'GATT and trade in services: how we can resolve the north–south debate', *Financial Times*, 27 November.
—— (1986) 'Economic perspectives on trade in professional services', *Chicago Legal Forum* 1 (1) (March).
—— (1987) 'International trade in services and its relevance for economic development', in O. Giarini (ed.) *The Emerging Service Economy*, Services World Economy Series 1, New York: Pergamon.
GATT (1989) Document MTN.TNC/11, 21 April.
Hill, T.P. (1977) 'On goods and services', *Review of Income and Wealth*, (December).
Hindley, B. (1982) *Economic Analysis and Insurance Policy in the Third World*, London: Trade Policy Research Centre.
—— (1987) 'Trade in services within the European Community' in H. Giersch (ed.) *Free Trade in the World Economy*, Tubingen: J.C.B. Mohr (Paul Siebeck).
—— (1988) 'Service sector protection: considerations for developing countries', *World Bank Economic Review*, (May).
—— and Smith, A. (1984) 'Comparative advantage and services', *World Economy*, (December).

Samson, G. P. and Snape, R.H. (1985) 'Identifying the issues in trade in services', *World Economy*, (June).
UNCTAD Secretariat (1985) *Production and Trade in Services: Policies and their Underlying Factors Bearing upon International Service Transactions*, TD/B/941, New York: United Nations.

Part III
Foreign investment

8 Foreign direct investment and intra-firm trade: evidence from Japan

Leo Sleuwaegen and Hideki Yamawaki[1]

INTRODUCTION

One of the most remarkable developments in the post-war period is the strong growth in the activities of multinational corporations (MNCs). Within this process firms are operating more and more on a global scale and pursue an optimal international spread of their activities. In most cases this implies international intra-firm specialization, by which vertically related activities are geographically dispersed across national boundaries. Consequently, intra-firm trade becomes increasingly important in international transactions. It was estimated that in the early 1980s MNCs already represented, excluding the centrally planned economies, about 80–90 per cent of world trade with about two-fifths of all international trade transactions through intra-firm transfers (Clairmonte and Cavenagh 1982: 3; United Nations Centre on Transnational Corporations 1988).

MNCs can hardly be described as ordinary mobile factors of production. Technological know-how, marketing expertise and organizational experience are key elements in the bundle of resources that are transferred between the multinational parent companies and their subsidiaries abroad. The intangible and firm-specific nature of these operations poses specific problems in analysing the behaviour of MNCs. Recently trade theorists have started to integrate the specific nature of the operations of MNCs into general equilibrium models. In doing so, Helpman and Krugman (1985) show how MNCs and intra-firm trade will develop under specific international structures of factor endowments. Wilfred Ethier (1986) further develops the new theory in endogenizing the decision to internalize transactions within the company. Contrary to Helpman and Krugman he finds that, the more similar are factor endowments between countries, the more multinational companies will develop and the more intense intra-company trade will take place.

However, as Ethier in his innovovative paper admits, some of the results may be specific to the way he has modelled the internalization decision.

In this paper we do not try to adopt an integrative approach, but illustrate from a partial equilibrium point of view some key elements behind the intra-firm trade decisions of Japanese MNCs. In the second section the basic motives to integrate vertically across national boundaries are discussed. Among other market imperfections, protectionism by national governments may play an important role in intra-firm trade, as is illustrated within the confines of a formal model in the Appendix.

The importance and main characteristics of intra-firm trade by Japanese MNCs are then discussed and intra-firm trade by Japanese corporations is studied in relation to Japanese direct investment in distribution.

VERTICAL INTEGRATION AND THE REGULATION PARADOX

Intra-firm trade basically reflects integration of vertically linked activities within the firm across national borders. The theory of vertical integration explains the advantages and disadvantages of internalizing transactions and markets within the firm. It explains why the internal co-ordination of different stages of production and distribution is preferred above the co-ordinating role of an open market. It follows that, when upstream or downstream activities are optimally located in different countries, vertical integration will lead to the development of MNCs and to intra-firm trade in intermediate products and services (Baldwin 1988). In essence, the theory states that vertical integration will occur when total profits from two or more stages of production and distribution integrated within one firm are higher than when these different stages are performed by independent firms. Formally

$$\max_{x,y} [\pi(x) + \pi(y)] > \max_x \pi(x) + \max_y \pi(y) \qquad (8.1)$$
$$\text{subject to } y = F(x,z)$$

where π is profit, x and y are intermediate and final product respectively and z represents all other inputs.

Following this logic, Blair and Kaserman (1983) describe five basic motives for vertical integration: optimal appropriation of quasi-rents from the exploitation of firm-specific assets, avoiding incomplete contracts, eliminating abuse of sequential market power, obtaining implicit insurance and minimizing transaction costs. These motives will typically occur with transactions dealing with intangible or complex goods or services, such as the (un-embodied) results of past (sunk) R&D investments. From these observations it is not surprising that vertical integration and the development of MNCs is typical in technology-intensive and resource-intensive industries.

While the foregoing motives could be typified as natural market imperfections there exists an equally important number of unnatural government-created market imperfections which give rise to vertical integration. International differences in profit tax rates and tariffs, and in laws concerning patents, licensing or direct investment regulations such as *inter alia* local content requirements or enforced joint ventures, may substantially affect the international (vertical) integration decision of MNCs. Through intra-company trade with transfer prices different from arm's length prices MNCs can exploit – or defend against – these international differences.

Similarly, with strict regulations or enforced joint ventures, transfer prices become an important instrument for MNCs to extract the maximum of profits from the regulated operations. As a consequence, intra-firm trade strategies by MNCs may lead to trade behaviour very different from open market trading (Goldsborough 1981). This leads to a regulation paradox. With governments starting to regulate part of the operations of an MNC; they may stimulate intra-firm trading, necessitating more and more specific regulation of transfer prices. These regulations may counteract (macro-economic) adjustment flexibility and lead to trade reactions by MNCs whereby they move further and further away from the welfare optimum that was originally envisaged by the local government.

In addition to tariff or tax measures many non-tariff barriers to international trade exist that may equally stimulate intra-firm trade. Typical examples are the different technical barriers embedded in national regulations on products. These different regulations imply international differences in standards and certification. As a consequence of these barriers, international corporations are forced to adapt their product to local conditions, necessitating in many cases the set-up of assembly plants in the different countries. Similarly, government procurement policies may favour companies with production activities located in the country concerned. In short, these various tariff and non-tariff barriers stimulate intense intra-firm trade and/or lead to specific direct investments in the different countries. This is formally developed within the framework of an oligopoly model in the Appendix. The model assumes that non-tariff trade barriers increase the costs of exporting companies through making it necessary to undertake extensive investments in downstream distribution or service activities in the foreign country. Depending on the nature of the trade barriers, increased protection may lead to a substitution of exports for direct investment in the protective country. The model emphasizes the role of the potential market in this substitution process. The faster the market grows and the higher are trade barriers, the more exports will be substituted by local manufacturing in the foreign country. As a consequence, intra-firm trade linked with foreign market protection will change and reduce in magnitude.

THE IMPORTANCE AND PATTERNS OF INTRA-FIRM TRADE

MNCs dominate world trade. For instance, in the USA they accounted for over three-quarters of US exports and for almost one half of US imports in 1983. In the UK MNCs were responsible for over 80 per cent of exports in the early 1980s. Not all this trade is intra-firm trade.

Table 8.1 The importance of intra-firm trade

Country	Share of intra-firm trade (percentage) in national trade		
	Country based MNC (1)	Foreign based MNC (2)	All MNC (3)
USA			
Exports			
1977	26.7	2.6	29.3
1982	21.9	1.1	23.0
1985	29.0	2.0	31.0
Imports			
1977	21.7	20.5	42.2
1982	17.1	21.3	38.4
1985	15.1	24.0	40.1
Japan			
Exports			
1980	24.1	1.7	25.8
1983	30.6	1.2	31.8
Imports			
1980	31.5	10.6	42.1
1983	18.4	11.9	30.3
UK			
Exports			
1981	16.0	14.0	30.0

Source: United Nations Centre on Transnational Corporations (1988)

The share of intra-firm trade is substantially below the share of open market trade for home country MNCs in the USA, UK or Japan. In these countries intra-firm exports associated with all MNCs centre around 30 per cent of all exports Table 8.1, (column 3). The share of intra-firm imports is markedly higher in the USA which seems to be primarily a result of the growing US market penetration by foreign investors. For US-based MNCs the share of intra-firm imports is falling.

As can be seen in Table 8.2 intra-firm trade tends to concentrate in high-technology industries and in those producing complex manufactures.

Table 8.2 Share of intra-firm trade in exports and imports associated with home-country transnational corporations, early 1980s

Industries	USA (1982)		Japan (1983)		United Kingdom (1981)
	Exports	Imports	Exports	Imports	Exports
	%	%	%	%	%
All industries	32.9	40.8	23.7	27.7	27.0
Petroleum	23.4	24.1	42.4[a]	28.8[a]	–
Mining	–	–	4.5	11.5	–
Manufacturing	38.6	63.0	29.9	20.9	–
Foods and beverages	19.3	22.0	18.3	2.3	27.4
Textiles	–	–	2.7	5.2	–
Wood, paper and pulp	–	–	0.4	22.0	–
Chemicals	36.4	–	19.5	8.0	48.1
Metals	16.7	–	2.2[b]	1.8[b]	21.5
Non-electrical machinery	51.4	74.2	12.8	20.0	–
Electrical machinery	32.5	55.7	24.8	41.9	–
Transport equipment	43.6	–	45.3	34.3	49.8[c]
Precision instruments	–	–	38.7	32.1	–
Other manufacturing	36.2	42.8	–	–	18.3
Wholesale trade	12.2	12.8	18.2	30.6	–
Other industries	24.6	49.4	12.3	22.1	21.2

Source: United Nations Centre on Transnational Corporations (1988), based on official national sources
Notes:
[a]Petroleum and coal products.
[b]Iron and steel.
[c]Motor vehicles.

These categories of goods require important after-sales service, which explains why they are marketed through wholesale subsidiaries of the exporting companies.

A good proportion of intra-firm trade is in parts and components of more complex goods, and relates to a new international division of labour. According to the nature of the activity and to take maximum advantage of economies of scale, production of a particular component is concentrated in one (attractive location) country from where the component is shipped to plants in the home country or other countries where further manufacturing takes place. Given that they are in a more advanced stage of the transnationalization process, this new division of labour would indeed seem to be more typical for US-based MNCs than for Japanese MNCs.

The share of intra-firm imports in total imports by US MNCs is substantially higher than for Japanese MNCs. The rising importance of foreign affiliates in the global operations of US-based MNCs may also be derived from Table 8.3, which shows the importance of exports by parent companies and foreign affiliates in terms of world exports. These findings suggest that US-based corporations are increasingly operating on a global scale, and use their competitive advantages in conjunction with comparative advantages present in the different countries in which they operate (see also Lipsey and Kravis 1985). The data for the US contrast with those for Japan, where companies recently started to expand production across national frontiers much more. A recent study by Dunning and Pearce (1985) found that, for a rationalized sample of firms in 1982, the overseas market sourcing ratio (i.e. the share of foreign production in total foreign sales) of Japanese MNCs was only 19 per cent while for US MNCs the figure was 84 per cent.

Table 8.3 Exports of manufactures by transnational corporations in the USA and Japan, as a percentage of world exports of manufactures

Year	USA			Japan		
	MNC-related exports	Parents' exports	Affiliate exports	MNC-related exports	Parents' exports	Affiliate exports
1966	17.7	11.0	6.7	–	–	–
1974	–	–	–	7.4	6.6	0.8
1977	17.6	9.2	8.4	–	–	–
1983	17.7	9.1	8.6	9.9	9.3	0.6
1984	18.1	9.2	8.9	–	–	–

Source: United Nations Centre on Transnational Corporations (1988)

Table 8.4 Exports of foreign subsidiaries to Japanese parents, (a) as a percentage of total sales of parents and (b) as a percentage of sales by foreign subsidiaries in the different regions, 1984

Industry	Location of subsidiary							
	USA		EC		Asia		World total	
	(a)	(b)	(a)	(b)	(a)	(b)	(a)	(b)
Food	0.4	22.1	0.0	0.2	0.1	8.6	0.6	16.0
Textiles	0.0	0.1	0.0	0.0	0.5	3.9	0.5	3.0
Wood and paper products	0.5	49.6	–	–	0.3	35.0	3.5	44.3
Chemicals	0.2	40.1	0.0	2.0	0.1	4.6	0.4	9.7
Iron and steel	0.0	3.3	0.0	0.0	0.2	7.3	0.2	4.0
Non-ferrous metal	0.0	0.0	0.0	2.3	0.0	0.3	2.4	21.2
Machinery	0.0	0.8	0.0	0.0	0.2	13.5	0.2	10.6
Electrical machinery	0.7	1.1	0.0	4.1	0.5	16.0	0.6	6.0
Transportation equipment	0.0	0.1	0.0	0.0	0.1	3.7	0.7	2.6
Precision instruments	0.0	0.2	0.0	3.1	0.9	27.9	2.0	19.6
Others	0.0	0.3	0.0	0.1	0.2	5.3	0.2	2.7
Manufacturing total	0.1	4.8	0.0	1.2	0.2	8.1	0.6	9.7

Source: Ministry of International Trade and Industry, *Kaigai toshi tokei soran No 2* (The 2nd Statistical Report on Foreign Investment), Tokyo: Keibunshuppan, 1986

Table 8.4 shows indeed that Japanese intra-firm imports as a per-centage of total sales of parent firms are very small, mostly less than 1 per cent. The ratio is higher in natural-resource-intensive industries such as the wood and paper and non-ferrous metal industries. The role of Asian subsidiaries in machinery and precision instruments is also noteworthy and reflects a growing international division of labour within the Japanese MNCs.

Table 8.5 Imports by foreign affiliates in the USA, major sector by country or region of origin, 1986

	Share of sector in US imports by foreign affiliates belonging to MNC based in		
	Canada	Europe	Japan
Manufacturing	0.54	0.29	0.05
Wholesale trade	0.36	0.58	0.95
Other	0.10	0.13	–
Share of country in total imports by foreign affiliates	0.06	0.35	0.51

Source: US Department of Commerce (1986)

Another distinctive pattern of Japanese intra-firm trade is that Japanese manufacturers use local distribution subsidiaries more extensively to market their products. As Table 8.5 indicates, US distribution subsidiaries of Japanese firms act as a major channel for intra-firm trade.

JAPANESE DIRECT INVESTMENT IN DISTRIBUTION

As McCulloch (1988) and Yamawaki (1989) have observed, one of the most interesting characteristics in the pattern of Japanese direct investment abroad is its emphasis on distribution or wholesale trade activities. This is particularly important in the US and European Community (EC) markets. Table 8.6 shows the distribution of Japanese subsidiaries across industries by region measured as the number of Japanese subsidiaries in distribution as a percentage of the total number of Japanese subsidiaries in each region. Thus, in the US markets, 49 per cent of the Japanese

Table 8.6 Distribution of Japanese subsidiaries across industry, 1986, by region

Industry	Location of subsidiary			
	USA	EC	Asia	Worldwide
	%	%	%	%
Agriculture	0.8	0.3	1.1	1.5
Mining	1.3	0.4	0.6	2.0
Construction	3.1	0.8	5.0	3.6
Manufacturing	28.5	25.7	61.1	42.0
Food	2.5	0.8	2.3	2.2
Textiles	0.8	0.9	5.7	3.2
Wood and paper	0.2	0.0	1.2	0.9
Chemicals	3.6	4.2	9.6	6.0
Iron and steel	1.4	0.1	3.2	2.2
Non-ferrous metals	1.2	0.3	1.4	1.1
Machinery	3.4	4.7	4.1	3.7
Electrical machinery	7.2	8.7	13.8	10.0
Transportation equipment	3.4	1.6	7.7	5.1
Investments	1.1	1.2	2.4	1.5
Others	3.8	3.2	9.7	6.1
Distribution	49.1	63.1	22.0	37.1
Service	7.1	2.9	5.5	5.3
Other industries	9.5	6.9	4.6	8.6
	100.0	100.0	100.0	100.0

Source: Ministry of International Trade and Industry (ed.), *Dai 16-Kai Wagakuni Kigyo no Kaigai Jigyo Katsudo* (The 16th Report on the Foreign Activity of Japanese Corporations), Tokyo: Keibunshuppan, 1988, Table 3–2, p. 15
Note: Japanese subsidiaries which are 50 per cent and more controlled by their parent are included in the calculation.

subsidiaries are in the distribution sector, and in the EC markets, 63 per cent of the Japanese subsidiaries are in the distribution sector. By contrast, in the Asian countries, the importance of direct investment in distribution is lower, while the importance of direct investment in manufacturing is higher. Thus, the fraction of total employees in Japanese subsidiaries engaged in distributional activities in the US and the EC is larger than that worldwide (Table 8.6). This distinctive pattern of Japanese direct investment in US and EC markets implies that the subsidiary of the Japanese MNC not only produces the parent's goods for the local markets but also organizes a distribution system and provides customer service in the local markets. The relatively high concentration of Japanese direct investment in distributional activities may reflect Japanese firms' organizational strategy in their home market. In fact, Williamson and Yamawaki (1989) have found that Japanese manufacturers have integrated forward into wholesaling more strongly than typical US firms in pharmaceuticals, electrical machinery and household appliances, professional and scientific instruments, pottery, and furniture. Japanese automobile companies, meanwhile, show the highest forward integration into wholesaling of any industry in Japan (Table 8.7).

Table 8.7 Share of wholesale trade performed by manufacturer subsidiary, the USA and Japan

Industry	USA	Japan
	%	%
Fabric	45.3	14.8
Women's and children's apparel	26.5	19.1
Furniture	17.8	40.5
Paper and allied products	48.5	26.3
Chemicals	74.0	36.0
Pharmaceuticals	0.7	61.6
Pottery	5.7	22.5
Fabricated metal products	17.1	18.7
Machinery	44.4	45.5
Household appliances	59.6	66.9
Other electrical machinery	34.0	51.5
Automobiles and parts	48.9	70.1
Other transportation equipment	41.5	38.7
Instruments	30.8	41.1
Toys and sporting goods	40.6	31.7
Average	35.7	39.0

Source: Adapted from Williamson and Yamawaki (1989), Table 1, p. 2

Having found the distinctive pattern of Japanese direct investment, we now seek its determinants, focusing on the choice between local production and imports through local distribution subsidiaries. A survey conducted by the Ministry of International Trade and Industry in Japan and summarized in Table 8.8 shows that 'to deal with trade friction' is the major reason why Japanese MNCs set up production subsidiaries in industrialized countries, whereas low production costs are the most important incentive to produce in developing countries.

Table 8.8 Motives for Japanese firms seeking production bases overseas

	Motives [a]					
	1	*2*	*3*	*4*	*5*	*6*
	%	%	%	%	%	%
Industrialized countries						
Office equipment	96.7	3.3	–	–	–	–
Machine tools	77.1	14.3	–	–	5.0	3.6
Home electric appliances	53.6	13.6	10.7	14.3	2.8	5.0
Electronics	30.0	32.1	11.3	10.8	8.8	7.1
Automobiles	66.0	24.0	–	–	–	10.0
Developing countries						
Textiles	16.5	10.4	5.0	60.4	2.7	5.0
Chemicals	13.9	10.9	10.0	46.1	5.0	14.1
Ferrous/non-ferrous metals	12.5	12.5	13.8	50.0	1.8	9.4
Home electric appliances	15.0	18.8	2.4	58.8	5.0	–
Electronics	10.8	15.4	27.9	38.5	2.4	5.0

Source: Ministry of International Trade and Industry, 1986, as reproduced in Dicken (1988)
Note: [a]Companies were asked to rate motives for seeking production sites overseas, assuming 100 per cent as their total motives. Results were then summed by industry and by region. The motives are coded as follows: 1, to deal with trade friction; 2, to secure or expand overseas market for reasons not related to trade friction; 3, to respond to moves overseas by customer companies; 4, to take advantage of lower production costs overseas; 5, to hedge risks related to exchange rate fluctuations; 6, others.

These motives are consistent with the pattern of intra-firm trade discussed in the previous section. To identify the determinants of the choice between local production and imports through local distributional subsidiaries, we use a statistical model that regresses the share of employment in US distribution by Japanese MNCs on a set of explanatory variables. These variables are explained in Table 8.9 and in the Appendix. The major hypothesis to be tested is that the presence of trade barriers encourages local production and discourages imports through local distributional subsidiaries.

Table 8.9 Variable definition, mean and standard deviation ($n = 43$)

Symbol	Variable	Mean (Standard deviation)
DISTJ	Employment in Japanese distribution subsidiaries in USA/Total employment in Japanese subsidiaries in USA, 1986	0.489 (0.372)
EXPJUS	Japanese exports to USA/Total US sales, 1986	0.075 (0.131)
KLJ	Gross fixed assets/Total employment, Japan 1984	5.287 (4.528)
GRUS	Change in shipments 1976–84/Shipment 1976, USA	0.901 (0.742)
RDUS	Cost of company R&D/Sales, USA 1977	0.022 (0.020)
ADUS	Media advertising expenses/Sales, USA 1977	0.017 (0.019)
HUFB	Hufbauer's (1970) proxy for product differentiation: the coefficient of variation of unit values of US exports among various destination countries, 1965	0.972 (0.360)
TARIFF	Nominal rate of tariff protection, post-Tokyo Round, USA	4.107 (3.275)
TRNUS	Weiss's (1972) proxy for transportation costs mile radius within which 80% of industry shipments were made	0.940 (x 10^3) (0.310) (x 10^3)
NONTAR	Non-tariff barrier index, USA, *ad valorem* equivalent, 1984	1.500) (3.889)
QDUM	Dummy variable equal to one if the industry is subject to quantitative trade restrictions	0.140 (0.351)
CDUM	Dummy variable equal to one if the industry is judged to sell primarily consumer non-convenience goods	0.372 (0.489)
SEM	Sales divided by employment in US manufacturing, 1982 ($million)	1.055 (0.069)
SED	Sales divided by employment in US distribution 150, 1982 ($million)	4.116 (3.575)

By using the share of employment in US distribution as the dependent variable we are not suggesting that local manufacturing does not require investment in distribution. However, because local manufacturing requires less investment in distribution and in view of the fact that the denominator comprises employment in Japanese subsidiaries in distribution as well as in manufacturing, the dependent variable strongly reflects the substitution of exports for local production in the US industry.

Table 8.10 reports the regression results. In line with the theoretical model in the Appendix, a growing market in the USA and high transportation costs favour local production more than imports through local distributional subsidiaries. Since the model is designed to explain the relative importance of distributional activity in total Japanese direct investment in the USA, by using employment as a proxy for investment, there should be a control for technological differences between the manufacturing and distribution activities. However, the three control variables, KLJ, SEM and SED, are not statistically significant.

Table 8.10 Regression results (dependent variable, DISTJ)

CONSTANT	0.034	−0.067
	(0.334)	(0.317)
TRNUS	0.492**	0.441**
	(0.200)	(0.212)
KLJ	−0.014	−0.007
	(0.013)	(0.014)
GRUS	−0.235**	−0.274**
	(0.093)	(0.101)
EXPJUS	−0.983**	−0.821*
	(0.436)	(0.474)
SEM	−0.083	−0.089
	(0.08)	(0.086)
SED	0.0079	0.012
	(0.015)	(0.016)
RDUS	3.966	6.845*
	(3.411)	(3.581)
HUFB	0.457***	0.382**
	(0.165)	(0.165)
ADUS	−5.448*	−5.458*
	(2.905)	(3.159)
CDUM	0.346**	0.275*
	(0.139)	(0.148)
TARIFF	−0.039*	
	(0.022)	
NONTAR	0.044**	
	(0.021)	
QDUM	−0.433***	
	(0.159)	
R^2	0.558	0.408
Adjusted R^2	0.360	0.223
$F(n = 43)$	2.821	2.206

Notes:
Standard errors are in parentheses
*   5 per cent significance in a two-tailed *t* test.
** 10 per cent significance in a two-tailed *t* test
*** 1 per cent significance in a two-tailed *t* test.

The recent finding by Yamawaki (1989) that distributional activities promote exports from Japan to the US market, together with the argument that distributional activities are subject to substantial scale economies (Williamson and Yamawaki 1989), suggests that there will be relatively less investment in distribution as the ratio of Japanese exports to total US sales becomes larger. Thus, EXPJUS has a negative coefficient.

Technological intensity and Hufbauer's measure of product differentiation are positively correlated with the degree of Japanese investment in US distribution relative to manufacturing. Industries producing primarily non-convenience consumer goods also display relatively more investment in distribution. However, with other product differentiation features controlled for, industries characterized by high advertising in the USA display relatively less Japanese investment in distribution. As to the role of trade friction variables, non-tariff trade barriers mostly involve specific adaptations to local market conditions and require specific servicing. Consequently, the higher are these trade barriers, the larger are the investments in distribution activities encompassing these service activities. Different from the effect of the non-tariff variable, high nominal tariffs and import quantity restrictions lead to a substitution of exports from Japan in favour of local production in the US market. This result is clearly in line with our *a priori* hypothesis about the effects of trade restricting measures. Table 8.10, second column, shows the impact on the estimation results of leaving out trade friction variables. Only the coefficient of R&D changes markedly and becomes significantly different from zero, suggesting collinearity between R&D intensity and the various protective measures.

CONCLUSION

In this paper intra-firm trade was explained as the result of vertical integration of firms across national boundaries. In looking at the different motives for vertical integration it was argued that government intervention may lead to important 'unnatural' market imperfections which stimulate firms to use intra-firm trade as a mechanism to take advantage or defend against these imperfections.

By contrasting data on Japanese intra-firm trade with intra-firm trade data for US firms, it was found that Japanese parent firms import relatively less from their foreign affiliates and strongly direct their intra-firm exports to their foreign distribution subsidiaries in the USA and Europe. Empirical evidence for Japanese subsidiaries in the USA suggests that this kind of intra-firm trade reduces in magnitude and becomes substituted by local manufacturing when the market grows, transportation costs become more important and trade restrictions increase.

Finally, most of the Japanese intra-firm trade pattern can be explained by the fact that the expansion of Japanese firms in global markets is of much more recent origin than is the case for US or European firms. It is very probable that this pattern will change in the future and converge to the situation within US or European firms along with further world integration of markets.

APPENDIX

The model we propose presents a simple characterization of protectionism within the context of an oligopoly model. By its simple nature the model allows us to make explicit some basic effects of protectionistic measures upon economic variables, such as price, distribution of market shares, the importance of intra-firm trade and the extent of foreign direct investment in the industry.

In line with Richard Baldwin (1988) we envisage protectionism in relation to two kinds of cost-raising measures: those which raise the marginal cost of supplying the product or service and those which raise the fixed cost of controlling a foreign firm (such as the various regulations concerning direct investment). The first category may include import tariffs, but also various kinds of non-tariff barriers, such as *inter alia* the different kinds of technical regulations on products or services for which local adjustment necessitates the location of downstream services in the foreign country which raises marginal supply costs. In the model these marginal cost-raising barriers are denoted by τ, while the specific fixed cost incurred in local production by foreign companies is denoted by F. Most of the non-tariff barriers are not intended to raise government revenue. With trade barriers present, trade will be internalized within firms and foreign firms will face constant marginal costs $c_i(1 + \tau)$ for these export transactions. To keep the model simple, we assume that the relevant marginal cost is also c_i if they produce locally in the foreign market. However, in the latter case they incur a (recurrent) specific cost F, because of possible discriminating measures against foreign producers and the various expenses associated with operating in an unfamiliar environment.

The model assumes Cournot–Nash equilibrium outcomes for N producers. The Nash equilibrium in quantities is defined as

$$\pi_i(q_i^*) > \pi(q_i^*,\dots, q_{i-1}^*,q_i,\dots, q_N^*) \qquad \text{A}q_i, \text{A}i \qquad (8.\text{A}1)$$

Define three sets of firms: S_D the set of the domestic producers, S_X the set of the exporters and S_F the set of all foreign producers with local production in the market. Profit functions are

$$\pi_i = P(Q)q_i - c_i q_i \qquad\qquad A i \, \epsilon \, S_D \qquad (8.A2)$$

$$\pi_i = P(Q)q_i - c_i(1 + \tau)q_i \qquad\qquad A i \, \epsilon \, S_X \qquad (8.A3)$$

$$\pi_i = P(Q)q_i - c_i q_i - F \qquad\qquad A i \, \epsilon \, S_F \qquad (8.A4)$$

where

$$Q = \Sigma \quad q_i$$
$$i \, \epsilon \, S_D \, \cup \, S_X \, \cup \, S_F$$

With only import tariffs present, the MNC will choose marginal cost c_i as the optimal transfer price, given that this is the lowest possible transfer price tax authorities will accept. It is also important to notice that in the decision process S_X and S_F are the same. Assuming constant marginal costs, the equilibrium implies corner solutions with either exports or foreign production equal to zero. Therefore, in discussing the equlibrium conditions, only active exporters from the set S_X and active foreign producers from S_F will be considered. These subsets are denoted by S_X^+ and S_F^+. Active domestic producers are denoted by S_D^+. By imposing the restriction that $P' < 0$, $P''q_i < 0$ it has been shown that there exists a stable and unique Cournot–Nash equilibrium (Dierickx *et al.* 1987). At any equilibrium point $q_i^* > 0$ we have

$$P + \frac{\partial P}{\partial Q} q_i^* - c_i = 0 \qquad\qquad \forall \, i \, \epsilon \, S_D^+ \, \cup \, S_F^+ \qquad (8.A5)$$

$$P + \frac{\partial P}{\partial Q} q_i^* - c_i(1 + \tau) = 0 \qquad\qquad \forall \, i \, \epsilon \, S_X^+ \qquad (8.A6)$$

These conditions can be reformulated as follows:

$$P(1 - \frac{s_i}{\eta}) - c_i = 0 \qquad\qquad \forall \, i \, \epsilon \, S_D^+ \, \cup \, S_F^+ \qquad (8.A7)$$

$$P(1 - \frac{s_i}{\eta}) - c_i(1 + \tau) \qquad\qquad \forall \, i \, \epsilon \, S_X^+ \qquad (8.A8)$$

where $s_i = \dfrac{q_i^*}{Q}$, the market share of firm i.

Summing over the active firms, and using the constraint $\Sigma\, s_i = 1$, yields the following price equation:

$$P = \bar{c} \left(\frac{\eta}{\eta - \dfrac{1}{N}} \right). \tag{8.A9}$$

where

$$\bar{c} = \frac{1}{N} \left[\sum_{i \,\in\, S_D \cup S_F} c_i + \sum_{i \,\in\, S_X} c_i(1 + \tau) \right]$$

and N is the number of active suppliers in the market. In words, $\bar{c}$ is the (unweighted) average marginal cost of all suppliers. Inserting (8.A9) into (8.A7) and (8.A8) we obtain the following market share functions:

$$s_i = \eta - \left(\eta - \frac{1}{N} \right) \frac{c_i}{\bar{c}} \qquad \forall\, i \in S_D^+ \cup S_F^+ \tag{8.A10}$$

$$s_i = \eta - \left(\eta - \frac{1}{N} \right) \frac{c_i(1 + \tau)}{\bar{c}} \qquad \forall\, i \in S_X^+ \tag{8.A11}$$

From condition (8.A9) it can be verified how the trade barriers summarized in τ increase price, restrict demand and, as equation (8.A11) shows, take away market share from exporters. The equilibrium conditions also enable us to calculate 'effective' measures of protection, in the sense that they totally impede export penetration by foreign producers. With a given number N of domestic firms, characterized by average marginal cost $\bar{c}$, exports will effectively be impeded as long as

$$P - c_i(1 + \tau) < 0 \tag{8.A12}$$

or, given price equation (8.A9),

$$\left(\frac{\bar{c}}{c_i} + \frac{1}{N} \right) \left[\frac{N\eta}{(N+1)\eta - 1} \right] < 1 + \tau \tag{8.A13}$$

for all potential exporters. Condition (8.A13) implies that (non-) tariff barriers have to be high enough to compensate for the higher marginal cost of domestic firms *vis-à-vis* any potential foreign exporter. For demand elasticities larger than unity, the more elastic the demand curves become, the less protection will be needed. The effect of changing the number of firms depends on the magnitudes of the cost differential and demand elasticity.

As an alternative way of penetrating the market, foreign companies might decide to invest and produce locally in the market. In this case protectionism would still have to focus on making specific adjustments or servicing of the product necessary, or on increasing the specific cost F that foreign investors incur in operating foreign plants. In order to operate on a profitable scale, MNCs need to attain a market share large enough to compensate for this specific cost F. Formally, if profitability (profits π_i divided by revenues R_i) has to be positive, it is necessary that

$$\frac{\pi_i}{R_i} = \frac{(p - c_i)q_i}{pq_i} - \frac{F}{pq_i} > 0 \qquad (8.A14)$$

which implies, using (8.A7),

$$\frac{s_i}{\eta} - \frac{F}{pq_i} > 0 \qquad \text{or} \qquad s_i > \left(\frac{F}{pQ}\right)^{\frac{1}{2}\eta} \qquad (8.A15)$$

where pQ is the size of the market.

Formula (8.A15) can be further developed by calculating potential market share s_i from (8.A10) and total market size from (8.A9), with the provision that $\bar{c}$ now includes the marginal cost c_i of the potential foreign firm and with the number of firms extended to $N+1$. Given this information F, which effectively impedes entry by a foreign firm, can be calculated. It is important to note from condition (8.A15) that the size of the market as summarized in pQ is an important determinant for direct investment to take place. With the assumptions made in this model, foreign production will always yield larger market shares and larger price–marginal cost margins than exporting to the protected market. It follows that the timing of foreign direct investment to substitute exports in this model is basically explained by the growth of the foreign market. Obviously, the model could be extended by introducing different marginal cost conditions in the home and the foreign country for the MNC, and by allowing for fixed costs for domestic as well as for foreign firms. These extensions would undoubtedly refine the analysis, but they would not alter the basic insights obtained so far.

Japanese direct investment in US distribution: selection of samples

The matched manufacturing industries used in this paper were selected on the basis of the standard industry classification system in Japan and the USA. The level of industry classification is comparable with the three-digit US Standard Industrial Classification (SIC). The forty-three industries in our sample were those industries where Japanese MNCs control (50 per cent or more) their distribution subsidiaries in the USA.

Sources of data

DISTJ was constructed from Toyokeizal (ed.), *Kalgalshlnshulsn Klgvu soran: 1988* (*Directory of Japanese Multinational Corporations 1988*) (Tokyo: Tokyokeizai). This data source publishes the number of employees in each subsidiary in the USA by line of business. Thus the number of employees in Japanese subsidiaries at the industry level was constructed by aggregating the figure for the line of business. EXPJUS was constructed from Japan External Trade Organization (JETRO), *White Paper on International Trade Japan*. KLJ and total Japanese shipments were obtained from Japan, Ministry of International Trade and Industry, *Census of Manufactures*. GRUS was constructed from US Bureau of Census, *Census of Manufactures*, and RDUS and ADUS were obtained from US Federal Trade Commission, *Annual Line of Business Report*, 1977. HUFB was obtained from G.C. Hufbauer, 'The impact of national characteristics and technology on the commodity composition of trade in manufactured goods', in R. Vernon (ed.) *The Technology Factor in International Trade* (New York: National Bureau of Economic Research, 1970). NONTAR, TARIFF were obtained from Alan V. Deardorff and Robert R. Stern, 'The effects of the Tokyo Round on the structure of protection', in R.E. Baldwin and A.O. Krueger (eds) *The Structure and Evolution of Recent U.S. Trade Policy* (Chicago, IL: University of Chicago Press, 1984) and Alan V. Deardorff and Robert R. Stern, 'Alternative scenarios for trade liberalization', Seminar Discussion Paper 217, Department of Economics, University of Michigan, Ann Arbor, Mi. The data were available for only twenty-one broadly defined industries and so we assumed that the value for each was common for each of the forty-three industries included within it. Finally, TRNUS was obtained from Leonard W. Weiss, 'The geographic size of markets in manufacturing', *Review of Economics and Statistics* 54 (August 1972): 243–57, and is a weighted average of the four-digit shipping radius, SEM and SED were obtained from the US Census of Industry, 1982 and the 1982 Census of Wholesale Trade respectively.

NOTES

1 Partial financial support of the Research Fund of the KU Leuven (OT/89/5) is gratefully acknowledged. The paper benefited from comments by Jagdish Bhagwati, Peter Dicken, Theo Peeters and Luc Soete.

REFERENCES

Baldwin, R. (1988) 'Factor market barriers are trade barriers: gains from trade in 1992', Columbia Business School, mimeo.

Bhagwati, J. (1988) *Protectionism*, Cambridge, MA. MIT Press.

Blair, R. and Kaserman, D. (1983) *Law and Economics of Vertical Integration and Control*, New York: Academic Press.

Clairmonte, F. and Cavenagh, J. (1982) 'The ever-grasping drive', *Development Forum* (November): 3–4.

Dicken, P. (1988) 'The changing geography of Japanese foreign direct investment in manufacturing industry: a global perspective', *Environent and Planning A* 20: 633–53.

Dierickx, I., Matutes, C. and Neven, D. (1987) 'Indirect taxation and Cournot equilibrium', INSEAD, mimeo.

Dunning, J.H. and Pearce, R.D. (1985) *The World's Largest Industrial Enterprises*, Farnborough: Gower Press.

Ethier, W. (1986) 'The multinational firm', *Quarterly Journal of Economics* 101: 805–33.

Goldsborough, D. (1981) 'International trade of multinational corporations and its responsiveness to changes in aggregate demand and relative prices', IMF *Staff Papers* 18: 573–99.

Helpman, E. and Krugman, P. (1985) *Market Structure and Foreign Trade*, Cambridge, MA: MIT Press.

Lipsey, R.E. and Kravis, I.E. (1985) 'The competitive position of U.S. manufacturing firms', *Banco Nazionale del Lavoro* (153): 127–54.

McCulloch, R. (1988) 'Japanese investment in the United States', paper presented at the Tenth Annual Middlebury College Conference on Economic Issues.

United Nations Centre on Transnational Corporations (1988) *Transnational Corporations in World Development*, United Nations Publications E.88.II.A.7.

Williamson, P. and Yamawaki, H. (1989) 'Distribution, Japan's hidden advantage', Discussion Papers FS IV, 89–11, Wissenschaftszentrum, Berlin.

Yamawaki, H. (1989) 'Exports and direct investment in distribution, evidence on Japanese firms in the United States', Discussion Papers FS 111, Wissenschaftszentrum, Berlin.

9 *Quid pro quo* foreign investment and policy intervention

Elias Dinopoulos and Kar-yiu-Wong

INTRODUCTION

Among Bhagwati's recent contributions to the political-economy-theoretic analysis of international economic phenomena is his identification and analysis of a novel form of direct foreign investment (DFI). It occurs with the purpose of reducing and even eliminating, rather than circumventing, the threat of protection. Bhagwati (1985) christened this phenomenon *quid pro quo* DFI to capture the following process: DFI occurs in the first period at an economic loss (from the point of view of myopic one-period profit maximization), with a view to defusing the threat of future protection and consequently increasing profits in the second period by maintaining access to product markets, the latter gain being the *quid pro quo* for the former loss. *Quid pro quo* DFI differs from the conventional 'tariff-jumping' DFI: the former aims at reducing the threat of protection whereas the latter does not influence the level of protection but rather circumvents actual or anticipated protection which it takes as given. In reality both types of DFI coexist.

How does DFI defuse the protectionist threat? What is the mechanism of interaction between the threat of protection and DFI? Bhagwati (1985) focused on several political-economy and strategic aspects. Noting that threats and enactment of protection typically result from 'demands' by producers, i.e. corporations and unions, and 'supply' by the Congress and Executives in democratic countries, Bhagwati suggested that DFI could be the instrument used to co-opt these demanding and supplying agents into a less protectionist stance and actions. 'Chiefly, [the moderation of the protectionist threat] can occur because DFI is regarded, and can be exploited by lobbies on behalf of the exporting country, as a helpful phenomenon that "saves jobs" in the importing country whereas the imports are "costing jobs" instead' (Bhagwati 1987: 10–11). While this "goodwill" effect operates mainly on those who supply protection,

DFI could also, through the creation of jobs, reduce union pressures for protection if the jobs are created where the import-competition-affected plants are located. It can reduce corporate pressures for protection as well if the DFI is a joint venture with the adversely impacted corporations, as was the Toyota–General Motors venture in the USA that preceded the conversion of General Motors to free trade in autos (Bhagwati 1985, 1987).[1]

Corresponding to this diversity of possibilities in the importing country to which the *quid pro quo* DFI is taken, the analysis can be differentiated for the country of origin of the DFI as well. Thus, in oligopolistic industries, individual firms may see the advantage of *quid pro quo* DFI themselves. Alternatively, especially in competitive industries, the government itself may encourage, through subsidies or threats, equity investments abroad: Japan's Ministry of International Trade and Industry (MITI) may urge Toyota to invest in the USA, not for its own *quid pro quo*, but 'for Japan'. Evidently, different combinations of possibilities for modelling *quid pro quo* DFI are thus open.

They have in fact been explained in diverse ways in the existing formal analyses. Thus, Bhagwati *et al.* (1987) use the popular general equilibrium 2 × 2 model of international trade theory to analyse the exporting country's optimal policy intervention in a two-period framework when first-period investment by the exporting country in the importing country can moderate an exogenously specified threat by the latter country to impose protection in the second period. The exporting country acts as a Stackelberg leader in this analysis which is built on the Bhagwati and Srinivasan (1976) earlier two-period analysis of market disruption such that reduction in the first-period exports moderates the probability that protection is imposed in the second period. The model, given the atomistic nature of the firms, evidently does not permit them to undertake *quid pro quo* DFI for their own advantage. The investment occurs only under government initiative, implying a corresponding subsidy policy to create the optimal level of such investment. Correspondingly, the protectionist threat in this 2 × 2 model is against the exporting country rather than industry specific (in any meaningful sense since there is only one importable good and one exportable good).

But both the industry specificity of the protectionist threat, and its endogeneity in the model, have been introduced in later analyses that work with partial equilibrium models that admit imperfect competition. Thus, Dinopoulos and Bhagwati (1986) and Dinopoulos (1989) have analysed the industry specific *quid pro quo* DFI and examine how, even in the absence of governmental intervention, oligopolistic firms themselves will undertake such investment and adjust their exporting appropriately. Moreover, Dinopoulos has analysed the free-rider problem systematically: the larger the number of exporters, the smaller is the level of *quid pro quo* DFI, in consequence of the free-rider problem.

On the other hand, Wong (1989a) has endogenized the protectionist threat, modelling labour union behaviour in an industry with endogenous unemployment which can respond to import protection lobbied for by the union. Following Brock and Magee (1978), he determines the optimal trade restriction and lobbying effort by the union in this model. Acting as Stackelberg leader, the foreign government-cum-firms choose the optimum level of *quid pro quo* DFI, which, by affecting the unemployment, can lead to altered choices of lobbying effort by the union and resulting protection.

In the analysis below, the Wong model is used to develop the implications for policy intervention beyond the limited analysis offered earlier. In the next section we briefly discuss the essentials of the Wong model. The following section develops the welfare implications under *laissez faire*. In the section entitled 'Policies for the importing country' we consider the effects of alternative policy interventions of the importing country, while those of the exporting countries are analysed in the penultimate section. Concluding remarks are offered in the last section.

THE OPTIMAL PROTECTIONIST THREAT AND *QUID PRO QUO* DIRECT FOREIGN INVESTMENT

Following Wong (1989a), consider two countries labelled E (exporting) and M (importing) and two periods of time labelled 1 and 2 in which the preferences, technologies and endowments of the two countries remain unchanged. There are three groups of competitive firms in the two countries producing a homogeneous good A. First, there are firms located in country E and owned by residents of country E. They are called foreign (parent) firms, Second, there are firms, called foreign subsidiaries, located in country M which are subsidiaries of the foreign firms. Third, there are firms located in country M which are owned by residents of country M which are called domestic firms. The factor markets in both countries are characterized by flexible prices and full employment, except that in industry A in country M there exists a labour union which sets a downward rigid wage rate $\bar{W}$ for the domestic firms and foreign subsidiaries.[2] All variables for country E are asterisked. In both periods, good A is imported from country E by country M. The analysis is in partial equilibrium, with production of other goods omitted from view.

Let us first describe the production and consumption of good A in country E in each period. The foreign firms are endowed with a fixed amount of capital, $\bar{K}^*$ of which k is invested through their subsidiaries in country M, with the rest, $\bar{K}^*-k$, in country E. The optimal choice of k by the foreign firms will be discussed below so that, for the time being, k is treated as a a parameter. Assume the existence of a differentiable, strictly increasing and strictly concave production function for the industry given by $Y^* = f^* (\bar{K}^* - k)$, where Y^* is the output of the foreign firms and where inputs other than capital are deleted from the function either because they are fixed or because their changes are not significant. Using the production function, we define the (restricted) profit function of the industry as $\Pi^*(P^*,\bar{K}^* - k)$, where P^* is the price of good A in the foreign country. The profit function is differentiable, strictly increasing and strictly convex in P^*, and has the following derivatives:

$$\frac{\partial \Pi^*}{\partial P^*} = Y^*(P^*,\bar{K}^* - k) \qquad (9.1a)$$

$$\frac{\partial \Pi^*}{\partial k} = r^*(P^*,\bar{K}^* - k) \qquad (9.1b)$$

where $Y^*(P^*,\bar{K}^* - k)$ and $r^*(P^*,\bar{K}^* - k)$ are the supply function and the rental rate of capital respectively in country E. Strict convexity of the profit function implies that the supply function is positive sloped, i.e. $\partial Y^*/\partial P^* > 0$.

We now turn to the production of good A in country M, the importing country. Assuming the existence of a sectoral production function for the domestic firms, define the corresponding profit function as $\Pi(P,\bar{W})$, where P is the price of good A in country M. By the envelope theorem the derivatives of the profit function are

$$\frac{\partial \Pi}{\partial P} = Y(P,\bar{W}) \qquad (9.2a)$$

$$\frac{\partial \Pi}{\partial \bar{W}} = - n (P,\bar{W}) \qquad (9.2b)$$

where $Y(P,\bar{W})$ is the supply schedule of the domestic firms in country M and $n(P,\bar{W})$ is the derived demand for labour. If the profit function is strictly convex in P, the supply schedule is positively sloped, i.e. $\partial Y/\partial P > 0$

The profit function of the foreign subsidiaries can be defined in the same way as $\pi^*(P,k,\bar{W})$ which is differentiable, strictly increasing and strictly convex in P. The derivatives of the profit function are

$$\frac{\partial \pi^*}{\partial P} = y^*(P,k,\bar{W}) \tag{9.3a}$$

$$\frac{\partial \pi^*}{\partial k} = -r(P,k,\bar{W}) \tag{9.3b}$$

$$\frac{\partial \pi^*}{\partial \bar{W}} = -n^*(P,k,\bar{W}) \tag{9.3c}$$

where $y^*(P,k,\bar{W})$ is the output of foreign subsidiaries, $n^*(P,k,\bar{W})$ is the derived demand for labour and $r(P,k,\bar{W})$ is the rental rate in country M. Convexity of the profit function implies that the supply schedule is positively sloped, i.e. $\partial y^*/\partial P > 0$.

We can now turn to the consumption side of the two countries. Assume that the preferences of countries E and M can be represented by two differentiable and downward-sloping demand schedules $D^*(P^*)$ and $D(P)$ respectively, where $dD^*/dP^* < 0$ and $dD/dP < 0$. Note that we abstract from income and cross-price effects because of the partial equilibrium approach of the present model.

Free trade equilibrium

In this subsection we establish the free trade equilibrium. Since the countries have fixed endowments, technologies and preferences in periods 1 and 2, the following analysis applies to both periods.

Treating the level k of DFI as a parameter, we have the free trade equilibrium conditions

$$D^*(P^*) + D(P) = Y^*(P^*,k) + y^*(P,k,\bar{W}) + Y(P,\bar{W}) \tag{9.4a}$$

$$P = P^* \tag{9.4b}$$

which require zero excess demand for good A in the world and price equalization across countries. These equations can be solved for the free trade equilibrium price $P_i(k)$, with $\bar{W}$ dropped from the function for simplicity. Differentiate (9.4) and rearrange the terms to calculate the effect of DFI on P_f:

$$\frac{dP_f}{dk} = \frac{Y_k^* + y_k^*}{D_p^* + D_p - Y_p^* - y_p^* - Y_p} \tag{9.5}$$

where subscripts p and k on the right-hand side denote partial derivatives; e.g. $Y_k^* = \partial Y^*/\partial k$. Using the assumptions about the slopes of the demand and supply schedules, $D_p^* + D_p - Y_p^* - y_p^* - Y_p < 0$, which is in fact the condition for Marshallian stability. Thus, more DFI will increase or decrease the free trade price of good A depending on whether $Y_k^* + y_k^*$ is negative or positive.

We can now explain how k is determined endogenously. Suppose that foreign firms choose the optimal level of DFI in order to maximize the sum of profits of parent firms and subsidiaries,[3] i.e.

$$\max_k \ [\Pi^*(P^*,\bar{K}^* - k) + \pi^*(P,k,\bar{W})] \text{ subject to } P^* = P \qquad (9.6)$$

Differentiate the expression in (9.6) with respect to k, making use of (9.1) and (9.3) and rearranging the terms to give the equilibrium condition for DFI.[4]

$$r(P,k,\bar{W}) = r^*(P^*,\bar{K}^* - k) \qquad (9.7)$$

which is the equalization of rental rates. Because of diminishing marginal product of capital, $\partial r/\partial k < 0$ and $\partial r^*/\partial k > 0$. Using function $P_f(k)$, condition (9.7) can be solved for the equilibrium k. Denote the equilibrium value by k_f, and call this amount the income–differential-induced DFI. Thus, the free trade equilibrium price of good A is $P_f(k_f)$. Once the equilibrium values of P and k are known, the production and consumption of the good in the two countries can be determined. For example, the export level of country E equals $Y^*[P_f(k_f),k_f] - D^*[P_f(k_f)]$. Given the rigid wage rate $\bar{W}$, free trade DFI k_f and price $P_f(k_f)$, the total demand for labour of the domestic firms and foreign subsidiaries is given by

$$l^f = n^*(P_f(k_f),k_f,\bar{W}) + n(P_f(k_f),\bar{W}) \qquad (9.8)$$

Lobbying and trade restriction threat

In order to explain sector–specific unemployment, assume that there is a fixed amount $\bar{L}$ of labour in the sector, which may be because of labour immobility across sectors, at least in the short run. Further assume that under free trade the demand for labour given in (9.8) is less than the available amount of labour, so that there exists unemployment in the first period given by

$$U = \bar{L} - l^f > 0 \qquad (9.9)$$

All the workers in the industry, whether employed or unemployed, are represented by a labour union. The labour union wants to eliminate the unemployment using a trade restriction in the form of a tariff.[5] Let us first derive the appropriate tariff required to remove the unemployment before we examine how the labour union lobbies for the trade restriction.

If we suppose that an *ad valorem* tariff τ is imposed on the imported good A, the restricted trade equilibrium in (9.4) is described by

$$D^*(P^*) = D(P) = Y^*(P^*,k) + y^*(P,k,\bar{W}) + y(P,\bar{W}) \qquad (9.10a)$$

$$P = P^*(1 + \tau) \qquad (9.10b)$$

which can be solved for the restricted-trade equilibrium price $P_t(r,k)$ of good A in country M and for $P_t^*(r,k)$ in country E, where $\bar{W}$ is dropped from the functions for simplicity. Substituting (9.10b) into (9.10a) and totally differentiating the latter gives

$$\left[D_p - y_p^* - Y_p + \frac{(D_p^* - Y_p^*)}{1 - r} \right] dP = (Y_k^* + y_k^*)\ dk + \frac{P(D_p^* - Y_p^*)}{(1 + \tau)^2}\ d\tau \qquad (9.11)$$

By the assumptions about the slopes of the demand and supply schedules, we obtain $\partial P_t / \partial r > 0$. If we assume inefficient allocation of DFI under trade restriction, we have $Y_k^* + y_k^* < 0$, meaning that a transfer of capital from country E to M, under unchanged prices, lowers the total production of good A in the world. This implies that $\partial P_t / \partial k > 0$. Similar arguments can be used to show that $\partial P_t^* / \partial \tau < 0$ and $\partial P_t^* / \partial k < 0$.[6] The value of the tariff rate required to eliminate unemployment is given by the solution to the following equation:

$$\bar{L} = n^*\ [P_t(\tau,k),k] + n\ [P_t(\tau,k)] \qquad (9.12)$$

Denote the required tariff rate by $r_t(k)$. We assume that $r_t(k)$ is not prohibitive. Totally differentiate (9.12) and rearrange the terms to give the effect of DFI on the full-employment tariff rate;

$$\tau' \equiv \frac{dr}{dk} = - \frac{n_k^* + (n_p^* + n_p)\partial P_t / \partial k}{(n_p^* + n_p)\partial P_t / \partial \tau} < 0$$

where it is assumed that labour and capital used by foreign subsidiaries are substitutes and that the marginal product of labour is diminishing, implying that $n_k^* > 0$.

Suppose now that in period 1 the labour union lobbies the government for passing a law which imposes a tariff of $\tau_t(k)$ on the imported good A. We assume that passing a law has to go through all political channels and processes, and it takes time. This means that in period 1 trade remains free and that the protectionist law, if passed, will take effect at the beginning of period 2.

We assume that the probability of passing the protectionist law, denoted by $\theta \in [0, 1]$, depends on the lobbying of the labour union, *ceteris paribus*. The labour union will choose the optimal lobbying to maximize the net benefit of lobbying.

To derive the optimal lobbying, we postulate that the cost of lobbying in period 1 can be represented by the function $\tilde{C}(\theta,\tau)$, which depends on the probability of passing the law and the tariff rate. Following Wong (1989a), we assume that

$$\frac{\partial \tilde{C}}{\partial \theta}, \frac{\partial \tilde{C}}{\partial \tau} > 0$$

Call $\partial \tilde{C}/\partial \theta$ the marginal cost of lobbying. We further assume that the marginal cost of lobbying is increasing with θ and approaches infinity when θ approaches unity owing to 'diminishing returns' to lobbying. In the following analysis, it is more convenient to define a new lobbying cost function $C(\theta,k) \equiv \tilde{C}[\theta,\tau_t(k)]$. We have $\partial C/\partial \theta = \partial \tilde{C}/\partial \theta > 0$, and $\partial C/\partial k = (\partial \tilde{C}/\partial \tau)\tau' < 0$.

Consider now the benefit of lobbying which is defined as the discounted expected income in the two periods of the workers who get employed as a result of the lobbying and protectionist threat. Either in period 1 or in period 2 if trade is not restricted, the change in employment is

$$l(k) = n^*[P_f(k),k] + n[P_f(k)] - l^f \tag{9.13}$$

If trade is restricted in period 2, employment is improved by U which is given in (9.9). As a result, the benefit of lobbying can be defined as

$$B(\theta,k) = \bar{W}l(k) + \omega[\theta U + (1 - \theta)l(k)]$$

where ω is the present value of $\bar{W}$ using an exogenously given discount rate.

Differentiate (9.13) with respect to k to give

$$\frac{dl}{dk} = \frac{dn^*}{dk} + \frac{dn}{dk} = \left(\frac{\partial n^*}{\partial P_f} + \frac{\partial n}{\partial P_f}\right)\frac{dP_f}{dk} + \frac{\partial n^*}{\partial k} > 0 \tag{9.14}$$

Equation (9.14) implies that the threat itself improves employment in both periods even if trade remains free in period 2. As shown below, k will not be great enough to remove all unemployment. This means that, if free trade exists, $l < U$.

The derivatives of the benefit of lobbying are given as follows:

$$\frac{\partial B}{\partial \theta} = \omega[U - l(k)] > 0 \tag{9.15a}$$

$$\frac{\partial B}{\partial k} = [\bar{W} + \omega(1 - \theta)]\frac{dl}{dk} > 0 \tag{9.15b}$$

$$\frac{\partial^2 B}{\partial\theta\partial k} = -\omega\,\frac{dl}{dk} < 0 \qquad (9.15c)$$

$$\frac{\partial^2 B}{\partial\theta^2} = 0 \qquad (9.15d)$$

We are now ready to derive the optimal protectionist threat. Suppose that the labour union takes the investment of the firms in country E as given and spends resources on lobbying in order to maximize the net benefit of lobbying, $N(\theta,k)$. Formally, the problem of the labour union can be stated as

$$\max_{\theta} N(\theta,k) = B(\theta,k) - C(\theta,k)$$

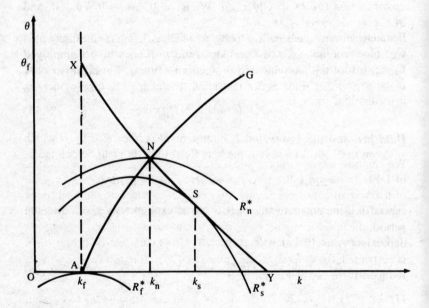

Figure 9.1

The first-order condition states that the marginal benefit of lobbying equals the marginal cost of lobbying:

$$B_\theta(\theta,k) = C_\theta(\theta,k) \qquad (9.16)$$

where the subscripts represent partial derivatives. The second-order condition is also satisfied, because

$$B_{\theta\theta} - C_{\theta\theta} = - C_{\theta\theta} < 0$$

Equation (9.16) can be solved for the probability $\tilde{\theta}(k)$ of passing the protectionist law, which can be called the reaction function of the labour union when k is taken as given. The reaction function is plotted graphically in Figure 9.1 as schedule XNSY. Note that the reaction schedule is defined when $k \geq k_f$, the DFI under free trade. The slope of the reaction function is obtained by differentiating (9.16) and rearranging the terms:

$$\frac{d\tilde{\theta}}{dk} = \frac{B_{\theta k} - C_{\theta k}}{C_{\theta\theta}}$$

Because of the nature of the problem at hand, we assume that $B_{\theta k} > C_{\theta k}$, meaning that the employment effect of DFI is significant. Since $C_{\theta\theta} > 0$, the reaction schedule is negatively sloped. The slope of the reaction schedule is in fact the crucial feature of the model, because it means that more DFI will lower the threat of trade restriction.

Quid pro quo direct foreign investment

We can now explain *quid pro quo* DFI and compare it with other types of DFI. In period 1 the foreign firms choose the allocation of capital of a fixed amount between the two countries. Once the allocation of capital is decided, it remains fixed for at least two periods.[7] In each period, the optimal production of the foreign parent firms and subsidiaries depends on the allocation of capital and, in period 2, on whether trade is restricted. To determine the optimal DFI, define the following four reduced-form profit functions:

$\Pi_f^*(k) = \Pi^*[P_f(k), \bar{K}^* - k]$, profits of parent firms under free trade;

$\Pi_f^*(k) = \Pi^*\{P_t^*[\tau_t(k),k], \bar{K}^* - k\}$, profits of parent firms under restricted trade;

$\pi_f^*(k) = \pi^*[P_f(k),k]$, profits of subsidiaries under free trade;

$\pi_f^*(k) = \pi^*\{P_t[\tau_t(k),k],k\}$; profits of subsidiaries under restricted trade.

Since trade is free in period 1 but may be restricted in period 2, the discounted expected income, or the discounted expected profits, of foreign firms over the two periods is given as

$$R^*(\theta,k) = \Pi_f^*(k) + \pi_f^*(k) + \tilde{\sigma}^*\{\theta[\Pi_t^*(k) + \pi_t^*(k)] + (1 - \theta)[\Pi_f^*(k) + \pi_f^*(k)]\}$$
(9.17)

where $\tilde{\sigma}^*$ is foreign firms' discount rate, which is assumed to be fixed. The derivatives of the expected income are

$$\frac{\partial R^*}{\partial \theta} = \tilde{\sigma}^*[\Pi_t^*(k) + \pi_t^*(k) - \Pi_f^*(k) - \pi_f^*(k)] < 0$$
(9.18a)

$$\frac{\partial R^*}{\partial k} = \Pi_f^{*\prime}(k) + \pi_f^{*\prime}(k) + \tilde{\sigma}^*\{\theta[\Pi_t^{*\prime}(k) + \pi_t^{*\prime}(k)] + (1 - \theta)[\Pi_f^{*\prime}(k) + \pi_f^{*\prime}(k)]\}$$
(9.18b)

The sign of $\partial R^*/\partial \theta$ is due to the fact that protection hurts the firms. The sign of $\partial R^*/\partial k$ is ambiguous, depending on the values of $\tilde{\sigma}^*$, θ and k. Figure 9.1 shows three possible schedules which are defined by (9.17) and correspond to the expected income levels of R_f^*, R_n^*, and R_s^* where $R_f^* > R_s^* > R_n^*$. These schedules are called iso-expected-income (IEI) schedules.

We can now examine two types of strategies of the foreign firms. The first, a Nash–Cournot strategy, is to take the protectionist threat as given and choose the optimal k to maximize the expected income, i.e. to maximize $R^*(\theta,k)$ with respect to k, taking θ constant. The first-order condition of the problem is given by

$$\frac{\partial R^*}{\partial k} = 0$$

which can be solved for the reaction function $k(\theta)$ of the foreign firms. In Figure 9.1, the reaction function is represented by schedule ANG, which is assumed to be positively sloped. The slope of schedule ANG captures the property that the foreign firms react with more DFI to a more severe protectionist threat. The horizontal intercept of the reaction schedule, point A, represents the income-differential-induced DFI that exists under free trade when no protectionist threat exists. If only the income-differential-induced DFI exists, the labour union will lobby for protection with a probability of success given by θ_f, the vertical height of the labour union's reaction schedule above point A. The figure also shows the Nash equilibrium, which occurs at the point of intersection N between the two reaction schedules. Given the slopes of the two reaction schedules, it can be seen that the protectionist threat causes an inflow of capital which lowers the protectionist threat. Denote the corresponding DFI as k_n. The difference, $k_n - k_f$, can be called the protectionist-threat-responding DFI.

The protectionist-threat-responding DFI is akin to the familiar tariff-jumping DFI, but two differences between them can be noted. First, the protectionist-threat-responding DFI occurs before trade restriction, if any, exists in period 2. In fact, trade may remain free in period 2. Second, for protectionist-threat-responding DFI, the protectionist threat is endogenously determined, and may diminish when more DFI flows in. In the conventional theory of tariff-jumping DFI, protection is assumed by the firms to be given exogenously.

The second strategy available to the foreign firms is to act as a Stackelberg leader *vis-à-vis* the labour union. To employ this strategy successfully, it is assumed that the government of country E or an appropriate industry association co-ordinates the investment decisions of the foreign firms.[8] The strategy is expressed formally as

$$\max_{k} R(\theta,k) \qquad \text{subject to } \theta = \tilde{\theta}(k)$$

The solution to the problem occurs at the point of tangency S between the labour union's reaction schedule and an IEI schedule of the foreign firms. Denote the corresponding DFI by k_s. The difference between k_s and k_n is what we call *quid pro quo* DFI, because this investment takes place with the view to defusing the protectionist threat.

In the case shown, both the protectionist-threat-responding DFI and *quid pro quo* DFI would cause a decrease in the protectionist threat. However, they have one major difference. Foreign firms engage in protectionist-threat-responding DFI when they are reacting to protectionist threat in a Nash fashion, while they use *quid pro quo* DFI to defuse the protectionist threat as a Stackelberg leader. Both the analyses and Figure 9.1 show that, by defusing the protectionist threat, foreign firms increase their expected discounted income. In the special case in which the reaction curve of the labour union is horizontal, the *quid pro quo* DFI is zero because the protectionist threat is fixed from the point of view of foreign firms.

WELFARE EFFECTS OF TRADE RESTRICTION AND *QUID PRO QUO* DIRECT FOREIGN INVESTMENT

In this section we shall examine how *quid pro quo* DFI affects the welfare of the two countries. Let us first look at country M. In period 1, in response to the protectionst threat more foreign investment arrives, but production and price remains unchanged. In period 2, whether or not trade is restricted, the price of the commodity changes and the welfare of consumers, producers and the labour union will change. If trade is restricted, the government will receive tariff revenue which is assumed to be distributed in a lump-sum fashion to consumers. Neglecting issues related to income distribution, national welfare can be represented by the sum of the consumer surplus, producer surplus, the net benefit of lobbying and the tariff revenue.[9] Let us first define the following two functions:

$$\zeta_f(k) = - \int_{P_0}^{P_1} D(P)dP + \Pi(P_1) - \Pi(P_0) \tag{9.19a}$$

$$\zeta_t(k) = - \int_{P_0}^{P_2} D(P)dP + \Pi(P_2) - \Pi(P_0) + (P_2 - P_2^*)[D(P_2) - Y(P_2)] \tag{9.19b}$$

where $P_0 = P_f(k_f)$, $P_1 = P_f(k)$, $P_2 = P_t[\tau_t(k),k]$ and $P_2^* = P_t^*[\tau_t(k),k]$. In equation (9.19), the integration of the demand schedule represents the change in the consumers' surplus, and the profit function of domestic firms is a measure of the producer surplus. In (9.19b), the tariff revenue $(P_2 - P_1^*)[D(P) - Y(P)]$ is included. Thus, $\zeta_f(k)$ and $\zeta_t(k)$ measure the sum of the changes in consumer surplus, producer surplus and tariff revenue under free trade and restricted trade respectively. The two welfare measures depend on DFI in the following way:

$$\zeta_f'(k) = - [D(P_1) - Y(P_1)] \frac{dP_1}{dk} < 0 \tag{9.20a}$$

$$\zeta_t'(k) = - [D(P_2) - Y(P_2)] \frac{dP_2^*}{dk} + (P_2 - P_2^*) \left(\frac{dD}{dP} - \frac{dY}{dP} \right) \frac{dP_2}{dk} < 0 \tag{9.20b}$$

The sign of ζ_f' and ζ_t' comes from the fact that *quid pro quo* DFI tends to hurt world output of good A and raise prices P_1, P_2 and P_2^* because it flows from country E with a higher rental rate to country M with a lower rental rate.

The expected national welfare in both periods discounted to the beginning of the first period is

$$V(\theta,k) = \zeta_f(k) + \sigma[\theta\zeta_t(k) + (1 - \theta)\zeta_f(k)] + B(\theta,k) - C(\theta,k) \tag{9.21}$$

where σ is the exogenously given social discount rate. The welfare in (9.21) includes the properly discounted consumer surplus, producer surplus in both periods, the tariff revenue in period 2 if trade is restricted, and the net benefit of lobbying. The derivatives of the welfare measure are given by

$$\frac{\partial V}{\partial \theta} = \sigma \left[\zeta_t - \zeta_f\right] + B_\theta - C_\theta \tag{9.22a}$$

$$\frac{\partial V}{\partial k} = \zeta_f' + \sigma[\theta\zeta_t' + (1 - \theta)\zeta_f'] < 0 \tag{9.22b}$$

If the labour union chooses the optimal lobbying, $B_\theta = C_\theta$ and $\partial V/\partial \theta = \sigma(\zeta_t - \zeta_f)$. Assume that the trade restriction, if imposed, does not improve the terms of trade of country M much so that it is detrimental, implying that $\zeta_t < \zeta_f$ and $\partial V/\partial \theta < 0$.

Based on the signs of the derivatives of V, the total welfare impact of the *quid pro quo* DFI is given by

$$\frac{dV}{dk} = \frac{\partial V}{\partial k} + \frac{\partial V}{\partial \theta}\frac{d\tilde{\theta}}{dk} \tag{9.23}$$

where $d\tilde{\theta}/dk < 0$ is the slope of the labour union's reaction schedule in Figure 9.1. The sign of dV/dk is ambiguous because *quid pro quo* DFI lowers the probability of trade restriction in period 2.

We now turn to the effects on the welfare of country E. Again, we represent the welfare of consumers and producers by the consumer surplus and producer surplus respectively. Note that no welfare loss due to any unemployment is considered because it is assumed that factors are always fully employed.[10] Producer surplus can be represented by the expected total income of foreign firms defined in (9.17). Measure the consumer surplus under free trade and that under restricted trade by the following functions:

$$\zeta_f^*(k) = - \int_{P_0}^{P_1} D^*(P^*)dP^* \tag{9.24a}$$

$$\zeta_t^*(k) = - \int_{P_0}^{P_2^*} D^*(P^*)dP^* \tag{9.24b}$$

Using (9.24), the welfare of country E can be represented by

$$V^*(\theta,k) = \zeta_f^*(k) + \sigma^*[\theta\zeta_t^*(1-\theta)\zeta_f^*(k)] + R^*(\theta,k) \tag{9.25}$$

The welfare of country E is affected by the protectionist threat and the capital outflow in the following way:

$$\frac{\partial V^*}{\partial \theta} = \sigma^* [\zeta_t^* - \zeta_f^*] + \frac{\partial R^*}{\partial \theta} = -\sigma^* \int_{P_1}^{P_2^*} D^*(P^*) dP^* + \frac{\partial R^*}{\partial \theta} < 0 \tag{9.26a}$$

$$\frac{\partial V^*}{\partial k} \zeta_f^{*'} + \sigma^*[\theta \zeta_t^{*'} + (1-\theta) \zeta_f^{*'}] + \frac{\partial R^*}{\partial k}$$

$$= -D^*(P_1) \frac{dP_1}{dk} - \sigma^* \left[\theta D^*(P_2^*) \frac{dP_2^*}{dk} + (1-\theta) D^*(P_I) \frac{dP_1}{dk} \right] + \frac{\partial R^*}{\partial k} < 0 \tag{9.26b}$$

The sign of $\partial V^*/\partial \theta$ in (9.26a) is due to the fact that both producers and consumers are hurt by the protectionist threat, while that of $\partial V^*/\partial k$ comes from the assumption that more *quid pro quo* DFI hurts the discounted expected income but tends to raise prices. As a result, country E is hurt by the protectionist threat and capital outflow, *ceteris paribus*.

The total effect of *quid pro quo* DFI on country E's welfare, however, is ambiguous, because

$$\frac{dV^*}{dk} = \frac{\partial V^*}{\partial k} + \frac{\partial V^*}{\partial \theta} \frac{d\tilde{\theta}}{dk}$$

As in the case of country M, *quid pro quo* DFI may or may not be detrimental to the welfare of country E because of its defusion of the protectionist threat.

POLICIES FOR THE IMPORTING COUNTRY

The welfare analysis of the protectionist threat and *quid pro quo* DFI on the exporting and importing countries has important implications for commercial policy. In this section we shall examine policies which can be employed by the government of the importing country to improve its national welfare.

In the preceding two sections we assumed that in country M trade policies such as imposing a tariff are decided by the legislative branch of the government. The members of the legislative branch are elected by the voters and subject to re-election, and thus are often influenced by the lobbying of interest groups.[11] In Western democratic countries, the executive branch of the government is usually controlled by a different group of people with different objectives for choosing policies. Although the executive branch does not have the power to pass a law, it has tremendous power, through political party discipline, persuasion, appeals to the voters, flexibility in executing laws and so on, in influencing the choice of trade policies.

An interesting observation is that the executive branch is usually more interested in national welfare while the legislative branch is more interested in regional welfare. For the case of the USA, Baldwin (1985) pointed out that the President tends to be more liberal on trade matters than the Congress. Being the only government official elected by voters across the nation, and having unparalleled opportunities to communicate and appeal to the voters of the nation, the President is usually more concerned with national welfare and acts more autonomously, i.e. more independently of the pressure from lobbying groups.

Thus, in this section, we concentrate on the policy options available to the executive branch of the government of country M in period 1 before lobbying of the labour union occurs. Four policies will be analyzed: capital inflow restriction, counter-lobbying, production subsidy and employment subsidy. The objective of these policies is to improve national welfare measured by function $V(\theta,k)$ in (9.21). In analysing these policies it is assumed that the government has full information about the preferences and technologies of domestic and foreign firms, and also about the reactions of the labour union and foreign firms. It is also assumed that the foreign government does not react with its own policies.

A capital inflow restriction

Represent the welfare of country M by function $V(\theta,k)$ which is the sum of national welfare in the first period and the expected discounted national welfare in the second period. Suppose that the executive branch of the government can use administrative rules, or without incurring any cost can persuade the legislative branch to regulate the amount of DFI in the economy in the first period. The problem of the government can be stated as

$$\max_{k} V(\theta,k) \quad \text{subject to } \theta = \tilde{\theta}(k)$$

where $\tilde{\theta}(k)$ is the reaction of the labour union. The policy requires the choice of an optimal amount of DFI which, when measured along the reaction curve of the labour union, gives the highest utility level. By totally differentiating $V(\theta,k)$ with respect to k, the first-order condition for an optimal DFI is given as

$$\frac{\partial V}{\partial \theta} \frac{d\tilde{\theta}}{dk} + \frac{\partial V}{\partial k} = 0$$

which can be arranged to give

$$\frac{d\tilde{\theta}}{dk} = -\frac{\partial V/\partial k}{\partial V/\partial \theta} \qquad (9.27)$$

Denote the amount of DFI which solves (9.27) by k_q. We assume that unrestricted *quid pro quo* DFI is harmful in the sense that $k_q < k_s$, suggesting that an appropriate quota on DFI can be beneficial.

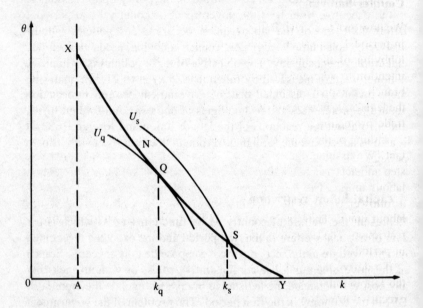

Figure 9.2

The problem of the government can be illustrated graphically. Figure 9.2 shows the reaction curve XNQSY of the labour union and several indifference curves of country M represented by $V(\theta,k)$. Indifference curves closer to the origin represent higher utility levels. $d\tilde{\theta}/dk$ is the slope of the labour union's reaction curve while the slope of an indifference curve is equal to $-(\partial V/\partial k)/(\partial V/\partial \theta)$. Thus condition (9.27) suggests that the optimal DFI occurs at the point of tangency between the reaction curve and an indifference curve. Denote the point of tangency by Q and the corresponding social utility level by U_q. The second-order condition for maximum welfare requires that the indifference curve touches the reaction curve from below.

Given the assumption that the reaction schedule of the labour union is downward sloping, the restriction on DFI will raise the protectionist threat, i.e. the possibility of trade restriction in period 2. This is because, in the presence of a smaller amount of foreign capital, the labour union will lobby more in order to raise the chance of future protection. The policy generally hurts aggregate profits of foreign firms and subsidiaries and thus the welfare of country E.

Counter-lobbying

We now turn to another policy: counter-lobbying by the executive branch in period 1 against any trade restriction in the next period. Counter-lobbying of the executive branch includes the announcement of its intention to veto any protectionist proposals passed in the legislative branch, personal campaigns such as intensive talks with members of the legislative branch and direct appeals to the voters in the nation against trade protection.

Timing of the steps taken by different players in the game is important. We assume that in period 1 the executive branch takes the first step and acts as a Stackelberg leader *vis-à-vis* the foreign firms and the labour union. The foreign firms then take the second step, acting as a follower *vis-à-vis* the executive branch but as a leader *vis-à-vis* the labour union. The labour union takes the third step and lobbies for trade restriction. The legislative branch then decides whether trade is restricted in period 2.

To derive the equilibrium of the game, consider first the choice of the labour union. Denoting the counter-lobbying expenditure of the executive branch by G, the cost of lobbying of the labour union can be written as $\hat{C}(\theta,k,G)$. Note that, when $G = 0$, the above function reduces to the cost-of-lobbying function used in the previous two sections, i.e. $\hat{C}(\theta,k,0) \equiv C(\theta,k)$. Since effective counter-lobbying will raise the cost of lobbying, we have $\partial \hat{C}/\partial G > 0$.

The labour union takes the level of DFI and counter-lobbying as given, and chooses the optimal expenditure on lobbying to maximize the net benefit of lobbying. The first-order condition is similar to that given by (9.16), and the optimal protectionist threat is a function of the level of DFI and counter-lobbying, $\theta = \hat{\theta}(k,G)$. Using the argument and assumptions in the second section, we again have $\partial \hat{C}/\partial k < 0$. The effect of G on the protectionist threat at any level of k can be obtained by differentiating the first-order condition and rearranging the terms to give

$$\frac{\partial \hat{\theta}}{\partial G} = \frac{\hat{C}_{\theta G}}{B_{\theta\theta} - C_{\theta\theta}}$$

Assuming that more intensive counter-lobbying will increase the marginal cost of lobbying, i.e. $\hat{C}_{\theta G} > 0$, then $\partial \hat{\theta}/\partial G < 0$, meaning that more intensive counter-lobbying will lower the probability of trade restriction in the next period.

The foreign firms take the counter-lobbying of the government as given and choose the optimal level of foreign investment subject to the reaction of the labour union. Their maximization problem is similar to that described in the second section. The optimal *quid pro quo* DFI can then be expressed as $k = \hat{k}(G)$. In general, the sign of its derivative $\hat{k}'(G)$ is ambiguous.

Before we explain how the optimal counter-lobbying is determined, we can illustrate its effects graphically. In Figure 9.3 XSY is the reaction curve of the labour union in the absence of any counter-lobbying. An expenditure of G on counter-lobbying will lower θ. This means that, when the government spends an amount $G > 0$ on counter-lobbying the reaction curve will shift down to X'S'Y', for example.[12] The new

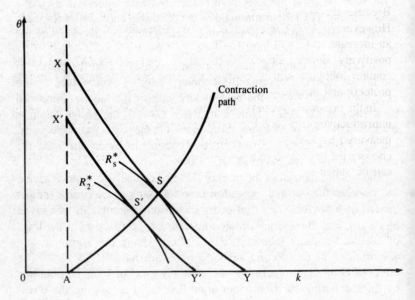

Figure 9.3

Stackelberg point, at which foreign firms obtain the maximum discounted expected income, is depicted by point S', at which the reaction curve touches an iso-expected-return schedule.

A different expenditure level of the executive branch on counter-lobbying usually leads to a new reaction curve and Stackelberg point. Call the locus of the Stackelberg points due to different counter-lobbying expenditures the *contraction path*. The slope of the contraction path is given by

$$\left.\frac{d\theta}{dk}\right|_{CP} = \theta_k + \frac{\theta_G}{\hat{k}'} \tag{9.28}$$

Since $\hat{\theta}_k < 0$ and $\hat{\theta}_G < 0$, (9.28) implies that if the foreign firms react positively to the executive branch's counter-lobbying the contraction path is negatively sloped, and that if the contraction path is positively sloped the foreign firms must react negatively to the counter-lobbying.

The total effect of counter-lobbying on the probability of a protectionist threat is given by

$$\frac{d\hat{\theta}}{dG} = \hat{\theta}_k k' + \hat{\theta}_G = \hat{k}' \left(\left.\frac{d\hat{\theta}}{dk}\right|_{CP} \right) \tag{9.29}$$

Because the sign of $\hat{k}'(G)$ is ambiguous, so is the sign of $d\theta/dG$. However, if $\hat{k}'(G)$ is positive, by (9.29) $d\theta/dG < 0$, meaning that an increase in G will lower at least θ or $\hat{k}$. If the contraction path is positively sloped, i.e. $d\theta/dk \mid_{CP} > 0$, then by (9.28) and (9.29) counter-lobbying will discourage both the *quid pro quo* DFI and the protectionist threat.

In the presence of counter-lobbying, which is treated here as a directly unproductive profit-seeking (DUP) activity, national welfare has to be measured by $V(\theta,k) - G$. We then assume that the executive branch chooses the optimal G to maximize $V(\theta,k) - G$. Formally, the problem can be stated as

$$\max_{G}[V(\theta,k) - G] \qquad \text{subject to } \theta = \hat{\theta}(k,G) \text{ and } k = \hat{k}(G)$$

The first-order condition is given by

$$\frac{\partial V}{\partial \theta} \left(\frac{\partial \hat{\theta}}{\partial k} \frac{\partial \hat{k}}{\partial G} + \frac{\partial \hat{\theta}}{\partial G} \right) + \frac{\partial V}{\partial k} \frac{\partial \hat{k}}{\partial G} - 1 = 0$$

Except in the singular case in which the optimal G is zero, this policy will discourage the lobbying of the labour union, *quid pro quo* DFI or both.

Production subsidy

In this subsection we examine another policy of the government, a production subsidy, which is given in periods 1 and 2 to all domestic firms and foreign subsidiaries while the wage rate is still fixed at $\bar{W}$. The subsidy, which is financed by lump-sum taxes, will lower the cost of production, encouraging employment and production. In order to highlight the implications of unemployment, we assume in this and the next subsections that the importing country is a small one without external monopoly power. Thus, $P^* = \bar{P}^*$, where $\bar{P}^*$ is given exogenously. This means that the rigid wage is the only distortion in the economy.

Denoting the specific subsidy rate by s, the producer price P^{p} equals $P + s$, where P is the price faced by the consumers. We assume that both the labour union and the foreign firms will take the production subsidy as given. Employment in the presence of the subsidy is

$$l^{\mathrm{p}}(P^{\mathrm{p}},k,\bar{W}) = n(P^{\mathrm{p}},\bar{W}) + n^*(P^{\mathrm{p}},k,\bar{W}) \tag{9.30}$$

The improvement in employment is then given by $l^{\mathrm{p}} - l^{\mathrm{f}}$, where l^{f} is the employment level without any government intervention or trade restriction threat. We shall show that the optimal subsidy is the one which brings full employment under free trade. To show this, let us examine the effects of the subsidy in the absence of any lobbying and with no *quid pro quo* DFI. The free-trade equilibrium is described by

$$D^*(P^*) + D(P) = Y^*(P^*,k) + y^*(P^{\mathrm{p}},k,\bar{W}) + Y(P^{\mathrm{p}},\bar{W}) \tag{9.31a}$$

$$P = P^* + \bar{P}^* \tag{9.31b}$$

where (9.31b) reflects price equalization under free trade and the exogeneity of the foreign price. Using (9.31b), totally differentiate (9.31a) and use $dP^{\mathrm{p}}/ds = 1$ to give

$$\frac{dk}{ds} = -\frac{y_{\mathrm{p}}^* + Y_{\mathrm{p}}}{y_k^* + Y_k^*} > 0 \tag{9.32}$$

The sign of dk/ds in (9.32) is due to the assumption that at and beyond the no-intervention equilibrium a transfer of capital from the foreign country to the home country decreases the world's output. Using (9.32), the employment effect of the subsidy can be obtained:

$$\frac{dl^p}{ds} = \frac{\partial l^p}{\partial P^p} + \frac{\partial l^p}{\partial k}\frac{dk}{ds} > 0 \qquad (9.33)$$

Because of no lobbying and *quid pro quo* DFI, and since the consumer price does not change, national welfare relative to that in the absence of government intervention can be measured by the change in producer surplus and the income of the originally unemployed workers. Therefore the present value of national welfare in the two periods can be given by

$$V^p(s) = (1 + \sigma)\left[\Pi(P^p) - \Pi(\bar{P}^*) + (l^p - l^f)\bar{W}\right] \quad (9.34)$$

Totally differentiate (9.34) to give

$$\frac{dV^p(s)}{ds} = (1 + \sigma)\left(Y\frac{dP^p}{ds} + \bar{W}\frac{dl^p}{ds}\right) > 0$$

where (9.33) has been used. Since imposing a production subsidy improves national welfare, the optimal production subsidy is the one which brings full employment under free trade. With full employment, there is no lobbying or trade restriction threat.

The full-employment subsidy can be obtained from the following condition:

$$n(P^p,\bar{W}) + n^*(P^p,k,\bar{W}) = \bar{L} \qquad (9.31c)$$

Using the exogeneity of the foreign price, (9.31a) and (9.31c) can be used to solve for the optimal production price and capital inflow, P^p and k. The subsidy rate is equal to $P^p - \bar{P}^*$.

Employment subsidy

Yet another policy is to subsidize employment directly. We again assume that the country does not have external monopoly power and that both the labour union and the foreign firms take the subsidy as given. The domestic price is then $\bar{P}^*$. The specific rate of wage subsidy can be written as $\bar{W} - W^e$, where W^e is the effective wage rate to domestic firms and foreign subsidiaries. The subsidy expenditure is financed by lump-sum taxes.

Since a production subsidy imposed on average-cost pricing firms can be regarded as employment subsidies of the same *ad valorem* rates imposed on all employed factors, the effects of a labour employment subsidy are qualitatively the same as those of a production subsidy. Thus, using the same argument as in the previous subsection, we can conclude that a labour employment subsidy will improve employment, increase production price and encourage DFI. Furthermore, an optimal labour employment subsidy is one which achieves full employment.

The required employment subsidy and full employment are given by the following conditions:

$$n(P,W^e) + n^*(P,k,W^e) = \bar{L} \tag{9.35a}$$

$$D^*(P^*) + D(P) = Y^*(P^*,k) + y^*(P,k,W^e) + Y(P,W^e) \tag{9.35b}$$

$$P = P^* = \bar{P}^* \tag{9.35c}$$

Using the exogeneity of the price level, (9.35a) and (9.35b) can be solved for the effective wage rate and the level of DFI. The employment subsidy rate is then given by $\bar{W} - W^e$.

Policy ranking

The above four policies can be ranked by making use of the principle of optimal policy intervention discussed by Bhagwati (1971). As mentioned, we assume that the country does not have any external monopoly power. This means that the rigid wage rate is the only source of distortion in the present framework. In the absence of any active policy intervention, the labour union spends resources to seek protection in order to reduce unemployment. At the same time, foreign firms counteract the protectionist threat by engaging in *quid pro quo* DFI. Since the employment subsidy attacks the distortion directly and eliminates the misallocation of resources due to the lobbying of the labour union and the *quid pro quo* DFI, it creates the least cost in achieving the employment objective, and is thus the first-best policy. Production subsidy is inferior to employment subsidy since it unnecessarily subsidizes the employment of factors other than labour at the same time.[13]

Employment subsidy and production subsidy are superior to capital inflow restriction and counter-lobbying, because the trade restriction threat under the last two policies creates inefficient allocation and because counter-lobbying by the government is a DUP activity. In general, capital inflow restriction and counter-lobbying cannot be ranked (uniquely) *vis-à-vis* one another.

POLICIES FOR THE EXPORTING COUNTRY

We now turn to country E and analyse its policy options. In order to concentrate on analysing the effect of different policies for country E, we assume in this section that the government of country M does not impose any policy. Two policies for country E will be discussed: capital outflow restriction and counter-lobbying.

For simplicity, we concentrate on the economic effects of these policies and abstract from the analysis of any political economic factors in country E. This means that interest groups and their lobbying activities in the country, if any, are not considered, and that the capital outflow restriction policy can be passed in the appropriate government branch and implemented without any significant cost. These assumptions, which can be relaxed by introducing relevant political economic elements of the country into the model, will allow us to bring out the economic factors that the government has to consider in choosing the policies.

We again assume that the government knows the reactions of the labour union in country M and those of the firms, and acts as a Stackelberg leader, while both the labour union and the firms take the policies as given. It will be clear that these two policies available to the government of the exporting country are symmetric to the two corresponding policies of the government of the importing country. By applying the analytical techniques developed in the previous section, we can greatly simplify the following analysis.

Capital outflow restriction

Recall that the welfare of country E is represented by $V^*(\theta,k)$, which is affected negatively by the protectionist threat and capital outflow, as shown by conditions (9.26) and based on the assumptions given. According to (9.25), $V^*(\theta,k)$ is in general different from $R^*(\theta,k)$. This means that the amount of *quid pro quo* DFI chosen by foreign firms to maximize their total profits is in general not the optimal amount from the viewpoint of the country. This suggests that the government may be able to improve national welfare by quantitatively restricting the amount of capital outflow. Formally, the problem of the government is

$$\max_{k} V^*(\theta,k) \qquad \text{subject to } \theta = \tilde{\theta}(k)$$

This policy is similar to the policy of capital inflow restriction by country

M. Graphically, the solution can be obtained by first constructing indifference curves of country E in Figure 9.2 and then finding the point of tangency between the labour union's reaction curve and an indifference curve. The second-order condition for a maximum is that the indifference curve touches the reaction curve from below.

Counter-lobbying

Some countries, like the USA, allow the existence of lobbying activities of foreign countries. This has been a phenomenon of growing significance.[14] In this subsection we assume that lobbying activities of the firms and government of country E in country M are possible.

As explained in the third section, protectionist threat from country M and *quid pro quo* DFI may hurt country E. Thus, country E has an incentive to counter-lobby for freer trade. Effective lobbying can lower the protectionist threat and *quid pro quo* DFI.

Formally, the policy of counter-lobbying can be analysed by denoting the probability function of protection as $\theta(C,G^*)$, where G^* represents the resources spent by country E's government on counter-lobbying. When the government varies G^*, both the action of the foreign firms and the reaction of the labour union in country M will be affected. We assume that the counter-lobbying of the government is effective in the sense that $\partial\theta/\partial G^* < 0$. In terms of Figure 9.2, the counter-lobbying will have the effect of shifting the labour union's reaction curve toward the origin, and the more the government spends, the further the reaction curve will shift. In the presence of the expenditure on counter-lobbying, national income of country E can be represented by $V^*(\theta,k) - G^*$. Suppose that the government has full information about the action of the foreign firms and the reaction of the labour union, it can choose the optimal G^* to maximize national income. The optimal G^* can be derived using the techniques developed earlier. Again, by applying the principle of optimal intervention, from country E's point of view, capital outflow restriction and counter-lobbying cannot be ranked uniquely.

CONCLUDING REMARKS

By utilizing the model developed by Wong (1989a), we examined the formation of protectionist threat in the importing country and the use of *quid pro quo* DFI by firms in the exporting country for defusing the threat. The framework has allowed us also to analyse the effects of *quid pro quo* DFI. Using appropriately defined welfare functions, we have investigated several policies available to the importing and exporting countries for improving their welfare levels.

Quid pro quo DFI is a realtively new phenomenon. As protectionism is generally rising in many countries, we expect that this type of investment will grow both in level and in significance. The theoretical and empirical study of this phenomenon is still in its infant stage, and more research in this area is needed.

The present paper can be extended in two major directions. First, the interactions between the policies of the governments in the presence of protectionist threat and *quid pro quo* DFI can be examined. When both governments are active in choosing the optimal policies, different games between the governments can be analysed. Two possible games are worth close examination. The first is that the two governments are imposing the optimal restriction on capital movement. Then, following the arguments of Cheng and Wong (1990), a quantitative restriction may not be equivalent to income taxation. In fact, a quantitative restriction imposed by both governments strategically could lead to complete elimination of capital movement.[15] The second game is the simultaneous lobbying by the labour union and counter-lobbying by the executive branch of country M and the government of country E. An analysis of this game will lead to insight into the growing important phenomenon of foreign country counter-lobbying. So far, however, little work has been done in this area.

An alternative extension to the present paper is to introduce a third country. A three-country framework, which is needed to study cross-country spill-over effects, has empirical relevance. For example, protectionist threats in the USA might attract both protectionist-threat-responding and *quid pro quo* investment from Japan. Given limited resources of the Japanese firms, it is likely that they will invest less in other countries such as European countries. Furthermore, a three-country framework can be used to examine how two countries (such as France and Britain) can compete with each other for the investment from another country (such as Japan). When unemployment exists in two countries, and when protection is possible in the future, the exporting country may consider using foreign investment to defuse the protectionist threats. The question is how the optimal level of foreign investment from the exporting country is determined and how it is distributed between the two importing countries.

NOTES

1   For other evidence of Japanese *quid pro quo* DFI in the USA, see Wong (1989b).
2   Mezzetti and Dinopoulos (1989) develop a model in which employment and the wage are determined endogenously through efficient Nash bargaining between a domestic firm and a labour union.
3   Since endowments, technologies and preferences of both countries do change over time, it does not matter whether the foreign firms are maximizing the sum of the profits of the foreign firms and subsidiaries in each period, as equation (9.6) represents, or the sum of the present values of the profits in both periods.
4   In this paper, we are interested in interior solutions only.
5   The assumption that the labour union wants a tariff to eliminate the unemployment can be relaxed in two ways. First, the labour union may choose a trade-off between the tariff rate requested and the probability of a trade restriction in period 2. For an analysis, see Wong (1989a). Second, the trade restriction may take the form of a quota. If the quota is auctioned off in a competitive fashion by the government of country M, then a tariff is equivalent to a quota. If the quota takes the form of a voluntary export restraint, the government of country E may get most of the economic rent. The equivalence between a tariff and a quota breaks down, and the analysis has to take into account the income and price effects of the rent.
6   Substitute the value of P (9.10b) into (9.10a) and totally differentiate the latter to get

$$[D^{*\prime} - Y_p^* + (D' - y_p^* - Y_p)(1 + \tau)] \, dP^* =$$
$$- (D' - y_p^* - Y_p)P^* d\tau + (Y_k^* + y_k^*)dk$$

Rearranging the terms will give the result.
7   Bhagwati *et al.*(1987) make an identical assumption, while Dinopoulos (1989) assumes that firms can choose the level of trade and DFI each period.
8   For *quid pro quo* DFI in other types of market structures, see Dinopoulos (1989) and Bhagwati and Dinopoulos (1986).
9   We consider lobbying as a kind of direct unproductive (DUP) activity, and assume that it requires resources from other sectors where factors are fully employed. Thus, the cost of lobbying is also a social cost to the economy. Bhagwati (1982) argued that, in a general equilibrium framework with distortion, DUP activities can be welfare improving if the shadow prices of some factors are negative. These paradoxical cases are ignored here since we are considering a partial equilibrium framework.
10   If there are unemployed factors caused by capital outflow, the sum of the products of the shadow price of each factor and the amount of unemployment has to be deducted from function V^* defined in (9.25).
11   In another approach, Mayer (1984) assumed that trade policies are decided by all voters. The government does not have any active role

in the decision process.

12 It is possible that the curve rotates in a counterclockwise direction around point Y. In this case point Y' coincides with point Y.

13 If profit is zero and if there is only one factor, labour, employed in the industry, as in a Ricardian economy, an employment subsidy is equivalent to a production subsidy.

14 In the USA, Japan is the foreign country with the heaviest lobbying activities. For more details of Japan's lobbying in the USA, see, for example, Cohen (1988: 127–8).

15 It is because both governments have the incentive to impose a quota slightly smaller than that imposed by the other government in order to capture the economic rent due to the rental-rate differential across countries.

REFERENCES

Baldwin, R.E. (1985) *The Political Economy of U.S. Import Policy*, Cambridge, MA: MIT Press.

Bhagwati, J.N. (1971) 'The generalized theory of distortions and welfare', in J.N. Bhagwati, R.W. Jones, R.A. Mundell and J. Vanek (eds) *Trade, Balance of Payments, and Growth: Papers in International Economics in Honor of Charles P. Kindleberger*, Amsterdam: North-Holland.

—— (1982) 'Directly unproductive, profit-seeking (DUP) activities', *Journal of Political Economy* 90: 988–1002

—— (1985) 'Investing abroad', Esmee Fairbairn Lecture, delivered at the University of Lancaster.

—— (1987) 'VERs, *quid pro quo* DFI and VIEs: political-economy-theoretic analysis', *International Economic Journal* 1 (spring): 1–14.

—— (1988) *Protectionism*, Cambridge, MA: MIT Press.

—— and Srinivasan, T.N. (1976), 'Optimal trade policy and compensation under endogenous uncertainty: the phenomenon of market disruption', *Journal of International Economics* 6: 317–36.

—— Brecher, R., Dinopoulos, E., and Srinivasan, T.N. (1987) '*Quid pro quo* foreign investment and welfare: a political-economy-theoretic model' *Journal of Development Economics* 27: 127–38.

Brock, W.A. and Magee, S.P. (1978) 'The economics of special interest politics: the case of the tariff', *American Economic Review* 68: 246–50.

Cheng, L.K. and Wong, K.-Y. (1990) 'On the strategic choice between capital and labor mobility', *Journal of International Economics* 28 (May): 291–314.

Cohen, S.D. (1988) *The Making of the United States International Economic Policy*, New York: Praeger.

Dinopoulos, E. (1989) '*Quid pro quo* foreign investment', *Economics and Politics* 1: 145–60.

—— and Bhagwati, J.N. (1986) '*Quid pro quo* foreign investment and market structure', presented at the 61st Annual Western Economic Association International Conference, in San Francisco, CA.

Mayer, W. (1984) 'Endogenous tariff formation', *American Economic Review* 74: 970–85.

Mezzetti, C. and Dinopoulos, E. (1989) 'Domestic unionization and import competition', University of California, Davis, mimeo.

Wong, K.-Y. (1989a) 'Optimal threat of trade restriction and *quid pro quo* foreign investment', *Economics and Politics* 1: 277–30

——— (1989b) 'The Japanese challenge: Japanese direct investment in the United States', in K. Yamamura (ed.) *Japanese Investment in the United States: Should We Be Concerned?*, Seattle, WA: Society for Japanese Studies, pp. 63–96.

10 Export promotion, import substitution and direct foreign investment in less developed countries

V.N. Balasubramanyam and M.A. Salisu

INTRODUCTION

In his Ohlin lectures on *Protectionism*, Bhagwati observes that 'few economists have seriously doubted the significance of the influence of ideas on policy since Keynes wrote: "the ideas of economists and political philosophers, both when they are right and when they are wrong, are more powerful than is commonly understood"' (Bhagwati 1988: 17). Not many would dispute this observation.

Indeed, Bhagwati himself is a splendid example of the sagacity of Keyne's remark. A distinguished economist of international repute, he has been a storehouse of ideas. He would be the first to admit that his ideas are not necessarily infallible, but few can deny that many of his ideas have had a significant impact on policy. Foremost among these, in the fields of international trade and economic development, relate to the relative merits of import-substitution (IS) and export promoting (EP) development strategies and were developed in numerous articles and books written through the 1960s and 1970s. These contributions played a major role in convincing policy makers of the inefficiencies associated with the IS strategy and in educating them on the merits of the EP strategy.

Here, we focus on one of the many ideas relating to IS and EP strategies proposed by Bhagwati (1978). The proposition that we analyse in depth is that the magnitude of direct foreign investment (DFI) attracted by countries pursuing an EP strategy will be higher than that attracted by those pursuing the IS strategy.

At first sight, the proposition that EP countries are likely to be recipients of a larger volume of DFI relative to IS countries runs counter to conventional wisdom. There is certainly a strong presumption in the early literature that barriers in the form of tariffs and quotas on imports induce inflows of DFI, resulting in the pheonomenon known as 'tariff-jumping' DFI.[1] Underlying this thesis is the proposition that, in the face of barriers to exports, firms would choose to penetrate foreign markets through investment. They would also have the added advantage of investing in markets protected from import competition.

Protection, however, is but one amongst several location-specific factors that induce firms to invest abroad with a view to exploiting the ownership-specific advantages they possess. Moreover, it is not always possible to separate the influence of protection on DFI from that of other factors such as market size and growth potential of host countries. Indeed, the impact of protection, in the form for instance of the common external tariff imposed by the European Economic Community (EEC) countries, on DFI in these countries has been a matter of some dispute. It has been suggested that the enlarged size of the West European markets consequent upon the formation of the EEC and the growth potential of these markets were much more significant in attracting DFI than the protection afforded by the formation of the European Community (Scaperlanda 1967; Hufbauer 1975).

Bhagwati's proposition does not, however, deny the influence of protection on inflows of DFI. In his incisive Esmee Fairbairn Lecture on 'investing abroad' delivered at the University of Lancaster, Bhagwati acknowledges the influence of protection on DFI (Bhagwati 1985). He draws a distinction, however, between DFI propelled by market forces and that induced by policy measures. The latter includes both IS-induced DFI and EP-induced DFI. He draws a crucial distinction between the inducements provided by the two types of development strategies. In the case of the EP strategy, although policy-determined incentives such as tax concessions have played a role in attracting DFI, the major incentive, as Bhagwati puts it, 'has been simply the conjunction of cheaper costs and the EP orientation'. By contrast, in the case of the IS strategy, DFI has been almost exclusively policy driven. As Bhagwati puts it, 'the IS strategy, on both domestic investments and DFI, has been cut from the same cloth: protect your market and attract home based investments to serve that market'. The magnitude of IS-oriented DFI, he argues will not ultimately be as large as EP-oriented DFI for the simple reason that it would be limited by the host-country market which induces it in the first place.

This hypothesis is worth testing empirically as it has far-reaching policy implications for less developed countries, most of which are now seeking to attract increasing amounts of DFI, because of both the technology and know-how it provides and its contribution to investible resources.

THE HYPOTHESIS AND ITS LOGIC

The precise hypothesis states:

> With due adjustments for differences among countries for their economic size, political attitudes towards DFI and political stability, both the magnitude of DFI inflows and their efficacy in promoting economic growth will be greater over the long haul in countries pursuing the export promotion (EP) strategy than in countries pursuing the import substitution (IS) strategy.
>
> (Bhagwati 1978: 212).

Several features of Bhagwati's hypothesis must be noted.

First, the magnitude of DFI relative to the economic size that countries are able to attract, and not the absolute amounts of DFI they attract, is relevant. Admittedly, relatively large developing countries, measured by the size of their population or gross national product, such as Brazil, India and Indonesia have attracted substantial amounts of DFI in absolute terms. But when for instance the population size of the various developing countries is taken into account, it is the relatively small-sized countries such as Singapore, Hong Kong, Ivory Coast and Malaysia that appear to harbour relatively large amounts of DFI (Table 10.1).

Second, the hypothesis does not emphasize the influence of the type of development strategy on DFI to the exclusion of other factors. These include political stability and the attitudes of countries towards foreign enterprise participation in their economies.

Third, the hypothesis is careful to note that it is over the long haul that the EP countries are likely to attract relatively large magnitudes of DFI. It is conceivable that the IS strategy with its policy-oriented inducements will immediately attract large volumes of DFI. But whether or not such investment flows would be sustained over time is arguable. The IS strategy is likely to result in a mere relocation of investment from the home countries of the investors to the host countries, induced by the restrictions on imports in the home countries rather than by considerations of comparative advantage and location-specific advantages offered by the host countries. In contrast, DFI in EP countries is likely to be induced primarily by the location-specific advantages they offer, including the availability of relatively cheap labour and raw materials. In other words, EP-type DFI is likely to conform to the dictates of comparative advantage and market forces, resulting in a sustained inflow of investment over time.

Moreover, it is worth noting that, while policy-oriented incentives such as tariffs and quotas on imports, which delimit competition from

Table 10.1 Magnitude of direct foreign investment in developing countries

	DFI (US$ million)	DFI/P (US$)
Argentina	257.08	9.87
Brazil	1,109.80	10.85
Colombia	46.28	1.98
Costa Rica	4.54	2.16
Mexico	489.98	7.58
Uruguay	4.14	1.68
Peru	148.40	10.44
India	41.00	0.08
Malaysia	95.36	8.05
Philippines	109.32	2.49
Singapore	150.50	65.57
Sri Lanka	1.82	0.21
Thailand	43.63	1.00
South Korea	48.33	1.67
Hong Kong	165.61	36.87
Sudan	2.65	0.16
Tanzania	4.37	0.29
Turkey	7.13	0.22
Egypt	11.69	0.28
Ghana	2.99	0.36
Ivory Coast	6.48	0.86
Malawi	6.08	1.33
Tunisia	7.44	1.31
Chile	14.24	2.32
El Salvador	2.50	0.61
Haiti	0.63	0.13
Honduras	1.10	0.36
Jamaica	12.39	10.41
Nicaragua	0.32	0.16
Paraguay	2.10	0.77
Trinidad and Tobago	8.67	7.96
Ethiopia	0.58	0.02
Morocco	4.65	0.26
Uganda	1.10	0.09
Zambia	25.13	5.19
Indonesia	219.27	0.79
Kenya	247.36	2.06
Nigeria	413.18	1.58

Source: World Bank, *World Bank Tables*, Washington, DC, 1984; OECD, *Development Cooperation* (various years); UNCTAD, *Handbook of International Trade Statistics, Supplement*, 1986; IMF, *International Financial Statistics Yearbook*, 1988

imports, and subsidies and tax concessions do induce DFI under the IS strategy, such incentives are likely to be limited and artificial. They tend to be limited in the sense that they are confined to industries and products subject to import restrictions, and their continuation over time is subject to the whims of policymakers. Foreign firms weary of unexpected policy changes or the threat of potential competition from other investors are unlikely to invest in countries pursuing the IS strategy (Frank 1980). As Corden (1974) has noted, while firm A may be lured into setting up production facilities behind tariff walls, it is always open to the threat of competition from firm B which may be able to supply the product at relatively low price from its home base. And the host country may threaten to lower its tariffs and subject firm A to competition from firm B in order to wrest a larger share of the gains from firm A's investment. Also policy-induced incentives tend to be artificial in the same sense that they direct investments into activities in which the country does not possess a genuine comparative advantage. In many cases policy-oriented incentives offered to foreign firms by host countries may be no more than a compensation for their lack of location-specific advantages. Foreign firms may find such incentives an inadequate and uncertain form of compensation for investing in an environment none too conducive to efficient operations.

To conclude, there are good reasons to expect that the EP strategy will attract larger magnitudes of DFI, when economic size and political stability of countries are taken into consideration, than the IS strategy. Bhagwati's hypothesis is thus, despite its novelty, grounded in persuasive economic logic.

THE EXPORT PROMOTION AND IMPORT SUBSTITUTION STRATEGIES DEFINED

The crux of Bhagwati's hypothesis relates to the influence of the nature of the development strategy on DFI. It is therefore essential to define at the outset what is meant by the EP and IS strategies. Again, we owe a precise definition of the two strategies to Bhagwati (1978): an EP strategy is one which equates the average effective rate of exchange for exports (EER_x) with the average effective rate of exchange for imports (EER_m). This is what Bhagwati identifies as the trade-neutral or bias-free strategy. In contrast, the IS strategy is one in which the EER_x is less than the EER_m. And an ultra- export strategy is one in which the EER_x is greater than the EER_m. Effective exchange rate, in this context, is defined as the number of units of local currency actually received or paid for a dollar's worth of international transactions. If tariffs and quotas on imports, for instance, were not matched by subsidies on exports, the EER_m would be greater than the EER_x. In this case, relatively more units of local currency would have to be paid for one dollar's worth of exports; and the system of exchange rates would be biased in favour of production for the home market as opposed to production for the export market, i.e. the country in question would be pursuing an IS strategy.

It is important to note that the EP strategy does not preclude IS in particular industries or sectors. It is conceivable that an EP strategy may harbour activities for which the EER_m may exceed the average EER_x. The essential point to note, though, is that the EP strategy in general does not impart a bias against exports. It merely requires that there should be no significant difference between the average EER_x and the average EER_m. It is worth emphasizing the asymmetry between the EP and IS strategies that the definition implies. In the case of the IS strategy $EER_m > EER_x$. But in the case of the EP strategy $EER_m = EER_x$, and $EER_x > EER_m$ is not required.

The essential feature of the EP strategy, as defined by Bhagwati, is its neutrality (Bhagwati 1986). On balance, the policy-oriented incentives it provides favour neither production for the domestic market nor production for the international markets. The market orientation of production is determined entirely by market forces including factor endowments and entrepreneurial and managerial skills of the countries in question. This is not to say that the State should play no role in shaping and promoting entrepreneurial and managerial skills. In EP countries such as Singapore and South Korea the State does actively participate in promoting such skills through the provision of subsidies and technical assistance and in many cases participation in financial and production-oriented activities. But the role of the State is largely confined to remedying factor and product market distortions and strengthening the market signals. Indeed, a policy of incentive neutrality even requires the minimization of factor and product market distortions which otherwise would serve to destroy the desired neutrality.

EMPIRICAL VERIFICATION

The *a priori* arguments in favour of Bhagwati's hypothesis are certainly appealing. But an empirical verification of the hypothesis is beset with several problems, mostly relating to the absence of statistical data required to quantify many of the determinants of DFI that Bhagwati identifies. None the less we attempt a statistical verification, utilizing available data and employing a number of plausible quantifiable proxies for the various determinants of DFI.

The statistical exercise is confined to a sample of thirty-eight developing countries over the 11 year period 1970–80 for which relevant data on DFI flows are available. A sample of thirty-eight countries provides a fairly good mix of countries pursuing differing development strategies, and while an 11 year period may not amount to the 'long haul' referred to in Bhagwati's hypothesis, it represents a longish time period.

The method used to test Bhagwati's hypothesis is the frequently used weighted ordinary least squares multiple regression analysis.[2] The dependable variable in the regressions refers to annual average inflows of DFI per capita into each of the thirty-eight countries over the period 1970–80. The independent variables employed in the equations have been chosen to represent the various determinants of DFI identified by Bhagwati, including the type of development strategy pursued by the various countries. The estimated regression equations are of the following general form:

$$DFI/P = a + b\,GDP/P + c\,GDP/Pg + d\,A/P + e\text{WPI} + f\,M/\text{GDP} + g\text{WR}$$
$$(10.1)$$

$$DFI/P = a + b\,GDP/P + c\,GDP/Pg + d\,A/P + e\,\text{WPI} + f\text{DI} + g\text{WR}$$
$$(10.2)$$

where DFI/P is the annual average inflows of DFI per capita into each of the thirty-eight countries in the sample during the period 1970–80, GDP/P is the annual average per capita real income for the period 1979–80, GDP/Pg is the annual average growth rate of per capita real income for the period 1979–80, A/P is the annual average inflows of foreign aid per capita into each of the sample countries during the period 1970–80, (nominal values of aid flows in dollars have been deflated by the index of unit value of imports), WPI is the annual average rate of inflation, measured by the wholesale price index, in each of the sample countries during the period 1970–80, M/GDP is the annual average ratio of imports to gross domestic product (GDP) for each of the countries in the sample during the period 1970–80, (values of imports in local currency are deflated by the index of unit value of imports, and GDP in local currency is deflated by the GDP deflator), DI is the World Bank's estimates of the composite distortion index for each of the countries in the sample and WR is the annual average wage rate in the manufacturing sector in each of the countries in the sample, expressed in dollars.

In these equations, GDP/P and the growth rate of real GDP per capita are included to assess the influence of market size and the economic potential of the recipient countries on inflows of DFI. These two variables are identified as significant determinants of DFI in the literature. The former of the two variables also serves to identify the differences in the economic sizes of countries. The coefficients of these variables are expected to be positive in the estimated equations.

The type of development strategy (EP or IS) pursued by the countries, which forms the crux of Bhagwati's hypothesis, is the most difficult variable to quantify. Ideally, it should be quantified by estimating the ratio of EER_x to EER_m for each of the countries in the sample. The data required to estimate the two exchange rates included tariff rates, import quotas, subsidies on exports and nominal exchange rates. Unfortunately most of these data are not available from published sources on a time series basis. India is one of the few countries for which estimates of the two exchange rates are available. These estimates are based mostly on informed judgement concerning export subsidies, and in the absence of available data, they ignore the impact of quotas on the EER_m (Bhagwati and Srinivasan 1975). In the absence of data relevant to the estimation of the two exchange rates, we are forced to resort to various proxies for quantifying the type of development strategy pursued by the countries in the sample.

One such proxy employed in the estimated equations is the ratio of the real value of imports to real GDP. In the literature the rate of exports plus imports to GDP is often cited as a measure of the degree of openness of economies. However, we have chosen to employ only the ratio of imports to GDP as a proxy for the type of development strategy pursued by the countries in the sample for the following reasons. First, Bhagwati's hypothesis emphasizes the distortion-free economic environment that the EP strategy provides for foreign investors and not the degree of openness of the economy. It is the presumption that countries which exhibit a relatively high ratio of imports to GDP tend to be relatively free of policy-induced distortions, for restrictions on imports are likely to be a major source of policy-induced distortions. It is also likely that a relatively high ratio of exports to GDP may be the consequence of widespread export subsidies, which too would be a source of policy-induced distortions. Second, it is conceivable that in countries which exhibit a relatively high ratio of imports to GDP the EER_m is unlikely to diverge significantly from the EER_x for a relatively high level of imports would not materialize in the presence of a relatively high EER_m, and in the absence of a high EER_m there would be little need for artificial inducements in the form of subsidies to persuade entrepreneurs to produce for the export markets as opposed to the domestic markets. For these reasons, for countries experiencing a relatively high ratio of imports to GDP the EER_m is likely to approximate to the EER_x and they would be pursuing the EP strategy as defined by Bhagwati. It follows from this line of reasoning that in the case of countries exhibiting a relatively low ratio of imports to GDP the EER_m is likely to be greater than the EER_x.

Another proxy employed in this paper to quantify the development strategy variable is the composite distortion index devised by the World Bank (Agarwala 1983; World Bank 1984). This index takes into account a variety of policy-induced distortions in product and factor markets of developing countries, including distortions in the markets for foreign exchange, credit and labour. In this context distortions are said to exist when market prices of goods and services as well as capital and labour do not accurately reflect their true social opportunity cost. It is likely that countries pursuing either an IS strategy or a super EP strategy exhibit a higher degree of policy-induced factor and product market conditions than countries pursuing a neutral or EP strategy. It is an established fact that countries pursuing an IS strategy are rife with distortions in their product and factor markets (Bhagwati and Srinivasan 1975; Bhagwati 1978; Greenaway and Chong Hyun Nam, 1988). Equally, indiscriminate export subsidies which would be characteristic of a super EP strategy are likely to introduce widespread factor and product market distortions. As stated earlier, an EP strategy as defined by Bhagwati will probably be relatively free of such distortions and induce relatively high levels of DFI. Validation of the hypothesis requires the coefficient of the distortion variable in the regression equations to be negative.

The other important characteristic of countries pursuing the EP strategy identified by Bhagwati is the availability of relatively cheap labour. This too would induce relatively high levels of DFI into the EP countries. The average annual real wage rate per man variable included in the estimated regressions is intended to capture this impact of the development strategy on DFI. Validation of the hypothesis requires the estimated coefficient of the variable to be negative.

The other two variables included in the estimated regression equations – A/P and WPI together with GDP/P and GDP/Pg – are intended to capture the impact of political stability and attitudes of countries towards foreign investment on DFI, identified in Bhagwati's hypothesis. Several studies have tested the influence of political stability on inflows of DFI (Levis 1979; Root and Ahmed 1979; Schneider and Frey 1985). These studies provide a mixed bag of conclusions. Most confirm the influence of political factors on DFI, but differ in the emphasis they attach to political as opposed to economic factors as determinants of DFI. While studies by Root and Ahmed and Levis assign primacy to economic as opposed to political factors, the statistical analysis by Schneider and Frey suggests that political and economic variables are equally important in explaining the inflows of DFI into developing countries. Schneider and

Frey's conclusion is based on the fact that a model which incorporates both political and economic variables performs much better than either a model which incorporates only economic variables or a model which includes only political variables. On *a priori* grounds alone this conclusion may be unassailable. But the choice of variables to denote economic and political factors in statistical exercises poses several problems. Frey and Schneider identify four explicit political variables: foreign aid received from western countries, foreign aid received from communist countries, political strikes and riots, and political ideology of countries (right wing = 1, left wing = 0). The hypothesis is that the higher the percentage of aid per capita received from Western countries the higher would be the inflows of DFI, as it would indicate political dependence of countries on the western bloc. Conversely, the higher the percentage of aid received from the Communist bloc, the lower would be the inflows of DFI. The hypotheses centring on the other variables listed above are self-explanatory.

In the regression equations estimated by Frey and Schneider the coefficients of all these political variables are statistically significant and robust, and confirm the postulated hypotheses. But it is open to question whether these variables merely reinforce economic determinants of DFI or signify the sole and exclusive influence of political factors on inflows of foreign investment. Is it not likely that countries rife with political strikes and riots also tend to be economically weak in terms of their per capita income and growth rates! Is it not conceivable that countries dependent on the Communist bloc for aid are also relatively weak in economic terms? As Bhagwati remarks in his Ohlin lectures, economists are fond of the counterfactual, to the extent that when an economist was asked 'how is your wife?' he is supposed to have replied 'relative to what?' Thus true to the traditions of our profession it may be asked, supposing countries receiving aid from the Communist bloc were also economically strong in terms of per capita income and growth rates, would not multinational firms with an ever active nose for profits seek investment outlets in these countries through either DFI and joint ventures or licensing agreements? Indeed, how is one to explain the overtures of many American multinationals to East European countries recognized in the literature as early as the mid-1970's (Lauter and Dickie 1975). The point to note though is that political factors may be inseparable from economic factors as determinants of DFI, and what are frequently alluded to as political factors may be no more than a manifestation of economic factors.

For these reasons, we take the view here that, while political factors are significant determinants of DFI, an attempt to separate out their influence from that of economic factors may be futile. And economic factors such as per capita income, growth rate of national product, and the rate of inflation would suffice to capture the influence of political factors on economic stability and hence on inflows of DFI. It may not be far-fetched to argue that the economic performance of countries experiencing long-term political instability, measured by their per capita income, inflation rate and growth rate is unlikely to be impressive. In the estimated regression equations the coefficient of the inflation rate variable is hypothesized to be negative and that of the income variables positive.

As stated earlier, we also include foreign aid per capita as an independent variable in the regression equations. We regard this variable as an economic rather than an explicitly political variable. Admittedly, aid donors may be able to exercise leverage or political pressure on recipient countries to provide a favourable economic climate for the operations of their multinational firms. Equally, aid recipients may be expected to be friendly in their attitudes towards the multinationals from the donor countries. Even so it is open to question whether foreign firms would be enthusiastic investors in countries which are recipients of relatively high magnitudes of aid but are economically weak. It is also to be noted that foreign aid flows include a relatively high proportion of military aid. And there is no presumption that countries receiving relatively high magnitudes of military aid are also politically stable and economically strong – the two main interacting determinants of DFI. Unfortunately, readily available published data on aid flows do not distinguish military aid from developmental aid flows. For these reasons we cannot dismiss the hypothesis that recipients of relatively high levels of aid may also be relatively weak economies and may also exhibit a considerable degree of political instability. If the latter hypothesis is valid, the coefficient of the aid variable in the estimated regressions should turn out to be negative.

RESULTS OF THE STATISTICAL EXERCISE

The estimated regression equations on balance appear to lend considerable support to Bhagwati's hypothesis. Equation (1) in Table 10.2 relates to the estimates incorporating M/GDP as a proxy for the type of development strategy pursued by the countries in the sample. The coefficient of the M/GDP variable is positive and statistically signifi-cant and fortifies Bhagwati's hypothesis that EP countries are likely to be recipients of a relatively large volume of DFI. All the other coefficients with the exception of the coefficients of the growth rate and the aid

Table 10.2 Estimated regression equations (dependent variable, annual average inflows of direct foreign investment per capita for the years 1970–80)

Equation number	C	GDP/P	GDP/Pg	A/P	M/GDP	WPI	WR	DI	R^2	N
(1)	-1.08 (1.11)	0.007* (5.02)	-0.07 (0.58)	-0.13** (2.04)	0.12* (3.01)	-0.05* (5.26)	-0.02* (2.55)		0.65	38
(2)	7.17 (2.08)	0.010* (5.35)	-0.61 (1.40)	0.12*** (1.85)		-0.05* (2.98)	-0.03* (2.59)	-2.87** (2.11)	0.58	38
(2a)	6.80 (1.32)	0.010* (5.65)	-0.32 (0.78)	0.21 (1.04)			-0.002* (2.51)	-3.89*** (1.64)	0.60	38
(3)	-1.49 (1.88)	0.008* (5.92)	-0.004 (0.01)		0.73** (2.19)	-0.05* (5.27)	-0.02* (3.61)		0.63	38
(4)	6.13 (1.55)	0.009* (4.38)	-0.73*** (1.67)			-0.07* (3.45)	-0.01** (2.24)	-2.57 (1.38)	0.62	38

Notes: ***, **, *, significant at the 10 per cent, 5 per cent and 1 per cent level respectively.
Figures in parentheses are absolute values of t ratios of individual coefficients.

variable conform to the hypothesis discussed earlier. The coefficient
of the growth rate variable is not only negative but also statistically
insignificant. This result may in part be due to the observed relatively
high correlation between the M/GDP variable and the GDP/Pg variable
(Table 10.3). Deletion of the GDP/Pg variable as a method of correcting
for the observed collinearity between GDP/Pg and M/GDP did not
materially affect the sign and statistical significance of the coefficients
of the other variables. The coefficient of the aid variable is negative
and statistically significant at the 5 per cent level of significance. This
result appears to lend support to our hypothesis discussed earlier that
countries exhibiting a relatively poor economic performance receive
relatively large magnitudes of aid, and their poor economic performance
also deters inflows of large volumes of DFI. The estimated correlation
coefficients between the per capita aid and the two income variables
and that between DFI/P and A/P appear to support this conjecture
(Table 10.3).

Table 10.3 Matrix of correlation coefficients

	DFI/P	GDP/P	GDP/Pg	A/P	M/GDP	WPI	WR	DI
DFI/P	1.000							
GDP/P	0.727	1.000						
GDP/Pg	0.370	0.300	1.000					
A/P	−0.031	−0.088	−0.110	1.000				
M/GDP	0.828	0.656	0.330	0.259	1.000			
WPI	−0.106	0.283	−0.196	−0.266	−0.218	1.000		
WR	−0.265	0.678	−0.111	0.087	0.192	0.322	1.000	
DI	−0.409	−0.120	−0.659	−0.032	−0.355	0.315	0.167	1.000

Equation (10.2) which incorporates the composite distortion index
as a proxy for the type of development strategy pursued by the countries
in the sample also ratifies Bhagwati's hypothesis. The coefficient of the
distortion index is negative as hypothesized and is statistically significant.
It may be recalled that we have argued earlier that EP countries are
likely to provide a relatively distortion-free economic environment and
hence attract relatively large magnitudes of DFI. Most of the estimated
coefficients, including that of the wage rate variable, conform to the
postulated hypothesis. But as in the case of equation (10.1) the coefficient of GDP/Pg is negative and statistically insignificant. This again
may be due to the observed high correlation between the distortion index
and GDP/Pg (Table 10.3). The coefficient of the aid variable, however,
is positive and statistically significant at the 10 per cent level. We are
unable to provide an explanation for this result except to suggest that

Table 10.4 Estimated regression equations (dependent variable, annual average inflows of direct foreign investment per capita for the years 1970–80)

Equation number	C	GDP/P	GDP/Pg	A/P	M/GDP	WPI	WR	DI	R^2	N
(1)	−0.79 (0.82)	0.007* (4.66)	−0.08 (0.75)	−0.08** (2.23)	0.10* (2.37)	−0.04* (5.25)	−0.02* (2.83)		0.62	37
(2)	6.14 (1.97)	0.009* (4.91)	−0.52 (1.22)	0.10 (1.60)		−0.05* (2.93)	−0.02* (2.54)	−2.93** (2.00)	0.55	37
(3)	−0.86 (0.88)	0.008* (5.82)	−0.07 (0.57)		0.06*** (1.65)	−0.05* (5.56)	−0.02* (3.86)		0.60	37
(4)	5.91 (1.47)	0.008* (3.72)	−0.71*** (1.59)			−0.07* (3.78)	−0.01 (0.94)	−2.43 (1.33)	0.60	37

Notes: ***, **, *, significant at the 10 per cent, 5 per cent and 1 per cent level respectively.
Figures in parentheses are absolute values of t ratios of individual coefficients.

it may be due to the observed correlation between the distortion index and the other independent variables, especially that between the DI variable and the growth rate variable on the one hand and the DI variable and the rate of inflation variable on the other. Furthermore, there appears to be a weak but negative relationship between the aid variable and the DI variable. In order to redress the problems posed by the observed multicollinearity between the independent variables, we re-estimated equation (10.2) by deleting the inflation index variable with which the DI variable is correlated (Table 10.2), equation (2a). As stated earlier, the inflation index forms a part of the composite distortion index – hence our decision to delete the inflation index from the estimated equation. The estimated results for equation (2a) show that the coefficient of the distortion index is statistically significant at the 10 per cent level and it continues to be negative as hypothesized; the coefficient of the aid variable, although positive, turns out to be statistically insignificant.[3] Both the equations explain 60 per cent of the variation in DFI flows into the countries in the sample.

It is frequently argued that a few countries such as Hong Kong and Singapore tend to figure prominently in the list of EP countries and most of the propositions concerning the economic performance of such countries derive their strength from the experience of these special cases. We have attempted a test of this proposition by deleting Hong Kong from the sample of countries. Scatter diagrams of DFI/P on M/GDP and DFI/P on the distortion index showed Hong Kong to be the principal outlier. However, the estimated equations are very similar to the ones that included Hong Kong in the sample (Table 10.4). Thus, Bhagwati's hypothesis appears to survive comfortably even with the deletion of the outlier country from the sample and may have general applicability. In any case it may be perverse and paradoxical to exclude Singapore and Hong Kong from a statistical analysis designed to test the impact of the EP strategy on inflows of DFI for the simple reason that they are prime examples of EP countries. One might equally suggest the exclusion of India, Brazil and Indonesia, prime examples of countries pursuing the IS strategy, for most of the time period of our exercise, from the sample.

CONCLUDING REMARKS

In this paper we have elaborated upon Bhagwati's hypothesis that EP countries are likely to attract large volumes of DFI relative to IS countries. We have also subjected the hypothesis to a statistical test utilizing available data and quantifiable proxies for the EP and IS strategies cited in the hypothesis. The results of our statistical exercise lend support to Bhagwati's hypothesis.

The analysis needs to be undertaken afresh, however, when more appropriate indices of EP and IS strategies become available. It would also be useful to test Bhagwati's hypothesis in the context of a time series model for developing countries which have switched from an IS to an EP strategy in recent years.

NOTES

1 Bhagwati has also developed a different political-economy-theoretic notion of *quid pro quo* DFI where firms invest in period 1 with a view, not to jumping a current or anticipated trade restriction, but to reducing the probability of such a restraint being invoked in period 2. Elias Dinopoulos and Kar-yiu Wong discuss this idea of Bhagwati's in depth in their contribution to this volume.
2 The weighted least squares (WLS) estimator is used to remedy the problem of heteroscedasticity i.e. when the variance of the residuals in a regression equation differs across observations. WLS coefficients are simply ordinary least squares parameters for the regression with weighted data. The weighted data are computed by multiplying the original data by the square roots of the weights, the weights being the inverse of the variance of the residuals in the regression equation.
3 Deletion of both the inflation and the growth rate variables from equation (2), both of which are highly correlated with the distortion index, yields results similar to those of estimated equation (2a), however.

SOURCES OF DATA

1 Inflows of direct foreign investment: UN Center for Transnational Corporations, *Transnational Corporations in World Development*, Third Survey (New York, 1983).
2 GDP per capita and growth rate of GDP per capita: World Bank, *World Tables*, vol. I (Baltimore, MD, and London, 1984).
3 Ratio of imports to GDP: International Monetary Fund, *International Financial Statistics*, Yearbook, 1988.
4 Ratio of foreign aid to GDP: Organization for Economic Corporation and Development, *Development Cooperation* (various issues).
5 Inflation index: World Bank, *World Tables*, vol. I, (Baltimore, MD, and London 1984).
6 Distortion index: Agarwala, R., *Price distortions and growth in developing countries*; World Bank Staff Working Paper 575 Washington, DC, 1985.
7 Wage rate: World Bank, *World Tables*, vol. I (Baltimore, MD, and London, 1984).

REFERENCES

Agarwala, R (1983) 'Price distortions and growth in developing countries',

World Bank Staff Working Paper 575, Washington, DC, World Bank.

Bhagwati, J.N. (1978) *Anatomy and Consequences of Exchange Control Regimes*, vol. 1, Studies in International Economic Relations, No. 10, New York: National Bureau of Economic Research.

—— (1985) 'Investing abroad', Esmee Fairbairn Lecture, University of Lancaster.

—— (1986) 'Rethinking trade strategy', in J.P. Lewis and V. Kallab (eds) *Development Strategies Reconsidered*, New Brunswick, NJ: Transaction Books.

—— (1988) *Protectionism*, Cambridge, MA: MIT Press.

—— and Srinivasan, T.N. (1975) *Foreign Trade Regimes and Economic Development : India*, New York: Columbia University Press.

Corden, W.M. (1974) *Trade Policy and Economic Welfare*, Oxford: Oxford University Press.

Frank, I. (1980) *Foreign Enterprise in Developing Countries*, Baltimore, MD, and London: Johns Hopkins University Press.

Greenaway, D. and Chong Hyun Nam (1988) 'Industrialisation and macroeconomic performance in developing countries under alternative trade strategies', *Kyklos* 41 (3).

Hufbauer, G. (1975) 'The multinational corporation and determinants of foreign direct investment', in P.B. Kenen (ed.) *International Trade and Finance: Frontiers of Research*, London: Cambridge University Press.

Lauter, G.P. and Dickie, P.M. (1975) *Multinational Corporations and East European Socialist Economies*, New York: Praeger

Levis, M. (1979) 'Does political instability in developing countries affect foreign investment flows? An empirical examination', *Management International Review* 19.

Root, F. and Ahmed, A. (1979) 'Empirical determinants of manufacturing direct foreign investment in developing countries', *Economic Development and Cultural Change* 27.

Scaperlanda, A.E. (1967) 'The EEC and US foreign investment: some empirical evidence', *Economic Journal* 77: 22–6.

Schneider, F. and Frey, B.S. (1985) 'Economic and political determinants of foreign direct investment', *World Development* (February).

World Bank (1984) *World Development Report*, Washington, DC: World Bank.

International Co-operation

Part IV

International economic co-ordination

11 The obstacles to macro-economic policy co-ordination in the 1990s and an analysis of international nominal targeting

Jeffrey A. Frankel [1]

INTRODUCTION

The world has seen three phases of international economic policy-making, since the post-war system of fixed exchange rates and US economic hegemony came unravelled in 1973. First, in the 1970s, the prevailing model was Keynesian and the prevailing wind from Washington urged joint worldwide expansion in line with the 'locomotive theory'. Germany and Japan eventually succumbed to these urgings in 1978 when they agreed to undertake some expansion at the Bonn Summit. But by 1980 worldwide inflation had reached such high levels that the Keynesian model, the locomotive theory and the Bonn Summit – indeed, even co-ordination itself – had all acquired 'bad names'.

The second phase, 1980–4, constituted the triumph of monetarism. By the beginning of the 1980s, the central banks of the USA, the UK, Germany, Switzerland and Japan had all largely accepted the monetarist prescription of pre-committing to a fixed rate of growth of M1 or some other monetary aggregate in an effort to stop inflation. Supporting the switch in emphasis was the accession to power of Margaret Thatcher in Britain in 1979, Ronald Reagan in the USA in 1981 and Helmut Kohl in Germany in 1982.

It is perfectly possible for one to be a monetarist and yet to favour the international co-ordination of policy and management of exchange rates, as Ronald McKinnon shows us. Nevertheless, the monetarist view that in fact dominated was the anti-coordination one that came from Milton Friedman: each country chose its own independent macro-economic policies, and the market was allowed to determine exchange rates with little or no guidance from policymakers. During the first Reagan Administration (1981–4), the USA insisted that this decentralized system, which extended the *laissez-faire* principles of micro-economics to the platform of global macro-economic policy-making, worked the best. Other trading partners had their doubts, but could do nothing towards co-ordination without American participation.

If the inflation problem torpedoed the plans of the 1970s, then the overvaluation of the dollar and the resulting US trade deficit torpedoed the plans of the early 1980s. If excessive monetary expansion was identified as the cause of the problem of the 1970s, then the unusual US monetary–fiscal policy mix and resulting high real interest rates was identified as the cause of the problems of the early 1980s. If the passing of Democrat and Labour governments at the end of the 1970s facilitated the triumph of monetarism, the transition to the next phase in 1985 was a simpler matter of the turnover of some key officials in the US Treasury. The anti-cooperativeness and monetarism of Donald Regan and Beryl Sprinkel gave way to the pragmatism of James Baker and Richard Darman.

THE G7 CO-ORDINATION MECHANISM

The third phase, G7 co-ordination, was inaugurated at a meeting of Finance Ministers, at the Plaza Hotel in New York in September 1985. At the time, the membership was confined to the traditional G5 – the USA, Japan, Germany, France and the UK – and the focus was on exchange rates. The meeting produced the Plaza Accord, under which the USA agreed to co-operate with the others in bringing down the value of the dollar. At the G7 Summit Meeting the next year in Tokyo, the heads of state agreed to expand the membership of the G5 Finance Ministers' meetings to include Canada and Italy, and to expand the list of 'objective indicators' that the Ministers would focus on. Thenceforth the G7 would focus in their meetings on a set of ten variables: the growth rate of gross national product (GNP), the interest rate, the inflation rate, the unemployment, the ratio of the fiscal deficit to GNP, the current account and trade balances, the money growth rate, international reserve holdings and the exchange rate.

No pretence was made that the members would rigidly commit to specific numbers for these indicators, in the sense that sanctions would be imposed on a country if it deviated far from the values agreed upon. But the plan did include the understanding that 'appropriate remedial measures' would be taken whenever there developed significant deviations from the 'intended course'. This language would seem to suggest that the indicators were not intended to be merely national forecasts – that the system was intended to include some substantive bargaining over policies, rather than only the exchange of information.

The list of indicators has been further discussed, and trimmed down, at subsequent G7 meetings. By the time of the Venice Summit in June 1987, the list had apparently been reduced to six indicators: growth, inflation, trade balances, government budgets, monetary conditions and exchange rates.[2] Treasury Secretary James Baker, however, in October 1987 told the International Monetary Fund (IMF) Annual Meeting that 'the United States is prepared to consider utilizing, as an additional indicator in the coordination process, the relationship among our currencies and a basket of commodities, including gold. . .'. At the Toronto Summit of June 1988, 'the G-7 countries welcomed the addition of a commodity price indicator and the progress made toward refining the analytical use of indicators'.

As we enter the 1990s, the G-7 co-ordination process seems to be stalled. It is not that some specific new economic problem has replaced the US dollar as the topic of concern. The problem of US international over-borrowing will no doubt continue to condition international policy-making in the coming decade. But it is not clear what co-operative macro-economic tasks the existing G7 body will be called upon to accomplish in the 1990s.

In what direction will it be desirable for the G7 to agree to move the macro-economic policies of its members? The desirable direction for co-ordination depends entirely on what 'public good' is missing from the world equilibrium. International spill-over effects can render the non-cooperative ('Nash') equilibrium unsatisfactory in a variety of ways. A prime example is when the world is in a recession due to inadequate demand, with each country afraid to expand on its own for fear that its trade balance will deteriorate. Then, if they agree to expand simultaneously, they can attain higher levels of output and employment without any one partner suffering a deterioration in its trade balance. This was the logic behind the locomotive theory put forward by the USA at the Bonn Summit in 1978. An opposite sort of example is when the Nash non-cooperative equilibrium is overly inflationary, with no single leader willing to accept the role of supplying the 'public good' of a currency that is stable in purchasing power. This is often thought to be the logic that originally lay behind the founding of the European Monetary System.[3]

While it is not clear whether the 1990s will require co-ordinated expansion or co-ordinated discipline, I believe that it is clear that the present G7 mechanism is in some ways not well-designed to respond to future developments. The current mechanism of co-ordination is vulnerable to serious obstacles of three sorts: compliance, inflation-fighting credibility, and uncertainty. These obstacles are so severe that, if the system is not improved, the institution of international co-ordination is as likely to make the world economy worse off as better off.[4]

THREE OBSTACLES TO INTERNATIONAL MACRO-ECONOMIC POLICY CO-ORDINATION

The first obstacle to successful and meaningful co-ordination is the difficulty of ensuring compliance. If the member countries make commitments to attainable macro-economic targets that can be monitored – which requires that they be explicit, measurable and preferably public – then they are unlikely to cheat on them. But, under the current system, the presence of so many different indicators on the G7 list, the vagueness as to whether these variables are in fact forecasts, goals or commitments, and the secrecy surrounding the whole procedure, all imply that substantive enforceable agreements are unlikely to emerge from G7 meetings.

A primary drawback of the list is that it is too long to be practical. When each country has ten indicators but only two or three policy instruments, it is virtually certain that the indicators will give conflicting signals. Thus the national authorities will feel little constraint on their setting of policy instruments. In this light, a serious co-ordination scheme might *begin* in the 1990s by setting only one target, and then only progress to commitments to multiple variables when and if sufficient political consensus and confidence has developed to justify that degree of sacrifice of sovereignty.

The next drawback is that, on the G7 list, no distinction is made as to whether the variables are forecasts, goals or commitments. It is difficult to imagine a G7 meeting, for example, applying moral censure to one of its members for having experienced a lower rate of inflation during the year than had been agreed upon in the preceding meeting, or a higher rate of real growth. The third drawback of the G7 list is that explicit targets are not made public. How can any pressure be brought to bear on countries that stray from the agreed-upon targets – whether it is moral suasion, embarrassment, the effect on long-term reputations or outright sanctions – if the targets are kept secret?

To take an example, in the Baker–Miyazawa Agreement reached in San Francisco in September 1986 the Japanese apparently agreed to a fiscal expansion in exchange for a promise from the US Treasury Secretary that he would stop 'talking down' the dollar, plus the usual US promise to cut the budget deficit. In the months that followed, each side viewed the other as not fully living up to the agreement. The episode is described in Funabashi (1988). But it was difficult for anyone to verify the extent of compliance, because the precise terms of the original agreement had not been public.

The second danger that threatens the success of co-ordination efforts is the risk that co-operative agreements will be biased in favour of expansion, with the result that high inflation rates will re-emerge. The argument is that, if governments set up the machinery for joint welfare maximization period by period, the co-operative equilibrium in each period is likely to entail a greater degree of expansion than the Nash non-cooperative equilibrium, as countries lose the inhibitions of worsened trade balances. Governments may find this joint expansion advantageous within any given period, but in the long run it will undermine the governments' inflation-fighting credibility and result in a higher inflation rate for a given level of output. In this view, developed by Rogoff (1985), renouncing the machinery of co-ordination is one of the ways that governments can credibly pre-commit to less inflationary paths.

The implication of the credibility issue is that a scheme for co-ordination is more likely to produce gains in the long run if the plan has the national governments making not just commitments to each other on a period-by-period basis, but also some degree of commitment to a monetary or nominal anchor on a longer-term basis. There are four nominal variables on the G7 list of indicators: the money supply, the price level, the price of gold and the exchange rate. We must develop grounds for choosing among candidates for the nominal variable around which co-ordination should focus.

To review our conclusions so far, the compliance problem suggests that co-ordination should involve an explictly agreed and publicly announced intermediate target. The inflation-fighting credibility problem suggests that the intermediate target to which the governments commit should be a nominal variable. There exists a third obstacle to successful co-ordination: uncertainty. It leads to the suggestion that the nominal intermediate target to which the countries should best commit is one that does not even appear on the current G7 list at all: nominal GNP.

Uncertainty makes it difficult for each country to know what policy changes are in its interest. This difficulty arises whether the uncertainty centres on the initial position of the economy (the 'baseline forecast'), the desired policy targets (e.g. full employment) or the changes in monetary and fiscal policy necessary to produce desired effects (the multipliers). Major econometric models of the world economy disagree, for example, on whether a foreign monetary expansion has a positive or negative effect on domestic trade and output. All three kinds of uncertainty make it difficult for each country in the bargaining process to know even what policy changes it should want its partners to make. A number of pessimistic conclusions emerge. Given differing perceptions, the policymakers may not be able to agree on a co-ordination package; and even if they do agree, the effects may be different from what they anticipated.[5]

The standard German view of the joint expansion agreed upon at the 1978 Bonn Summit is that it turned out to have been undesirable because by 1980, as we have seen, the priority had shifted back to fighting inflation. One possible way to think of this view is as an example of uncertainty about the baseline position of the economy relative to the optimum: the 1979 oil price increase associated with the crisis in Iran moved the world economy to a more inflationary position than had been anticipated at the time of the Summit. Another way to think of it is as an example of disagreement over the correct model. In the model that the representatives of the USA and some smaller countries have in mind, a monetary expansion can raise output and employment, whereas in the Germans' model monetary expansion simply goes into prices.

Compliance can always be a problem for co-ordination, as noted above, because each country stands to benefit in the short run by deviating from an agreement and leaving its trading partners to carry the burden. But the problem is particularly great in the presence of uncertainty. This is true for two reasons. First, it is difficult to verify compliance if the 'performance criteria' that are used to monitor compliance are not directly enough under the control of the authorities, because they can always claim plausibly that failure to meet the targets that they agreed to was not their fault. For this reason, the inflation rate or price level is not a good candidate to be the nominal target to which countries commit. Secondly, a country may end up regretting *ex post* the target that it agreed to *ex ante* if it is not directly enough related to the goals that it ultimately cares about. For this reason, the money supply is not a good candidate to be the nominal target to which countries commit. A country that commits to a narrow range for the money supply will regret it if there is a shift in velocity.

To take an example from recent US history, the Federal Reserve, citing large velocity shifts, decided beginning in late 1982 to allow M1 to break firmly outside their pre-announced target zone. They did not publicly admit that they had abandoned monetarism until several years later. M1 grew 10.3 per cent per year from 1982:II to 1986:II. For four years the monetarists decried the betrayal of the money growth rule and warned that a major return of inflation was imminent. Nobody can doubt, in retrospect, that the Federal Reserve chose the right course. Even with the recovery that began in 1983 and continued through the 4 years and beyond, nominal GNP grew more slowly than the money supply: 8.0 per cent per year. Thus velocity declined at 2.3 per cent per year, in contrast with its past historical pattern of *increasing* at roughly 3 per cent a year. If the Federal Reserve had followed the explicit monetarist prescription of rigidly pre-committing to a money growth rate lower than that of the preceding period, such as 3 per cent, and velocity had followed the same path, then nominal GNP would have grown at only 0.7 per cent a year. This number is an upper bound because, with even lower inflation than occurred, velocity would almost certainly have fallen even more than it did. The implication seems clear that the 1981–2 recession would have lasted another five years!

THE PROPOSAL FOR NOMINAL GROSS NATIONAL PRODUCT TARGETING

It can be argued that, whatever the degree of pre-commitment to a nominal target, nominal GNP makes a more suitable target than the other nominal variables that have been proposed. The general argument has been made well by others.[6] In the event of disturbances in the banking system, disturbances in the public's demand for money or other disturbances affecting the demand for goods, a policy of holding nominal GNP steady insulates the economy; neither real income nor the price level need be affected. In the event of disturbances to supply, such as the oil price increases of the 1970s, the change is divided equi-proportionately between an increase in the price level and a fall in output. For some countries, this is roughly the split that a discretionary policy would choose anyway. In general, unless one believes that precisely equal weights should be placed on the two objectives of stabilizing inflation and real growth, fixing nominal GNP will not give precisely the right answer. But if the choice is among the available nominal anchors, nominal GNP gives an outcome characterized by greater stability of output and the price level. The inflation rate is too far outside the direct control of the authorities; the money supply is too distantly related to the price level, output or other objectives; and the exchange rate and the price of gold are too distant from *both* the control of the authorities and the objectives.

In an Appendix to this paper the problem is considered formally, for the special case where the objective function puts equal weight on percentage variation in output and variation in the inflation rate. No judgement is made on the desirable degree of pre-commitment to a nominal target, as long as it is greater than zero and less than infinity.[7] But whatever the degree of pre-commitment to a nominal target, nominal GNP (or nominal demand) makes a more suitable target than the other nominal variables that have been proposed.

The model of the economy to which the Appendix applies nominal

Table 11.1 World model: money rule

	1	2	3	4	5	s.e
A: Oil price shock (100%)						
US economy						
Output, %Y	−1.79	−0.53	0.29	0.76	0.99	3.05
Inflation, D	3.57	−2.15	−1.44	−0.89	−0.47	4.52
Money, %	0.00	0.00	0.00	0.00	0.00	
Japanese economy						
Output, % Y	−1.07	−0.07	−0.01	0.03	0.05	1.12
Inflation, D	2.84	−2.15	−0.58	−0.40	−0.24	3.64
Money, %	0.00	0.00	0.00	0.00	0.00	
German economy						
Output, %Y	−0.29	−0.24	0.03	0.32	0.58	3.63
Inflation, D	2.46	−1.08	−1.03	−0.78	−0.53	3.03
Money, %	0.00	0.00	0.00	0.00	0.00	
Rest OECD economies						
Output, %Y	−1.35	−0.28	0.25	0.55	0.71	2.34
Inflation, D	3.38	−1.92	−1.24	−0.78	−0.45	4.18
Money, %	0.00	0.00	0.00	0.00	0.00	
B: US money demand shock (5%)						
US economy						
Output, %Y	−1.21	0.20	0.02	−0.07	−0.11	1.26
Inflation, D	−0.92	0.48	0.29	0.16	0.08	1.09
Money, %	0.00	0.00	0.00	0.00	0.00	
Japanese economy						
Output, %Y	0.12	0.01	0.01	0.00	0.00	0.12
Inflation, D	0.18	−0.17	−0.04	0.02	0.02	0.25
Money, %	0.00	0.00	0.00	0.00	0.00	
German economy						
Output, %Y	0.36	−0.08	−0.01	0.05	0.09	0.49
Inflation, D	0.25	−0.16	−0.12	−0.05	−0.01	0.33
Money, %	0.00	0.00	0.00	0.00	0.00	
Rest OECD economies						
Output, %Y	0.26	−0.04	0.01	0.06	0.07	0.29
Inflation, D	0.30	−0.23	−0.11	−0.03	0.01	0.39
Money, %	0.00	0.00	0.00	0.00	0.00	
C: US real demand shock (1%)						
US economy						
Output, %Y	1.33	−0.25	−0.15	−0.07	−0.03	1.36
Inflation, D	0.52	−0.18	−0.14	−0.11	−0.07	0.58
Money, %	0.00	0.00	0.00	0.00	0.00	

Table 11.1 Continued

	1	2	3	4	5	s.e
Japanese economy						
Output, %Y	0.42	0.00	0.00	0.01	0.01	0.43
Inflation, D	0.33	−0.16	−0.10	−0.06	−0.04	0.39
Money, %	0.00	0.00	0.00	0.00	0.00	
German economy						
Output, %Y	0.54	−0.03	0.01	0.05	0.08	0.73
Inflation, D	0.36	−0.12	−0.14	−0.10	−0.07	0.43
Money, %	0.00	0.00	0.00	0.00	0.00	
Rest OECD economies						
Output, %Y	0.51	−0.04	−0.02	0.01	0.03	0.53
Inflation, D	0.40	−0.14	−0.13	−0.10	−0.06	0.46
Money, %	0.00	0.00	0.00	0.00	0.00	

GNP targeting is greatly oversimplified, consisting as it does of only one country and essentially only two equations (aggregate supply and money market equilibrium). It is able to show that targeting nominal GNP is superior to targeting the money supply, under fairly general conditions. But, in the absence of a full parameterized model, the Appendix does not contain enough information to choose between a targeting rule and discretion.

AN INTERNATIONAL ANALYSIS OF NOMINAL GROSS NATIONAL PRODUCT TARGETING

Warwick McKibbin and I have begun to apply the McKibbin–Sachs global (MSG) model to these problems. The MSG model fully articulates the household, firm, asset market, wage-setting, balance-of-payments and government sectors, and covers seven regions: the USA, Japan, Germany, the rest of the European Monetary System, the rest of the Organization for Economic Co-operation and Development (OECD), non-oil developing countries and the Organization of Petroleum Exporting Countries. It is state of the art in that it keeps track of the cumulating stocks of domestic and foreign debt over time, and assumes model-consistent (i.e. rational) expectations. Expositions and applications of the MSG model include those of McKibbin and Sachs (1986, 1989a,b).

We consider several alternative plans, in each case assuming that the three member countries (the USA, Japan and Germany) adopt the same policy regime. The rest of the OECD countries, which are reported as a unit, are assumed to leave their money supplies unaltered. We consider the same three shocks as in the Appendix: an increase in oil prices or other supply shock, a money demand shock and a goods demand shock. The tables report implications over the subsequent five years for three out of eight macro-economic variables, all of which are on the G7 list of indicators. We shall follow the Appendix in considering only the first two variables as ultimate objectives: output and inflation. All effects are reported as percentage deviations from baseline. The effects should then be squared for use in a quadratic loss function, where it is assumed that it is optimal to get as close as possible to the baseline path for output and inflation. The last column in the tables conveys the overall magnitude of the effect over time; it is the square root of the sum of the yearly squared effects. The quadratic loss function can be thought of as the sum of the number in the first row squared and the number in the second row squared (either for a given year or for the long run).

We consider first the comparison of the money supply rule and the nominal GNP rule. The experiment captures uncoordinated setting of target paths, though one could interpret the decision of the three countries to settle on nominal GNP (or the money supply) as the variable on which each will independently target as itself the outcome of a co-operative international decision.

Table 11.1, panel A, reports the effects of a doubling of the world price of oil under a money rule. All countries experience a sharp increase in the price level in the first year (roughly 3 per cent), and a somewhat smaller decrease in the level of output, with the largest effects (not reported in the table) felt in the USA. Since the monetary authorities hold firm, the interest rate rises. The contraction of output continues in the second year, and the price level begins to fall back towards its original level. In the long run, there is no effect.

Table 11.2, panel A reports the effects of the same-sized supply shock under a nominal GNP rule. The effects on output and inflation are equal in magnitude, approximately, and offsetting, so as to keep the effect on nominal GNP equal to zero. Achieving the outcome of a fixed nominal GNP requires a monetary contraction in each country. For each of the three large countries, the short-run output loss is greater than under the money rule (and by more on a percentage basis than the gain in inflation). But, assuming that equal weight is placed on the two objectives in the quadratic loss function, the nominal GNP rule's success at reducing inflation is enough to yield welfare gains in the long run, especially in the case of Germany.

Next we consider a 5 per cent increase in US money demand. The excess demand for money raises the interest rate in the first year, causing a fall in output and in the price level of roughly 1 per cent each in the USA. It is here that the superiority of the nominal GNP rule (Table 11.2, panel B), comes through most strongly. The US recession is avoided completely, as the money supply is automatically increased by 5 per cent to offset the increase in money demand. When the increase in money demand originates in Japan or Germany, similar results obtain in those countries (data omitted to save space, but available on request).

The choice is almost as clear-cut for the case of a 1 per cent increase in US real demand for goods. Under the money rule (Table 11.1, panel C), the impact is a rise in output and inflation. The US expansion is transmitted positively to the other countries via a US trade deficit. Under the nominal GNP rule (Table 11.2, panel C), in contrast, an automatic contraction of the money supply leads to much smaller changes in output and inflation. The reported fall in the price level on impact is somewhat greater than the rise in output, even though total nominal GNP is held constant. The explanation is that the inflation numbers that are reported refer to consumer price index (CPI), not the GNP deflator, and an appreciation of the dollar against the other currencies puts downward pressure on US import prices. Again, the results for an increase in goods demand that originates in Japan or Germany are available on request. In sum, the nominal GP rule seems to dominate the money rule, regardless of the origin of the disturbance.

Either sort of rule, nominal GNP targeting or money targeting, necessarily loses the advantage of discretionary policy that it can respond to the shocks. We can now consider how the nominal GNP rule fares against a regime of full discretion, which is shown in Table 11.3. The discretion is assumed to be exercised by a benevolent far-sighted government which maximizes a present discounted value of the objective function. We do not yet incorporate any 'inflationary bias', i.e. any temptation for the government to expand irresponsibly for the short-run gain or higher output.

Discretion for the oil-shock case is shown in Table 11.3, panel A. Even without a built-in inflationary bias, the government opts to take the supply shock more in the form of higher inflation than in the form of output loss. The recession lasts only one year, while it lasts two years in the case of the nominal GNP rule.

In the fourth and fifth years, however, output does not increase as much under discretion as it does under the nominal GNP rule. The squared loss function shows that the outcome under discretion is more desirable than the outcome under the nominal GNP rule, in the long run.

Evidently, the advantages of letting the optimizing government

Table 11.2 World model: INT with feedback on observed shocks

	1	2	3	4	5	s.e
A: Oil price shock (100%)						
US economy						
Output, %Y	−2.92	−0.71	0.48	1.00	1.12	3.81
Inflation, D	2.94	−2.18	−1.16	−0.52	−0.14	3.88
Money, %	−3.75	−1.67	−0.37	0.33	0.63	
Japanese economy						
Output, % Y	−2.14	−0.13	−0.05	0.00	0.03	2.16
Inflation, D	2.16	−1.98	−0.17	−0.09	−0.04	2.93
Money, %	−4.38	−1.04	−0.25	0.28	0.52	
German economy						
Output, %Y	−1.47	−0.50	0.06	0.34	0.50	2.86
Inflation, D	1.50	−1.07	−0.55	−0.28	−0.16	1.95
Money, %	−4.49	−2.36	−0.73	0.16	0.55	
Rest OECD economies						
Output, %Y	−0.98	−0.31	0.27	0.67	0.88	2.39
Inflation, D	4.15	−2.29	−1.66	−1.00	−0.48	5.14
Money, %	0.00	0.00	0.00	0.00	0.00	
B: US money demand shock (5%)						
US economy						
Output, %Y	0.00	0.00	0.00	0.00	0.00	0.01
Inflation, D	−0.01	0.01	0.00	0.00	0.00	0.01
Money, %	4.86	0.00	0.00	0.00	0.00	
Japanese economy						
Output, %Y	0.00	0.00	0.00	0.00	0.00	0.00
Inflation, D	0.00	0.00	0.00	0.00	0.00	0.00
Money, %	−0.06	0.01	0.00	0.00	0.00	
German economy						
Output, %Y	0.00	0.00	0.00	0.00	0.00	0.01
Inflation, D	0.00	0.00	0.00	0.00	0.00	0.01
Money, %	−0.10	0.00	0.00	0.00	0.00	
Rest OECD economies						
Output, %Y	0.03	0.00	0.00	0.00	0.00	0.03
Inflation, D	0.03	−0.02	−0.01	0.00	0.00	0.04
Money, %	0.00	0.00	0.00	0.00	0.00	
C: US real demand shock (1%)						
US economy						
Output, %Y	0.15	−0.03	−0.11	−0.14	−0.13	0.33
Inflation, D	−0.24	0.24	−0.10	0.03	0.00	0.35
Money, %	−4.55	0.12	0.05	0.01	−0.01	

Table 11.2 Continued

	1	2	3	4	5	s.e
Japanese economy						
Output, %*Y*	−0.05	−0.01	−0.01	−0.01	−0.01	0.06
Inflation, *D*	0.11	−0.10	0.01	0.00	0.00	0.15
Money, %	−1.99	−0.21	−0.03	0.00	0.00	
German economy						
Output, %*Y*	0.02	0.00	−0.06	−0.07	−0.06	0.19
Inflation, *D*	−0.12	0.13	0.04	0.00	−0.01	0.19
Money, %	−3.38	−0.08	0.02	0.03	0.02	
Rest OECD economies						
Output, %*Y*	0.85	−0.14	0.06	0.13	0.15	0.92
Inflation, *D*	0.97	−0.67	−0.27	−0.10	−0.02	1.21
Money, %	0.00	0.00	0.00	0.00	0.00	

respond to the oil shock are greater than the advantages of being able to reduce inflation by pre-committing to an intermediate nominal target.

In the case of a money demand shock, discretion (Table 11.3, panel B) is able to accomplish the same feat, insulation of the economy, as the nominal GNP rule (Table 11.2, panel B).

In the case of a real demand shock, the differences between the regimes are relatively small. The discretionary government responds with a first-year monetary contraction that is great enough to push the price level down rather than up (Table 11.3, panel C), the same thing that happens under the nominal GNP rule. The government is not able to nullify the effects of the demand shock altogether, apparently because of the appreciation of the dollar, which operates on the CPI relatively more than on output. But discretion succeeds in making the absolute effects on output and the price level (the CPI) even more nearly equal than does the nominal GNP rule, when the demand shock originates in the USA. The squared loss function makes discretion look a little better in the long run, though it makes the nominal GNP rule look slightly better on impact. When the demand shock originates in Japan or Germany (data not reported), however, the initial fall in inflation, and the subsequent rise, are exacerbated in those respective countries.

Summing up the results across the three shocks, the case in favour of pre-commitment to a rule is not clear-cut, *if* the alternative is discretion by a far-sighted government without an inflationary bias. Below, we shall build in an inflationary bias to the discretion regime, which will change the conclusions.

Table 11.3 World model: Optimal non-cooperative rule (discretion)

	1	2	3	4	5	s.e
A: Oil price shock (100%)						
US economy						
Output, %Y	−2.47	0.53	0.53	0.50	0.45	2.79
Inflation, D	3.09	−0.82	−0.81	−0.76	−0.68	3.45
Money, %	−4.27	3.33	2.65	1.90	1.14	
Japanese economy						
Output, % Y	−0.61	−0.03	0.00	0.01	0.02	0.62
Inflation, D	3.30	0.14	0.01	−0.08	−0.13	3.31
Money, %	−0.16	3.12	3.68	3.79	3.71	
German economy						
Output, %Y	−0.10	0.03	0.04	0.05	0.05	0.20
Inflation, D	2.44	−0.74	−0.99	−1.11	−1.16	3.17
Money, %	−1.70	1.64	1.53	0.74	−0.35	
Rest OECD economies						
Output, %Y	−1.15	−0.47	0.34	0.69	0.78	2.10
Inflation, D	3.57	−2.59	−1.25	−0.51	−0.14	4.61
Money, %	0.00	0.00	0.00	0.00	0.00	
B: US money demand shock (5%)						
US economy						
Output, %Y	0.01	0.00	0.00	0.00	0.00	0.01
Inflation, D	−0.01	0.00	0.00	0.00	0.00	0.01
Money, %	4.87	−0.01	0.00	0.00	0.01	
Japanese economy						
Output, %Y	0.00	0.00	0.00	0.00	0.00	0.00
Inflation, D	0.00	0.00	0.00	0.00	0.00	0.00
Money, %	−0.06	0.00	0.00	0.01	0.01	
German economy						
Output, %Y	0.00	0.00	0.00	0.00	0.00	0.00
Inflation, D	0.00	0.00	0.00	0.00	0.00	0.01
Money, %	−0.10	−0.01	0.00	0.01	0.01	
Rest OECD economies						
Output, %Y	0.03	0.00	0.00	0.00	0.00	0.03
Inflation, D	0.03	−0.02	−0.01	0.00	0.00	0.04
Money, %	0.00	0.00	0.00	0.00	0.00	
C: US real demand shock (1%)						
US economy						
Output, %Y	0.19	−0.10	−0.08	−0.06	−0.06	0.27
Inflation, D	−0.22	0.15	0.12	0.10	0.09	0.32
Money, %	−4.32	−0.24	−0.05	0.08	0.18	

Table 11.3 Continued

	1	2	3	4	5	s.e
Japanese economy						
Output, %Y	−0.02	−0.01	−0.01	−0.01	−0.01	0.03
Inflation, D	0.13	0.05	0.05	0.04	0.03	0.16
Money, %	−2.02	−0.11	0.16	0.27	0.32	
German economy						
Output, %Y	0.01	0.00	0.00	0.00	0.00	0.01
Inflation, D	−0.13	0.11	0.10	0.08	0.06	0.22
Money, %	−3.28	−0.35	0.01	0.18	0.26	
Rest OECD economies						
Output, %Y	0.84	−0.11	0.05	0.13	0.16	0.91
Inflation, D	0.96	−0.61	−0.31	−0.14	−0.04	1.19
Money, %	0.00	0.00	0.00	0.00	0.00	

None of the cases so far concerns international co-ordination, interpreted as joint policy-setting on a year-by-year basis. In Table 11.4 we consider co-ordination between the USA, Japan and Germany, or its equivalent, the maximization by a G3 central planner of a world objective function, which in this case weights the countries' individual objective functions by their shares of GNP.

Each country responds to the oil price shock (Table 11.4, panel A) with a more expansionary monetary policy than in the non-cooperative discretionary case or in the case of a nominal GNP rule. Apparently the non-cooperative equilibrium is handicapped by a tendency of each country to raise its interest rates in a (collectively futile) attempt to bid up the value of its currency and thereby attain lower import prices and a lower CPI. As a result, inflation is slightly higher and the initial fall in output slightly smaller in the co-operative equilibrium, for the USA, Japan, and Germany. The effect of co-ordination on the objective function, relative to non-cooperative discretion, is relatively small – a slight improvement for the USA, slight deterioration for Japan and Germany – both in the long run and in the short run. Evidently the standard advantage of co-ordination, that it allows each country to expand without fear of the implications for its external sector, is fully offset by the 'Rogoff' effect – the undermining of public expectations that the monetary authorities will hold the line against inflation.

The nominal GNP rule is better able to resist the temptation to inflate. But the impact on output is considerably larger. The objective function shows that co-ordination dominates in the long run, especially for the USA.

Table 11.4 World model: Optimal co-operative rule (discretion)

	1	2	3	4	5	s.e
A: Oil price shock (100%)						
US economy						
Output, %Y	−2.31	0.51	0.51	0.48	0.43	2.62
Inflation, D	3.19	−0.85	−0.85	−0.80	−0.73	3.58
Money, %	−3.69	3.40	2.67	1.86	1.06	
Japanese economy						
Output, % Y	−0.52	−0.02	0.01	0.02	0.03	0.53
Inflation, D	3.35	−0.33	−0.52	−0.61	−0.64	3.51
Money, %	0.54	3.04	3.03	2.60	1.98	
German economy						
Output, %Y	0.00	0.00	0.01	0.01	0.02	0.07
Inflation, D	2.52	−0.80	−1.07	−1.18	−1.23	3.33
Money, %	−1.12	1.69	1.49	0.61	−0.56	
Rest OECD economies						
Output, %Y	−1.20	−0.46	0.32	0.66	0.75	2.08
Inflation, D	3.48	−2.52	−1.21	−0.50	−0.13	4.49
Money, %	0.00	0.00	0.00	0.00	0.00	
B: US money demand shock (5%)						
US economy						
Output, %Y	0.01	0.00	0.00	0.00	0.00	0.01
Inflation, D	−0.01	0.00	0.00	0.00	0.00	0.01
Money, %	4.87	−0.01	0.00	0.00	0.01	
Japanese economy						
Output, %Y	0.00	0.00	0.00	0.00	0.00	0.00
Inflation, D	0.00	0.00	0.00	0.00	0.00	0.01
Money, %	−0.06	0.00	0.01	0.01	0.02	
German economy						
Output, %Y	0.00	0.00	0.00	0.00	0.00	0.00
Inflation, D	0.00	0.00	0.00	0.00	0.00	0.01
Money, %	−0.10	−0.01	0.00	0.01	0.01	
Rest OECD economies						
Output, %Y	0.03	0.00	0.00	0.00	0.00	0.03
Inflation, D	0.03	−0.02	−0.01	0.00	0.00	0.04
Money, %	0.00	0.00	0.00	0.00	0.00	
C: US real demand shock (1%)						
US economy						
Output, %Y	0.19	−0.10	−0.07	−0.06	−0.05	0.27
Inflation, D	−0.22	0.16	0.12	0.10	0.09	0.33
Money, %	−4.33	−0.22	−0.03	0.11	0.21	

Table 11.4 Continued

	1	2	3	4	5	s.e
Japanese economy						
Output, %Y	−0.02	−0.01	−0.01	−0.01	−0.01	0.03
Inflation, D	0.13	0.14	0.13	0.11	0.09	0.27
Money, %	−2.08	−0.06	0.30	0.48	0.59	
German economy						
Output, %Y	0.00	0.00	0.00	0.00	0.00	0.00
Inflation, D	−0.14	0.11	0.11	0.08	0.07	0.23
Money, %	−3.31	−0.34	0.02	0.19	0.28	
Rest OECD economies						
Output, %Y	0.84	−0.11	0.05	0.13	0.16	0.92
Inflation, D	0.96	−0.62	−0.31	−0.14	−0.04	1.20
Money, %	0.00	0.00	0.00	0.00	0.00	

In the case of the money demand shock, as usual, the regimes are all equally good except for the money rule, which, it will be recalled, produces a needless recession. The co-ordinated response to a US real demand shock involves monetary contraction in all three countries, just barely more so than the non-cooperative case. The effects are virtually identical.

We saw above that, even though the nominal GNP rule was superior to the money rule, rules in general did not fare well in comparison with discretion. But the regime evaluated was discretion by a benign far-sighted government that maximised the present discounted sum of future welfare. Those who argue the superiority of rules believe that governments left to themselves are in fact more inflation-prone than this, and thus need to be constrained from expanding. There are two natural ways of modelling the inflation bias under unconstrained discretion. The first is to assume that the government has a high discount rate – in the extreme that it cares only about *current* output and inflation – for example because it is only expecting to be in office a short time or because the electorate only reacts to the current state of the economy. The second is to assume that the target rates of output and employment that the political system produces are higher than the level of potential output and the natural rate of unemployment, for example because of the power of labour unions. Either approach can yield the result that a country will attain a higher value for its intertemporal objective function if the government is constrained from expanding.[8]

A credible constraint reduces public expectations of future inflation, thereby reducing the rate of actual inflation that corresponds to a given

Table 11.5 Optimal policy with inflationary bias

	1	2	3	4	5
US economy					
Output, %Y	0.75	0.63	0.57	0.52	0.47
Inflation, D	0.39	0.56	0.65	0.73	0.80
Money, %	1.47	1.58	2.02	2.61	3.31
Japanese economy					
Output, % Y	0.93	0.03	0.01	0.01	0.01
Inflation, D	0.65	5.50	5.64	5.64	5.60
Money, %	−0.58	2.80	8.69	14.45	20.11
German economy					
Output, %Y	0.99	0.99	0.99	0.99	0.99
Inflation, D	0.69	0.80	0.73	0.68	0.64
Money, %	1.60	2.36	3.04	3.69	4.31
Rest OECD economies					
Output, %Y	−0.12	0.06	0.13	0.14	0.14
Inflation, D	−0.45	−0.10	−0.01	0.02	0.03
Money, %	0.00	0.00	0.00	0.00	0.00

level of output. Of course this still leaves the fact that, if there are unanticipated future disturbances, a rule prevents the government from responding. The choice between rules and discretion depends on the relative advantages of inflation-fighting credibility and the ability to respond to future disturbances. It is ultimately an empirical question.

We now examine an inflationary bias that takes the form of the adoption of a target level of output that is 1 per cent above baseline. One can think of the experiment as the result of a change in political parties or of an increase in the power of labour unions. First we consider the effect of the inflationary bias in the case of non-cooperative discretion (by a government maximizing an intertemporal objective function with the same discount rate as above). Table 11.5 considers the bias in isolation (no disturbances). In each of the three countries, output initially goes up by almost 2 per cent, and the price level by somewhat less. In the USA, output comes back down slowly over time thereafter, while the price level continues to rise. This path is between the extremes of Japan, where output comes back down rapidly but the price level rises by 5.6 per cent, and Germany, where output stays high; the differences arise because the MSG model has market-clearing wages in Japan and hysteresis in Germany.

Now we consider the inflationary bias in conjunction with the same sorts of disturbances considered above. Because of linearity in the model, the effect of a given disturbance in the presence of the bias is simply the sum of the effect of the corresponding disturbance from Table 11.3 plus the effect of the bias in Table 11.5. In the case of the oil shock, for example, the result of the inflationary bias is that the discretionary government expands so that the fall in output (1.72 per cent) is smaller, and the increase in the price level (3.48 per cent) larger, than was the case when the political goal for output was the same as the baseline.

Unexpected changes in oil prices, money demand or goods demand can, of course, be negative as easily as positive. When we were evaluating the quadratic loss function that corresponded to the experiments in Tables 11.1–11.4, it did not matter whether the disturbance was positive or negative. This is because when the political goal – the value of the target variable in the absence of disturbances – coincides with the baseline path that is the reference point for the quadratic loss function, the absolute magnitudes of positive and negative deviations from the optimum value of the target variables are the same. But now that we are allowing the political goal to exceed the baseline, it is important to allow for negative shocks. A fall in goods demand in the presence of an inflationary bias, for example, might coincidentally look much better than a rise in goods demand. To find the effects of a negative oil shock, respectively, we *subtract* the corresponding effects in Table 11.4 from the output and inflation effects in Table 11.5, rather than adding them. Then, to evaluate the welfare under the discretionary regime, we average the two values of the loss function, to recognize that positive and negative shocks are equally likely.

In the presence of the inflationary bias, discretion is now considerably worse than the nominal GNP rule in the event of real demand shocks because the government is unable to resist the urge to inflate, whereas in the absence of inflationary bias, discretion was only slightly worse than the rule. In the event of real demand shocks, discretion is again considerably worse than the nominal GNP rule because the government is unable to resist the urge to inflate, whereas in the absence of inflationary bias the two were equivalent. Only in the event of supply shocks does discretion still dominate the nominal GNP rule, because the fall in output is small in the event of an increase in the price of oil. The superiority of discretion in the last case is relatively small, however. It seems less likely that if money demand or real demand shocks are at all important, then the nominal GNP rule would result in higher welfare overall.

The drawbacks of discretion in the presence of the inflationary bias change little when we allow the three countries to co-ordinate. (Table 11.6). Indeed, regardless of the disturbance, the loss function looks

Table 11.6 Co-operative policy with inflationary bias

	1	2	3	4	5
US economy					
Output, %Y	0.87	0.92	0.83	0.75	0.68
Inflation, D	0.46	0.91	1.06	1.18	1.28
Money, %	1.37	2.18	2.92	3.89	5.02
Japanese economy					
Output, % Y	1.49	0.02	−0.02	−0.02	−0.01
Inflation, D	1.15	9.19	9.40	9.37	9.26
Money, %	−1.16	4.59	14.46	24.05	33.44
German economy					
Output, %Y	0.95	1.04	1.05	1.05	1.05
Inflation, D	0.56	0.85	0.77	0.71	0.67
Money, %	1.22	2.44	3.16	3.83	4.47
Rest OECD economies					
Output, %Y	−0.09	0.07	0.18	0.21	0.20
Inflation, D	−0.50	−0.18	−0.03	0.03	0.04
Money, %	0.00	0.00	0.00	0.00	0.00

slightly worse than when the countries set their policies independently. The reason is that the Rogoff problem is exacerbated: the USA and Japan both inflate more than they do in the non-cooperative regime, where they are inhibited by the threat of depreciated currencies. The advantages of pre-committing to a nominal target as a way of resisting the temptation to inflate thus look even greater.

THE PROPOSAL FOR CO-ORDINATION BY INTERNATIONAL NOMINAL TARGETING

The version of nominal GNP targeting that we have evaluated in this paper is a restricted one. As with the version of money supply targeting that was evaluated, it was assumed that the countries eternally fixed their rate of nominal growth. There was no sense in which the setting of nominal GNP was co-operative unless one wished to think of the simultaneous decision by the USA, Japan and Germany to switch to a nominal GNP rule as a co-ordinated decision.

I have proposed a co-operative international version of a nominal GNP rule that I call INT (international nominal targeting) (Frankel, 1989). At each G7 meeting, the national authorities would (i) loosely commit themselves to broad target ranges for their collective and individual rates of growth of nominal demand, for 5 years into the future, and (ii) commit themselves to somewhat narrower targets for the coming year. It would be up to each country how to attain the target to which it committed, though the tools of monetary policy must presumably take precedence over the tools of fiscal policy for purposes of short-run adjustments. The targets would be publicly announced, in the manner that the Chairman of the Federal Reserve Board announced target ranges for the M1 money supply to the US until recently. If a country's rate of growth of nominal demand turned out to err significantly in one direction or the other, the fact would be noted disapprovingly at the next G7 meeting.[9]

The next step in future research is to add to the list of regimes the co-operative setting of nominal GNPs and the co-operative setting of money supplies. This could be done both using the theoretical context of the Appendix and using the simulation approach of the MSG model.

To study co-operative setting of targets in a way that is meaningfully distinct from co-operative discretion requires that we have the sort of long-lasting disturbances studied here that push the world economy away from its optimum goals, which governments then respond to in a discretionary way (with or without co-ordination), but also that we have subsequent short-term disturbances in addition. Only if there are disturbances subsequent to the co-operative agreement will it make a difference whether the decisions that are made at the first stage are expressed in terms of nominal GNP, the money supply or some other variable. The goal would be to show, when the long-term situation is one of recession for example, that if the G7 wish to reap the potential benefits of joint expansion they are better off seeking to do so by agreeing on expansion in terms of nominal GNP than in terms of M1, because the former strategy is much more robust to possible future disturbances.

APPENDIX

In this appendix we compare three possible policy regimes: (i) floating exchange rates, with full discretion by national policymakers (the current regime); (ii) a rigid money supply rule; and (iii) a rigid nominal GNP rule. The approach, incorporating the advantages both to rules and discretion, follows Rogoff (1985) and Fischer (1988a), who in turn follow Kydland and Prescott (1977) and Barro and Gordon (1983).

We assume an aggregate supply relationship:

$$y = y^* + b(p - p^e) + u \qquad (11.\text{A}1)$$

where y represents output, y^* potential output, p the price level, p^e the expected price level (or they could be the actual and expected inflation rates respectively) and u a supply disturbance, with all variables expressed as logarithms.

We represent economic welfare by a quadratic loss function in output and the price level,

$$L = p^2 + (y - ky^*)^2 \qquad (11.\text{A}2)$$

where we have assigned a unit weight to the inflation objective,[10] and we assume that the lagged or expected price level relative to which p is measured can be normalized to zero. We impose $k > 1$, which builds in an expansionary bias to discretionary policy-making.

$$L = p^2 + [y^*(1 - k) + b(p - p^e) + u]^2$$

Discretionary policy

Under full discretion, the policymaker each period chooses aggregate demand so as to minimize that period's L, with p^e given.

$$dL/dp = 2p + 2[y^*(1 - k) + b(p - p^e) + u]b = 0 \qquad (11.\text{A}4)$$

$$p(1 + b^2) = [- y^*(1 - k)b + b^2 p^e - bu] \qquad (11.\text{A}5)$$

Under rational expectations,

$$p^e = Ep = - y^*(1 - k)b \qquad (11.\text{A}6)$$

So we can solve (11.A5) for the price level:

$$p = - y^*(1 - k)b - u \, [b/(1 + b^2)] \qquad (11.\text{A}7)$$

From (11.A2), the expected loss function then works out to

$$EL = (1 + b^2) \, [(1 - k)y^*]^2 + \text{var} \, (u)/(1 + b^2) \qquad (11.\text{A}8)$$

The first term represents the inflationary bias in the system, while the second represents the effect of the supply disturbance after the authorities have chosen the optimal split between inflation and output.[11]

Money rule

To consider alternative regimes, we must be explicit about the money market equilibrium condition. (In the equations above, it was implicit that the money supply m was the variable that the authorities were using to control demand.)

$$m = p + y - v \qquad (11.A9)$$

where v represents velocity shocks. (We assume that v is uncorrelated with u.) If the authorities pre-commit to a fixed money growth rule in order to reduce expected inflation in long-run equilibrium, then they must give up on affecting y. The optimal money growth rate is the one that sets Ep at the target value for p, namely 0. Thus they will set the money supply m at Ey, which in this case is y^*. The aggregate demand equation thus becomes

$$p + y = y^* + v \qquad (11.A10)$$

Combining with the aggregate supply relationship (11.A1), the equilibrium is given by

$$\begin{aligned} y &= y^* + (u + bv)/(1 + b) \\ p &= \qquad (v - u)/(1 + b) \end{aligned} \qquad (11.A11)$$

Substituting (11.A2), the expected loss function is

$$EL = (1 - k)^2 y^{*2} + [2 \text{ var } (u)/(1 + b)^2 + (1 + b^2 \text{ var } (v)/(1 + 2)^2] \qquad (11.A12)$$

The first term is smaller than the corresponding term in the discretion case because the pre-commitment reduces expected inflation, but the second term is probably larger because the authorities have given up the ability to respond to money demand shocks and so var (v) enters. Which regime is better depends on how big the shocks are, and on how big b is.

Nominal gross national product rule

In the case of a nominal GNP rule, the authorities vary the money supply in such a way as to accommodate velocity shocks. Equation (11.A10) is replaced by the condition that $p + y$ is constant. The solution is the same as in the preceding case but with the v disturbance dropped. Thus the expected loss collapses from (11.A12) to

$$EL = (1 - k)^2 y^{*2} + 2 \text{ var } (u)/(1 + b^2)^2 \qquad (11.A13)$$

The expected loss in (11.A13) is less than that in (11.A12). We thus see the central theorem: the nominal GNP rule unambiguously dominates the money rule case. It is still not possible, without knowing var (u) and b, the size of the supply shocks and the flatness of the short-run supply relationship, to say that the rule dominates discretion (to compare the expected losses in (11.A8) and (11.A13)). For this question, we need the full model simulations described in the text.

It is quite likely, especially if the variance of u is large, that an absolute commitment to a rule would be unwisely constraining – hence the argument for a target zone rather than a single number, and for subjecting the central bank chairman to a mere loss of reputation if he misses the target rather than a firing squad. But it seems clear that, to whatever extent the country chooses to commit to a nominal anchor, nominal GNP dominates the money supply as the candidate for anchor.

NOTES

1 I would like to thank Warwick McKibbin: simulation results reported here draw on joint research.
2 This list did not appear in the communiqué but in comments to the press by the US Treasury's Assistant Secretary David Mulford. Funabashi (1988, esp. p. 130ff.) offers a fascinating account of the machinations of the G7 mechanism from 1985 to 1987.
3 For a review of the literature on international macro-economic policy co-ordination, see Fischer (1988b).
4 For sceptical views on international co-ordination, see Feldstein (1983, 1988) and Frankel (1988).
5 Frankel and Rockett (1988). See also Holtham and Hughes Hallett (1987).
6 In the domestic context, nominal GNP targeting has many adherents. In the international context, Williamson and Miller (1987) propose targeting nominal demand as part of their 'blueprint' for exchange rate target zones.
7 Analogously, in the context of international co-ordination, we take as given by the political process the degree of commitment to co-ordination.
8 For a review of the literature, see Fischer (1988a).
9 There is a reason for choosing nominal demand (defined as GNP minus

the trade balance) as the target variable in place of nominal GNP, even though the latter is a more familiar concept. In the event of a recession, countries need to be discouraged from the temptation to accomplish their expansion of output through net foreign demand – for example, through protectionist measures – as opposed to domestic demand.

10 The Appendix to Frankel (1989) allows the weights on the output and inflation objectives to differ.

11 Note that the higher *b* is, the greater the inflationary bias. The reason is that, under rational expectations, people know that the government will be more tempted to expand, the flatter the supply relationship is.

REFERENCES

Barro, R.J. and Gordon, D.B. (1983) 'Rules, discretion and reputation in a model of monetary policy', *Journal of Monetary Economics* 12 (July): 101–21.

Feldstein, M. (1983) 'The world economy', *The Economist* 11 June.

—— (1988) 'Distinguished lecture on economics in government: thinking about international economic coordination', *Journal of Economic Perspectives* 2 (2) (spring): 3–13.

Fischer, S. (1988a) 'Rules vs. discretion in monetary policy', NBER Working Paper 2518, February.

—— (1988b) 'International macroeconomic policy coordination', in M. Feldstein (ed.) *International Policy Coordination*, Chicago, IL: University of Chicago Press.

Frankel, J. (1988) 'Obstacles to international macroeconomic policy coordination', International Monetary Fund Working Paper 87/28, *Studies in International Finance* 64, Princeton University, December.

—— (1989) 'International nominal targeting (INT): a proposal for overcoming obstacles to policy coordination', in J. McCallum and R. Mundell (eds) *Global Disequilibrium*, forthcoming.

—— and Rockett, K. (1988) 'International macroeconomic policy coordination when policy-makers do not agree on the true model', *American Economic Review* 78 (3) (June): 318–40.

Funabashi, Y. (1988) *Managing the Dollar: From the Plaza to the Louvre*, Washington, DC: Institute of International Economics.

Holtham, G. and Hughes Hallett, A. (1987) 'International policy coordination and model uncertainty', in R. Bryant and R. Portes (eds) *Global Macroeconomics: Policy Conflict and Cooperation*, London: Macmillan.

Kydland, F.E. and Prescott, E.C. (1977) 'Rules rather than indiscretion: the inconsistency of optimal plans', *Journal of Political Economy* 85 (June): 473–92.

McKibbin, W. and Sachs, J. (1986) 'Comparing the global performance of alternative exchange rate arrangements', NBER Working Paper 2000, and *Journal of International Money and Finance* 7: 387–410.

—— and —— (1989a) 'The McKibbin–Sachs global (MSG2) model', Brookings Discussion Paper in International Economics 78 (August).

—— and —— (1989b) 'Implications of policy rules for the world economy: results from the McKibbin–Sachs global (MSG2) model', in R. Bryant,

D. Currie, J. Frenkel, P. Masson and R. Portes (eds) *Macroeconomic Policies in an Interdependent World*, Washington, DC: Brookings Institution.

Rogoff, K. (1985) 'International macroeconomic policy coordination may be counterproductive', *Journal of International Economics* 18 February: 199–217.

Williamson, J. and Miller, M. (1987) *Targets and Indicators: a Blueprint for the International Coordination of Economic Policy*, Washington, DC: Institute for International Economics, September.

12 Threats to the world trading regime: protectionism, unfair trade *et al*

Jagdish Bhagwati

INTRODUCTION

This volume contains papers by some of my many students, research associates and friends, made and cherished over three decades of a scholarly professorial life. Professor Loet Mennes organized an International Symposium in my honour, on the occasion of the award of an honorary doctorate to me by Erasmus University at its seventy-fifth Anniversary celebration; and many of the papers were presented on that occasion.

To him, his co-editor Ad Koekkoek, and the authors of this volume, I owe thanks, not merely for the excessive generosity of their sentiments but also for the excellence that characterizes their contributions and, equally so, for the relevance that these have in turn to my own scientific work and research interests. Indeed, the thoughtfulness in making their contributions appropriate to this volume by developing themes that are central to my interest makes it less arduous for me to respond to the editors' request to make a closing response.

The world trading system is at a crossroads. There are certainly encouraging signs. They revolve around the efforts being made at the Uruguay Round to strengthen and revitalize the General Agreement on Tariffs and Trade by introducing discipline into new sectors (e.g. services, discussed splendidly by Brian Hindley in this volume), and structural trends concerning investments and trade in the world economy that have produced a new political economy supportive of open markets. At the same time, the example provided by the spectacular success of the outward-oriented export-promoting developing countries, beautifully reviewed by James Riedel in this volume, has provided an impetus to the forces in favour of freer trade by gathering new converts among the hitherto sceptical developing countries.

Yet, it is too soon to celebrate success. There are disturbing signs as well. I concentrate on them below, not because they are likely to overwhelm the favourable trends just noted, but because of what I have called the Dracula principle: exposing evil to light helps destroy it. By focusing on these darker trends, we may encourage the awareness that is necessary to contain them.

PROTECTIONISM

The case for open markets has faced serious crises before now. The most dramatic such crisis was in the years after the Great Crash of 1929. The massive unemployment made it impossible at the time to sustain the case for free trade which requires, of course, that market prices reflect social costs. Thus arose policies to create employment by diverting demand from foreign to domestic goods: such employment-creating expenditure-switching policies would include tariffs and quotas. The dramatic conversion of Keynes to such an argument for protection is well known to any serious student of economics (though it seems to be strangely unknown to some of the younger trade theorists today who assert that the case for free trade has not been seriously challenged in theory until recently). Needless to say, the use of tariffs to create aggregate demand (through expenditure switching) for one's own good is only a second-best policy, aside from the inevitable danger that it leads to what Joan Robinson called beggar-my-neighbour policies that are mutually harmful. The applications of the theory of economic policy *à la* Tinbergen and Meade, and the policy assignment theory of Mundell, suggest that the optimal solution is to use macro policies to create adequate aggregate demand and to use (free) trade policy to reap gains from trade.

The recent threat to keeping markets open reflects both the growth of the protectionist pressures in the leading pro-free-trade country, the USA, and the combination thereof with the ignorant view that 'new' trade theories are 'finally' supportive of protection whereas earlier ones were exclusively supportive of free trade 'always' and *therefore* protection is now an acceptable, indeed a fashionable, 'with it' ideology to embrace. This combination of interests and ideas has led to strong pro-protectionist sentiments, both feeding the demand by lobbies for protection and cutting away at the ideas that help to reduce its supply.

The protectionist pressures grew in the USA in the 1980s, thanks to the serious overvaluation of the dollar, the intensified competition from the rising Far East, the 'double squeeze' imposed on manufactures which faced competition at the low-technology labour-intensive end from developing countries generally and at the high-technology end from the

Far East, and the consequent fear of 'de-industrialization' that bothered many politicians and policymakers and even a small handful of economists who became late converts to the sorts of pro-manufacturing views that Nicholas Kaldor had propounded for Britain several years earlier when he began writing on Britain's de-industrialization and its adverse effects.[1] Perhaps the overriding factor in changing the ethos among politicians in favour of protection appears to have been psychological: what I have called the 'diminished giant syndrome' in recent writings.[2] Confronting the rapid rise of the Far East, and the near-certain arrival of the twenty-first Pacific century, many Americans felt panic, and then succumbed to petulance and protectionism *vis-à-vis* the countries who were moving upscale so fast. It was a repeat performance of the trauma and drama that the British had gone through at the end of the nineteenth century as they witnessed and confronted the dramatic rise of Germany and the USA on the world economic scene.

UNFAIR TRADE

An important development has been the growing concern with whether trade is 'fair'. The concern in the USA partly reflects (as I noted earlier) the diminished giant syndrome, exactly as in Britain at the end of the ninteenth century. But two other factors, more universal and applicable to many countries beyond the USA, are involved too.

First, if protectionists demand protection, they will today confront politicians who are generally hesitant to supply it because it is not comfortable to be called 'protectionist'. However, if you cry 'foul' and allege that the foreign rival is resorting to 'unfair' trade practices and therefore you need protection, your chances of successful lobbying are much greater. Protectionists have increasingly come to appreciate this and to shift their style of complaints accordingly to 'unfair trade', opening this notion to ever more areas of concern (e.g. workers' rights enforcement by foreign countries).

Second, economists have observed that protectionists have increasingly captured even the main 'fair trade' mechanisms today, chiefly the countervailing duties against foreign subsidies and anti-dumping (the so-called CVD and AD mechanisms), to harass unfairly their successful foreign rivals and thus to *deter* fair competition and free trade. Thus, these legitimate institutions of fair trade, designed to complement and sustain free trade, have been increasingly captured for protectionist purposes.

The globalization of the world economy has also contributed to the growing concern with whether foreign traders resort to unfair trade policies. With substantial recent rises in ratios of trade to gross national product in virtually all countries, reflecting mostly the explosive criss-crossing of investments in the world economy, everyone is in everyone else's backyard, feeling the pinch of competition. The sense of vulnerability has also increased as exchange rates have become flexible and sometimes volatile. In this fiercely competitive and high-risk climate, concerns with fair trade have correspondingly increased.

The free traders today must therefore address forms of protectionism that are unusual and different from the traditional instruments such as tariffs and quotas.[3] They must explore questions such as the redesign of the conventional fair trade mechanisms (e.g. CVD and AD) to prevent their misuse by protectionists.

But deeper questions also arise from the concern with unfair trade. The itch to allege unfair trade has increasingly brought to the forefront the issue: is there anything like 'market-determined' comparative advantage? If differences in national institutions and policies can affect comparative advantage, as they surely can, and if these are now increasingly cited as sources of unfair trade (as they are), then we may be seriously eroding the possibility of free trade and leading towards 'managed trade' or towards free trade only when a great deal of policy harmonization has occurred (as in the European Community (EC)). This issue has come up in regard to the American concerns with foreign 'unfair trade' practices such as lack of workers' rights enforcement giving undue advantage to foreign rivals, the Japanese savings rates and land prices being 'too high', the Japanese distribution system being 'too inefficient', etc., these concerns having either been enshrined in legislation in the 1988 Trade Act or translated into actual negotiations as in the Structural Impediments Initiative talks with Japan.

If today South Korea can be accused of indulging in unfair trade because of its lax labour laws, and hence can be denied its GATT-defined access to US markets under the 1988 Trade Act, it is no longer fanciful to imagine that Bangladesh will be accused some day of unfair trade in exporting textiles with cheap labour because Bangladesh's population policy has led to too much population and hence to 'excessively' low wages.

I see in these recent tendencies, in the USA in particular, to see unfair trade in any policy and institutional differences elsewhere and to use muscle to deny the possibility of free trade as long as such differences continue, a real threat to the free trade regime as envisaged by the architects of the GATT. It is also an issue that poses an analytical puzzle to trade theorists: since all policies will inevitably affect (directly or indirectly) comparative advantage and (in this sense) there is therefore no purely 'natural' or 'market-determined' comparative advantage, where *should* one draw the line and say that autonomy in this set of policies is fine but not in others?

For instance, would we permit differences in *generalized* R&D subsidy, while ruling out *selective* R&D subsidy to specific industries? This sounds right only until one realizes that 'natural' comparative advantage may be shifted also by the former since it will affect favourably those industries that are R&D intensive. Similarly, an accelerated depreciation allowance appears to be neutral in its impact on comparative advantage but in fact differentially helps capital-intensive industries.

Only 'working' rules may be possible then, e.g. overtly selective interventions may be objected to, not indirectly selective interventions. We shall doubtless have to preoccupy ourselves with this question if we are to maintain open markets, on a multilateral basis, among countries with inevitably diverse institutions and policy agendas.

AGGRESSIVE UNILATERALISM

Yet another untoward development relates to the new willingness of the USA to use its considerable economic power to force on others its own views of what are unfair trade practices and to seek unrequited trade concessions (in contrast with the GATT-style mutually-balanced concessions as in successive tariff-cutting Rounds). Drawing on the original 1974 Trade Act's Section 301, considerably strengthened into a lethal weapon in Sections 301–10 of the 1988 Omnibus Trade and Competitiveness Act, the USA has now armed itself to practise such aggressive unilateralism by threatening tariff retaliation in case the American demands are not satisfactorily accommodated.

Since, in practice, such retaliation is GATT-illegal, and also because the demands are for unilaterally-specified and often unrequited trade concessions, this shift in American policy has provoked universal condemnation abroad. It certainly has served to undermine the perceptions of a firm American commitment to the GATT just as the Uruguay Round is drawing to a close and the American role there remains a matter of paramount importance.[4]

REGIONALISM

The question of regionalism has also risen to the forefront, posing itself in many eyes as the wave of the future and signifying the end of multilateralism as typified by the GATT. Indeed, as Professor Lester Thurow of Massachussetts Institute of Technology said recently, 'the GATT is dead'. The question then is: are we witnessing the end of the

GATT-focused multilateral trading system? If the answer were in the affirmative, it would certainly be a sad event. But I believe that this is not so, though the danger does exist. Let me elaborate.

Why did such sentiments take hold in the first place? The answer has to be found in the coincidence of two regional initiatives: Europe 1992 and the US–Canada Free Trade Area (FTA). These involved major actors in the world economy; and the FTA involved the USA which had, until very recently, refused to utilize Article XXIV of the GATT to go for such regional arrangements. Europe 1992 was only a continuation of what had started with the Treaty of Rome, finishing unfinished business, as indeed *required* by the terms of Article XXIV if we interpret them tightly. The impulse was *not* anti-multilateral-trade-regime, *not* therefore anti-GATT, nor was it protectionist as often feared. Rather, the impulse was to provide a boost to the EC and rekindle the boom mentality that the EC formation had generated earlier, to break therewith the stagnationist mentality and situation into which Western Europe seemed to have sunk since the 1970s. On the other hand, the FTA came from altogether different motivations, though they too did not have any anti-multilateral or protectionist impulses. The American frustration with getting a Round started at the GATT in November 1982, and the fear that if such a Round did not start then the protectionist sentiments in the Congress would get out of hand, were among the main motives behind the FTA: the US administration sought to convey a message to the GATT members that, if a Round did not start to address the issues of concern to the USA, then the USA would go the regional route and forget about multilateralism. Exit, rather than loyalty, would be the strategy used. There is little doubt that this message did play a role in getting the Uruguay Round started.

But the coincidence of Europe 1992 and the FTA suggested to many that multilateralism had no future and that the world was headed towards fragmentation into regional blocs. Unfortunately, such expectations can be self-fulfilling, even if objectively false. And there has been real danger of such an outcome, with the Pacific nations worrying about whether a Pacific bloc would not have to emerge if their trading interests were to be safeguarded. I, and others such as Michael Aho, my former student and now Director of Economic Research at the Council on Foreign Relations, have therefore urged that the USA explicity disavow any intentions of pursuing the regional route and reaffirm American commitment to the GATT and the multilateral route.

The proper answer to Thurow, paraphrasing the British sentiment when a monarch dies – The King is dead; long live the King – is: the GATT is dead; long live the GATT. The multilateral institution needs to be revitalized, extended and strengthened to take into account the changed world economy and the fact that the GATT is still not a full-scale institution like the International Monetary Fund or the World Bank but simply an agreement that has served as an institution, as best it can, in lieu of the International Trade Organization (ITO) that died unborn. That is precisely what the Uruguay Round is all about. To argue that the GATT should be forgotten or buried is to give up too soon, to lack the vision that builds international institutional structures that add up to socially productive regimes.

WILL THE MULTILATERAL OPEN TRADE REGIME SURVIVE?

What do these diverse threats to the open GATT-focused regime add up to? Will they devastate the vision of the great international economists, such as James Meade and Gottfried Haberler, whose cosmopolitan and reflective approach helped to shape the post-war multilateral regime that has served our interests so well and in whose footsteps I have been happy to follow during my scientific and policy career?

I do not think so. But I must confess to misgivings about the increased tendency on the part of my fellow-economists to rush into the public domain with instant opinions on subjects that require deeper reflection and a perspective and wisdom that only years of scholarship can yield. Economists readily attack the GATT, knowing little about the GATT but talking to influential columnists and Congressmen who know even less but are eager to find 'any good names' as their allies from the academic world. They ask for 'managed trade', militating against Japan's 'closed markets' on the basis of simplistic regressions, having little time to know that sophisticated econometric analysts divide on the issue and only demagogues have made up their minds on the question. The balloon keeps going up, filled with hot air. Gresham's law operates: the rubbish drives out the informed view.

It is time to remind these economists that professors are a public good and the least that might be asked of them is silence when they have no scholarship and creativity to define their competence in the area of public policy at issue. This was the earlier tradition in which my generation was brought up: and it certainly marked the Dutch tradition of integrity and responsibility that we associate with Professor Jan Tinbergen whose presence at the Symposium was a source of great pleasure to me. It is a tradition that needs to be restored as economists get increasingly into the public eye.

NOTES

1 I have developed and dissected these factors at some length in my Ohlin lectures (Bhagwati 1988) and in Bhagwati (1989).
2 The phrase was stated first in my joint paper with Douglas Irwin (Bhagwati and Irwin 1987) and widely picked up in articles by columnists in *The Economist*, *New York Times*, *Washington Post* etc. at the time.
3 Martin Wolf has wittily analysed voluntary export restraints in his contribution and I share his concerns, while concentrating on other issues.
4 The issues raised by the 301 legislation and actions are discussed in depth in Bhagwati and Patrick (1990). See especially the long papers by me (Chapter 1) and by Professor Robert Hudee (Chapter 4).

REFERENCES

Bhagwati, J.N. (1988) *Protectionism*, Cambridge MA: MIT Press.
—— (1989) 'The United States trade policy at the crossroads', *World Economy* 12 (4) 439–79.
—— and Irwin, D. (1987) 'The return of the reciprocitarians: US trade policy', *World Economy* 10 (2) 109–30.
—— and Patrick, H. (eds) (1990) *Aggressive Unilateralism: America's 301 Trade Policy and the World Trade Regime*, University of Michigan Press; Brighton: Harvester Wheatsheaf

Index